Mutual Gains

Mutual Gains

A Guide to
Union-Management Cooperation

Edward Cohen-Rosenthal
and
Cynthia E. Burton

PRAEGER

New York
Westport, Connecticut
London

Library of Congress Cataloging-in-Publication Data

Cohen-Rosenthal, Edward.
  Mutual gains.

  Bibliography: p.
  Includes index.
  1. Labor-management committees—United States.
2. Industrial relations—United States.
I. Burton, Cynthia E. II. Title.
HD6490.L33C64 1987   331'.01'12   86-25249
ISBN 0-275-92204-9 (alk. paper)

Library of Congress Catalog Card Number 86-25249
ISBN: 0-275-92204-9

First published in 1987

Praeger Publishers, 521 Fifth Avenue, New York, NY 10175
A division of Greenwood Press, Inc.

Printed in the United States of America

∞™

The paper used in this book complies with the Permanent Paper Standard issued by the National Information Standards Organization (Z39.48-1984).

10 9 8 7 6 5 4 3 2 1

Contents

PART TWO
Guide to Approaches for Union-Management Cooperation

7
Reorienting the Roots: Collective Bargaining and Grievance Procedures as Problem-Solving Tools

8
Building Linking Structures: Labor-Management Committees

Introduction

Union-management cooperation seems at some level almost paradoxical. After all, aren't they supposed to be at odds and fighting all the time? It really doesn't have to be that way; at the very least, it doesn't have to be that way all the time. They can cooperate broadly and still maintain integrity and advocacy. Many issues and concerns form the basis for joint action while respecting different perspectives. This book is about why and how to cooperate in ways that lead to mutual gains for both parties—union and management. We contend that union-management relationships are not quite as adversarial as they might seem in theory, but rarely have the beneficial possibilities that the union-management relationship can bring been fully tapped.

We believe in a system of industrial organization that balances the interests of management and unions. In the spirit of union-management cooperation, our goal is win-win. We are both pro-union and pro-management. By following the general prescriptions contained in this volume we feel that society, employees, and employers are best served when there is union representation at the workplace.

We recognize at the outset that not everyone will agree with this assessment. Some feel that unions are an unnecessary anachronism in dealing with today's challenges. We are less sanguine about the disposal of democracy and checks and balances to blind trust and questionable expertise. Some view unionization of the workplace as an evil to be avoided at all costs. They object to "third parties" interfering with the prerogatives of management. For us, a union is not a third party but an instrument of the workers in that location. The International union with which they are affiliated is no more an outsider than higher corporate levels. The vehemence of antiunion opposition underscores the need for a modifying force in the workforce. We do not believe that either side, union or management, holds any moral superiority or claim to rectitude. The union is far from perfect in practice, and management too rarely acts out the principles taught in business schools. We make our preference based on our personal experience and values as well as our professional judgment.

With this orientation laid bare, we do not provide extended rationalizations of the benefits of unionization or make caveats on its effectiveness. Nor do we describe how these principles could be applied in the nonunion setting. We leave that elaboration for others. We ask the reader to assume a unionized workplace and then look for the positive possibilities that brings. We do not naively believe that all situations can be positive, that conflicts don't occur, and that confrontation doesn't create caution. But our search is to find an affirmative answer to the collective bargaining equation that holds possibilities for growth of everyone involved.

The aim of this book is to uncover the breadth of application for union-management cooperation. Covering so much territory and linking areas that have never before been tied together in one place raise the danger of covering issues too lightly. As such, we have indicated additional resources for further reading in the footnotes and the end of most chapters. But our primary aim is to paint the broad picture of union-management cooperation from reorienting the roots to ventures for the future. The second emphasis of the book is that union-management cooperation isn't just a theory but a viable, practical alternative. Our writing comes out of our direct experience in working with a wide range of employers and unions to make cooperation real. This experience provides a filter to make sure that our prescriptions are workable.

The first part of this book provides a broad overview of the basis for union-management cooperation. It examines the definitions of cooperation and the particular perspectives of both the union and management. The history of union-management cooperation is presented to provide a perspective on where this approach comes from and its successes and its limitations. The range of experience in the United States and throughout the world demonstrates that cooperation is doable and flexible.

Part Two provides a panorama of the cooperative and participative possibilities. Starting from the basic agreement, it works its way outward. New ways to apply the negotiation setting and the grievance administration are discussed. A variety of ways to set up labor-management committees and worker participation in management are outlined. Finally, a consideration of marketing, product development, and investments illustrates ways to build together for the future based on an expanding revenue base.

Part Three provides insights on how to implement a joint program. A clear lesson of actual cooperative efforts teaches that while flexibility is needed, there are right ways and wrong ways to go about applying cooperation in practice. Important questions and structures are discussed in the areas of getting started, planning, design, training, governance, management, communications, monitoring, and evaluation. While particular applications may vary, these areas need to be addressed in each and every cooperative effort. This is not a cookbook or a how-to-do-it manual but a comprehensive view of the major factors and considerations.

Part Four looks at the connection between money and cooperation. Understanding financial rewards and the ways to structure pay to encourage cooperation and workplace change is a critical and often overlooked area. The potential role of collective bargaining and profit sharing is presented. Various individual and group incentive systems are outlined, including pay for knowledge and pay for performance. Productivity gain sharing and employee stock ownership plans, pros and cons, are highlighted. Yet finances sit within a context of other approaches. Pay alone is not enough to create a good workplace, and participation alone is not sufficient. Linked together in some fashion, they can have a strong impact in creating an overall better quality of life.

We want to thank William Batt, Robert Cole, Barry Cornwell, Harvey Samo, Susan Schurman, and John Simmons for their help in reviewing the manuscript and for their valuable comments. Our thanks are due to Roy Rosenthal for preparing the graphics. We particularly want to share our appreciation of our families, Raymond, Laura, Ellen, Janna, and Mollie for their forbearance and assistance in helping make this book possible. We dedicate this book to those who make our work worthwhile, the working women and men at all levels in the organizations we have worked with who recognize that it is better to struggle together than battle against each other. We have learned from them and drawn strength and inspiration.

I
Perspective on Union-Management Cooperation

1

What Is
Union-Management Cooperation?

WHAT UNION-MANAGEMENT COOPERATION IS AND IS NOT

Union-management cooperation in concept is really very simple. It is the union and management finding at least one thing in common they can work together on—and seeking ways to accomplish that goal jointly. From there, it gets more involved. They may have one goal or many goals in common. Union-management cooperation can and does address a broad range of issues in the workplace, from the handling of tools to strategic planning. It can and does take a wide variety of forms and manifests itself in manifold structures, including labor-management committees, quality circles, and self-managing work groups. It can and does take place at all levels, from the shop floor to the boardroom. This book describes the magnificent breadth of the possibilities of cooperation between managers and trade unionists. In some ways, it is easier to describe what union-management cooperation is *not*.

It is not a denial of the identity of either party. Too many descriptions of union-management cooperation paint it as if both sides were the Bobbsey twins off on a picnic. In real union-management cooperation, each party is clear about its interests and who it represents. They are working together because they believe it is in their own best interests, not out of altruism. Management has a responsibility to stockholders in the private sector and to taxpayers in the public sector. The union has an obligation to represent workers' interests.

It is not the absence of conflict. All organizations and interpersonal relations experience some degree of conflict. This is a healthy state of affairs because conflict brings out divergent opinions and perspectives. The question is the degree of conflict and how it is handled, not its existence. Some conflict continues to exist in organizations even after a successful, broad-ranging union-management cooperation effort has been implemented. What will be different is how that conflict is managed and the ways in which it is creatively channeled towards common

3

improvement. True union-management cooperation is hard work directed toward finding and acting on mutually acceptable goals, not industrial pansyism.

The fact is that, even without the union, conflicting interests still exist inside a company or agency or between employees and management. Departments and sections of companies express different interests all the time. It is in the employer's interests to put these perspectives on the table. The best choices are made when informed by different views and when recognizing different pressures. The same is true with employees; there are at times conflicting goals held by employees and management regardless of the certification of a union. These can be about wages, hours, work expectations, and other similar topics. The union provides a forum for the expression of these concerns. Cooperative programs provide a better way to address them. To some, cooperation brings prophetic visions of the lion lying down with the lamb, the merger into one big happy family and the end of conflict. In the real world, cooperation harnesses the positive aspects of difference and conflict.

It is not laissez-faire. Union-management cooperation is not each side doing its own thing or leaving each other alone. It is joint, deliberate, and structured. Cooperative approaches often involve highly complex, intricate sets of social and organizational relationships and boundaries. A cooperative stance states that the two parties care enough about things in common that they are willing to work together on them. A cooperative environment is not one where neither party bothers the other very much; it is one where each bothers to bother constructively.

It is not an answer to all ills. To some, union-management cooperation is a salve for all that ails a company or agency. As such it is oversold. What the use of cooperation admits is that management is not always right *and* that the union is not always right. But they'll be more right working together than working apart. Cooperation does not guarantee good results because it is an internally driven process. Cooperation cannot necessarily control such outside forces as economic swings, political upheavals, or natural disasters, but it can help adjust better and faster to these conditions. And, as a *process*, it can provide a better *way* to get things done, but the substance of the decisions remains very important. While cooperation is not a panacea for everything, as a rule it can be a better way to generate solutions and commitment.

In combination with the adversarial approaches to union-management relations, cooperative strategies form a framework for industrial or workplace democracy. Union-management cooperation can lead to an improved quality of working life (QWL), but QWL programs and employee involvement as applied in unionized workplaces are subsets of this topic. Also subsumed are the many forms of worker participation in management.

Our aim is to approach the issues with realism and sobriety while generating imagination and hope in the collective bargaining relationship. Cooperation is not always possible or desirable. Even when the two parties agree to cooperate, too often the manner in which it is undertaken undermines possibilities for real accomplishment. And even when a reasonable approach is taken, there is no guarantee of positive outcomes. The effort may not be sufficient to the task or other variables may later enter the picture, thereby eroding the effectiveness of the cooperative strategy. Further, past successes don't ensure future continuation of efforts. The parties and the environment change over time. Unless the cooperation remains a dynamic and flexible process, it can wither with time. But done right, union-management cooperation can be nurtured to flower and sustain itself in important ways that will be to the mutual gain of each party.

THE INFLATED MYTHOLOGY OF ADVERSARIAL LABOR RELATIONS

In the popular conception, union-management relations evoke images of dueling gunfighters of the Old West. This general picture of union-management relations is formed by an unfortunately distorted media view created by frequent television and newspaper reports of strikes. Yet, in fact, the strike as an expression of conflict is rarely used. In 1984, according to the Bureau of Labor Statistics (BLS), there were only 62 major work stoppages involving 1,000 or more employees. This amounted to 4 days per 10,000 days worked (0.0004 percent) for a lost time rate—an all-time low. If placed in a different perspective, union workers in large companies were on the job 99.9996 percent of the time. A problem-solving mechanism that results in agreement more than 99.9 percent of the time is clearly effective in finding areas of common understanding. Rather than the image of labor as the Jesse James or management as the Wyatt Earp of American society, a better connection for them from the same century may be of Henry Clay, the Great Compromiser.

Arbitrations are another measure of union-management difficulties. While in some cases arbitrations are used as a neutral and preventive problem resolution tool in the event of impasse, most of the time it is a result of a failure to agree. Too often, this is a way for either party to avoid really dealing with the issues or to save face with constituents by not having to take responsibility for the "bad news." According to the American Arbitration Association (AAA), the association receives about 17,000 requests per year for labor arbitration. Half of these are settled by the parties without the arbitrator's award. While this may seem like a lot, it amounts to about one arbitration case per year per 1,000 union workers. According to the AAA and the Federal Mediation and Conciliation Services (FMCS), the number of interest arbitrations that settle outstanding issues in contract negotiations is very small. Arbitrations represent a tiny portion of the actual number of grievances filed. There are no national statistics on grievances. If arbitrations represented 1 percent of all grievances, and allowing that several grievances can originate from one person, then more than 90 percent of all union workers are not involved in a grieved dispute with management in any year and more than 99.5 percent of all grievances would have been settled internally.

Before the strike is the mediation process. A high level of requests for mediation would indicate great difficulty in even talking between labor and management. Yet this is not the case. The Federal Mediation and Conciliation Service receives between 100,000 and 120,000 notices of expiration of contracts in a year. Of these, mediators are called in for one or more sessions only 8 to 10 percent of the time. Let's rephrase that in the affirmative: More than 90 percent of the time the two parties can come to agreement themselves without the assistance of any outside party.

When one looks at the real world of labor relations, the battlefield decreases even more dramatically. On an informal basis, information is shared between each party that is critical to the operation of each. Unions often pass on ideas for improvement that they hear from the membership. In fact, labor people are often the greatest boosters of their products, and rivalries frequently occur within a national union between locals from different companies producing the same product. Many managers have worked their way up from the ranks and maintain strong ties from their earlier years. In legislative battles that affect the industry or the acquiring of a government contract, the union and management are often on the same side. To be sure, there are locations where the relationship is terrible and little if anything is shared. And in many ways, cooperation may not be extensive or the agreement totally satisfying, but the clash and conflict in the workplace are overstated.

In sum, when one looks at the traditional adversarial tools of grievance handling, arbitration, mediation, negotiations, and strikes, the picture of the American labor-management relationship is one incredibly successful at coming to agreements both sides can live with. Even where strikes occur, in an overwhelming number of cases there is an agreement reached acceptable to both parties. For every Phelps Dodge that displays an inability to reach agreement are tens of thousands of cases where agreements are reached. The adversarial side of labor relations is literally the tail that wags the dog. Cooperation, however, goes beyond agreement where there may be an armed or uneasy truce or arms-length relationship. To illustrate that agreement is so common negates the notion of the intractability or irreconcilability of the two parties.

Because the parties come to agreement so often, one might reasonably ask, why not leave it alone? The notion that they can agree leads to the possibilities that this can be an even more proactive, cooperative process. It is extremely important for workers, employers, and the general society to find ways to improve significantly the process on the way to agreement and to magnify the beneficial outcomes of cooperation.

In short, confrontation describes the iconography but not the topography of the union-management relationship. Most literature about labor history centers on strikes, lockouts, violence, and discord. Industrial relations texts focus largely on grievances, arbitrations, permissible topics of negotiation, recognition, and a whole host of legalisms. Usually ignored is the fact that the union-management relationship as the interplay of the interests of two parties comes before any legal relationship. In so much of society the contact between parties has become overly legalized to the point where legal fineries overtake concern for the quality of the overall relationship. While awareness of the legal framework is helpful, more necessary is an improved understanding of what occurs *most of the time*.

Although asserting that adversarial situations form the fringe of the labor-management relationship, we don't deny their importance. The ability to take an adversarial posture forms important boundary conditions that many times encourages more cooperation and agreement. The threat of a stike or a lockout helps the parties come to a compromise. The ability to file a grievance helps restrain violations of the contract and provides the protection of due process to all of the membership—even if they don't use it. The right for management to say no to unreasonable demands or to resist intimidation is important to help maintain a lid on the relationship. The right to stike, even if unexercised, provides a sense of power and self-determination to the union. There are times where cooperation is not possible and confrontation is called for. Cooperation does not mean capitulation to a one-sided deal. There are limits each side has that cannot be crossed, and when those limits are violated, each side has to stand up and fight.

Yet the latitude for real cooperation has not been adequately tested. Too often the parties are frozen in adversarial postures when a cooperative approach could work. In many cases the cooperation is too timid or too limited to meet its potential. In the absence of effective cooperation, adversarial strategies look inviting. Yet war always looks more promising and romantic in the abstract. The bloody casualties and realities of real confrontations take their toll on the lives of employees, union leadership, and managers and their organizations. Someone may win in a conflict, but at what price? The costs and benefits of an adversarial posture need to be weighed against the potential of cooperation. In general, the prospects for joint construction are better than mutual destruction.

A FRAMEWORK FOR UNION-MANAGEMENT COOPERATION

Figure 1-1 describes the basic positions of union-management relations. The vertical axis represents the strength of the parties and the horizontal the polar interests of management and labor. The goal in union-management cooperation is to come together at the top of the diagram where there is a strong management and a strong union. There is no comfort to a union in having a weak management that is unable to perform well. A weak and divided union is more trouble to management than strong representation. Posturing by either party leads to serious problems. Managment's relying on its rights clauses rather than being competent and correct leads to conflict and mismanagement. Union leadership's not responding to the merits of particular situations leads to gridlock and poor membership representation. When both occur at once the result is terrible conflict. When there are serious power imbalances between the parties, there is a danger of co-optation by the stronger party. Worse yet, weak management and a weak union lead to little energy or capability for problem solving.

Another way to view the situation is to look at the concept of overlapping interests, as in Figure 1–2. In our opinion the two sets will never be identical, but the degree of overlap determines the degree of the cooperation. Radical unionists focus solely on the differences, and naive organizational theorists only see the overlap. Both commonality and difference occur in all situations.

FIGURE 1-1
Basic Positions of Union-Management Relations

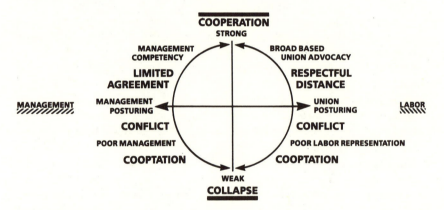

FIGURE 1-2
Overlapping Goals of Employers and Unions

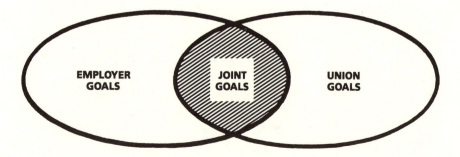

More than 30 years ago, a broad model was laid out excellently by Frederick Harbison and John Coleman of the University of Chicago. Based on field research, they examined the situations where agreements can be reached and divided them into three categories: armed truce, working harmony, and union-management cooperation. An initial category of confrontation precedes these three. The span of the model is illustrated in Figure 1-3. Their definitions of the categories are particularly instructive. "Armed truce" is defined as:

1. A feeling on the part of management that unions and collective bargaining are at best necessary evils in modern industrial society.
2. A conviction on the part of the labor leadership involved that the union's main job is to challenge and protest managerial actions.
3. Basic disagreement between the parties over the appropriate scope of collective bargaining and the matters which should be subject to joint determination.
4. Rivalry between management and the union for the loyalty of workers.
5. A frank admission on the part of both parties that settlements of major differences in collective bargaining are made on the basis of the relative power positions of the company vis a vis the union.
6. A mutual desire to work out an orderly method of containing conflict and compromising differences by living together under the terms of a collective bargaining contract.[1]

Though probably predominant, the best that can be said about this type of relationship is that there isn't open warfare. Management sticks to the letter of the agreement and the union uses the agreement as the sole foundation for a relationship. These organizations come to agreement over the contract, thereby avoiding strikes but only after adversarial posturing. The next level, "working harmony," is quite different and is also found in many organizations. Harbison and Coleman define it as follows:

1. A genuine acceptance of collective bargaining on management's part based on a conviction that the union is an asset as well as a liability in running the business.
2. A conviction on the union's part that attainment of its objectives is dependent in large measure on the continued prosperity and well-being of the company with which it bargains.
3. An awareness by both parties that, although their objectives are in conflict in important areas, it is possible to make compromises which allows each side to feel that it is advancing its interests thereby.
4. The retention by management of the sole responsibility for the carrying out of the core functions in running the business, while the union confines its activities to vigilant policing of managerial actions and to removing certain obstructions which lie in the path of efficient production.
5. A tendency continually to broaden the scope of matters subject to joint discussion and negotiation.
6. A recognition by each party of the complexities of the internal problems of the other coupled with a willingness to help in solving some of the thorny issues involved.[2]

FIGURE 1-3
A Continuum of Union-Management Relations

←——————————————————————————————————————→

Confrontation   Armed Truce   Working   Cooperation
                                            Harmony

   "Working harmony" organizations are characterized by the use of labor-management committees, quality circles, joint study teams, and other types of limited cooperative activities. The highest level of the relationship, and found in the least number of cases is "union-management cooperation." Cooperation is described in these terms:

1. A conviction on the part of management that the union as an institution is both willing and able to organize cooperative activity among employees to achieve lower costs and increased efficiency.
2. A willingness on the part of the company to share some vital managerial functions with the representatives of the union.
3. An eagerness on the union's part to be a production-boosting agency in return for tangible and intangible benefits for the union and its members.
4. A resulting relationship in which the parties assume joint responsibility for solving production problems and eliminating obstacles interfering with greater efficiency.
5. Outward manifestations of mutual trust and respect coupled with expressed confidence that the partnership of union and management "pays off" for both parties involved.[3]

   This statement, more than 30 years old, describes accurately the union-management cooperation being attempted today at the Saturn project of General Motors and the UAW and at the Shell-Sarnia plant working in conjunction with the Energy and Chemical Workers of Canada. The wisdom of these categories is not in the assignment of any one company and union to a category but the accuracy of the overall model to define areas for improvement in the labor-management relationship. In an updated version, our goal is to describe how employers and unions can shed an armed truce and arrive at effective examples of working harmony and union-management cooperation.

TRENDS MOTIVATING UNION-MANAGEMENT COOPERATION

Responding to Increased International and Domestic Competition

   Competition has probably been the biggest spur to union-management cooperation. The automotive industry clearly got serious about cooperative activities and joint sanctioning of participation after the imported auto threat hit home. Battered by imports, the same is true in the steel industry. Beleaguered by threats from foreign competitors, even staunch adversaries found that the differences between the union and management in any particular company paled before the threat of extinction. In many countries, union-management cooperation has been used successfully to compete more effectively in the international marketplace. Responding to that challenge requires more awareness and teamwork than ever before.

Yet the issue is not solely one of foreign competition. Union-management cooperation is also elicited by increased domestic competition. This is particularly true in deregulated industries. Excellent examples of cooperation are now found in railroads, telephone companies, and airlines. While some companies have responded to the pressure of competition by more authoritarian behavior, many have looked toward more cooperative approaches. As a rule, it can be said that the greater the competition, the more incentive for cooperation for mutual survival and gain. Conflict becomes a destructive luxury.

Cooperation increases during times of crisis, whether those be competitive, general economic downturns, corporate or agency retrenchment, or international conflict. It is a sad commentary that too often it takes real stress before most abandon their safe harbors and/or adversarial postures and consider cooperation.

Coping with a Changing Work Force

Reasons for change are also structural. The demographics of the U.S. work force are changing dramatically, and managements and unions need to respond better to this new composition of the workplace. The new work force is younger than ever before. As a result of the post–World War II baby boom, a large number of workers in the 1980s are between 25 and 35 years of age. In addition to sheer number, this generation has more schooling than any generation before and greater expectations on average than those before them. They want to use their talents and they want to do it now. Their demand is not only for good pay and benefits but also for a work life that respects them and their potential. On the other end of the scale, employees are retiring early, with the average age of retirement being 55 years of age. This means a declining stock of traditional managers who have staffed the hierarchical organization and a need to induce workers to stay beyond the age of possible retirement through making work more desirable. The squeeze on both ends is forcing a reexamination of the way work is organized to increase responsibilities at the lower levels and to find more collaborative and engaging ways to work.

In addition, both for reasons of economic necessity and increased equality, women have entered the paid work force in increasing numbers. Women demand new ways to work that can mesh with family responsibilities and that use more collaborative modes of problem solving. At the same time, with more racial and ethnic minorities involved in the work force, and at higher levels, new modes of management that stress acknowledging and using a diversity of backgrounds will be needed. Demographic trends accent the new ways of working, but workers of all ages, sexes, and races have expressed their desire to be included more in the management of the workplace.

The Dynamics of New Technology

Modern technology requires new modes of workplace organization. Because of the rapid pace of change, the useful life of capital equipment is relatively short. To justify investment and successful entry into new markets and to service new ones, new processes must be brought on stream quickly and the use of expensive equipment must be maximized. From the union perspective, new technology can have an enormous impact on the health, skill requirements, and job security of the membership, and new forms of involvement are required to understand and anticipate changes.

Also, the technology of a society provides a paradigm for its social life as well. Since Henry Ford, economics has been measured by the progress of the assembly line. Yet interrelationships of processes and supplies describe the computer age of production. The fundamentals have shifted from a manipulation of things to the processing of data and managing relationships. The new sociotechnical approach is far more team centered and emphasizes information and feedback loops. Union-management cooperation can be a better way to handle the scope, complexity, and effect of technological changes.

Flexibility as the New Management Imperative

During the 1960s, the world was treated to a bombast of concern about the pace of change. Today the concern is rarely discussed, only lived. In the lives of organizations, the way to respond to a rapid pace of change is to maximize flexibility in all areas. This is true in terms of technology, product, raw materials, markets, and a host of other issues. It is particularly important in the human and organizational sense. In many ways, profitability and survival are determined by how fast organizations can adapt and the quality of the transition.

Unionized organizations have to address these same issues. As such, management needs to work with the union to prepare for the future and to respond to changes in the business and political environments. In traditional adversarial labor relations, the union is often a drag on flexibility and change. In a cooperative environment, it helps lead. The union and management are looking together for operational, market, product, and technological answers necessary to achieve success.

The Demand for Employment Security

While corporations and agencies have become cognizant of the need for change, employees have become acutely aware of the need for employment security. As organizations change, the fear inside them is that many will be left by the wayside. Today the need for job security outweighs demands for pay and benefit increases, employees recognizing that the first step in quality of work life is work. Employees and their unions have learned that without their input, they can become casualties in the plans for change. Further, for organizations that do not plan for change, their survival can be threatened through lack of foresight. In short, in order to preserve jobs in the future, unions need to get involved with management in improving present operations and shaping the future to include continued employment.

CONCLUSION

Many forces have helped shape the increasing interest in union-management cooperation. As well there remain serious barriers, such as antiunionism and union busting of some management, isolationist views among some labor leadership, and short-term vision and the reluctance to change among both parties. Yet the conditions are in place that can support real growth in this area. The basis for any union-management cooperation is *respect* between the two parties. Management needs to recognize the union(s) as the legitimate representative of the members of the bargaining unit. The union needs to acknowledge management's responsibility to the shareholders or the taxpayers and its obligation to manage. Cooperation does not require that each party trust or even like each other to get started. What it does require is recognition of the respective responsibilities and a willingness to find and act on items of common concern for a better future. That collaboration can be an extensive and exciting opening for mutual gain.

ADDITIONAL RESOURCES

Axelrod, Robert. *The Evolution of Cooperation*. New York: Basic Books, 1984.
Batt, William L., and Edgar Weinberg. "Labor-Management Cooperation Today," *Harvard Business Review* 56 (January–February 1978): 96–104.
Harbison, Frederick, and John R. Coleman. *Goals and Strategy in Collective Bargaining*. New York: Harper & Brother, 1951.

Siegel, Irving, and Edgar Weinberg. *Labor-Management Cooperation: The American Experience*. Kalamazoo, Mich.: W. E. Upjohn Institute, 1982.

Skrovan, Daniel, ed. *Quality of Work Life: Perspectives for Business and the Public Sector*. Reading Mass.: Addison Wesley, 1982. See also Chapter 14, Edward Cohen-Rosenthal, "Worker Participation in Management: A Guide for the Perplexed."

"The New Industrial Relations." *Business Week*, May 11, 1981, pp. 85–98.

Walker, Kenneth. "Worker Participation in Management—Problems, Practice and Prospects." *International Institute for Labor Studies Bulletin*, No. 12 (1974).

2

The Union
Decision to Cooperate

THE EFFECT OF COOPERATION ON A UNION

Cooperation requires judgment. Each party has to weigh what it means for itself. For the union, the primary questions center on what a cooperative program will mean for the membership and what it will mean for the union as an organization. The judgments should take into account the short- and long-term effects of any initiative. For existing local unions, the prime areas for concern are briefly examined below.

Some unions decide that cooperation is not for them or that their situation makes it impossible. Yet mainstream trade unionists from Gompers to Kirkland have carefully examined the issues and have made a choice to try to make cooperation work to mutual advantage while warning against deceptive advertising on unilateral versions. In 1919, Samuel Gompers wrote, "Industry, like government, can only exist by the cooperation of all. . . . Every edifice, every product of human toil is the creation of the cooperation of all the people. In this cooperation it is the right of all to have a voice and to share in an equitable proportion of the fruits of these collective enterprises."[1] Lane Kirkland, president of the AFL-CIO, said in 1985:

> The element of difference—of conflict if you will—enters of course when we're negotiating a collective agreement or when we're engaged in an effort to organize a group of employees. Once a trade union is accepted as a negotiating partner, once collective bargaining exists, once a contract is in force, then there are numerous opportunities for a cooperative rather than a competitive or adversarial approach to a whole range of issues that affect the well-being of the firm and of the industry. And we are more than willing—we're anxious—to pursue those efforts.[2]

Impact on Contract Negotiation

The collective bargaining relationship as articulated in a written contract forms the foundation for cooperative projects. The contract establishes basic boundaries for the cooperation. The contract both responds to and structures the industrial relations and operational environment. This relationship means that collective bargaining as a process cannot be divorced from the cooperative proceedings. Directly or indirectly, the contract is the sanctioning document. It may lay out the mandate or framework of the cooperative effort or describe the gain-sharing plan. In the Relations by Objectives (RBO) program of the Federal Mediation and Conciliation Service, the difficulty in the labor-management contractual relationship is generally the springboard for examining cooperation. However, in most QWL and cooperative programs, the contract negotiations per se are held apart from the cooperative activities. As a general rule, the adversarial position takes precedence over the cooperative or participative approach. The parties retain the right to bring any issues to the bargaining table and to settle them through that process. The contract retains its binding nature subject to normal procedures for renegotiation. While it helps, cooperative activities are no guarantee of contract agreement. In fact, in companies with notable cooperative programs, such as AT&T and the Minneapolis *Star-Tribune*, there have been strikes over economic issues after the programs have been put in place. These examples demonstrate the ability to have a mature mix between cooperative and adversarial postures.

The more conflict-ridden the relationship, the more difficult are the negotiating sessions. If each side creates buffer zones to protect against incursions of the other, then there is less to give and take. If the employer manages poorly, then the union seeks more work rules for protection. If the coffer is low due to poor management, then the membership can get less. Both in terms of what is available and the nature of the relationship, cooperative union-management relations can yield better contract negotiations. In places with highly developed cooperation, the bargaining sessions become joint problem-solving and strategic planning sessions.

Impact on Contract Administration

A similar relationship exists between cooperation and contract administration. The right to file a grievance remains intact. The duty of fair representation remains in place. For several reasons, a cooperative working relationship makes contract administration easier. First, the parties are looking for areas of agreement, not opportunities to draw the line. There is less retaliation in a cooperative environment, which makes grievances less frequent and easier to settle. Grievances related to communications breakdowns fall off dramatically: in the

Tarrytown General Motors plant grievances went from 20 per week to 3 per month. It is interesting to note, though, that, even in workplaces with model cooperation, grievances almost never disappear completely. This illustrates that even reasonable persons can have different perspectives and that the backstop of an effective grievance procedure is necessary. Decisions on grievances can be important ways that the contract takes on clearer definition.

Because of the decline of the total number of formal grievances, those on the docket get faster and more complete attention. There are fewer arbitration and labor board appeals, which saves considerable resources that the union can better use elsewhere. In cooperative work settings, union officials file fewer formal grievances, but because of broader contact with the membership are just as busy (if not more so) helping solve the problems of the membership. Some argue that the effectiveness of the union is measured by how many grievances can be filed. This is wrong because the effectiveness of the union is in how many grievances can be *solved*. No member thinks his or her union is effective when it takes a long time to get a claim resolved or if legitimate beefs were traded off. In a cooperative work environment, the representational role of the union is retained but energies are spread across a broader range of approaches.

Impact on Membership Service

Many union members and outside observers have the perception that the union is for the 10 percent of employees who are "troublemakers." This is way off the mark because union-won wages and benefits are for everyone. However, in the day-to-day life of an agreement, the truth is that since the squeaky wheel gets the grease, a disproportionate share of time is spent dealing with the chronic problem employee or the frequent griever. The daily workplace concerns of the other 90 percent of the work force are also important to the union. A large proportion of the membership has few run-ins with management and files few grievances, if any. They too often become disaffected from the union.

Especially in "right-to-work" states, servicing all employees is critical to obtaining maximum membership. Many strategies can be used to broaden membership service outside the workplace, including holding social events and providing services in the legal, health, education, community service, and consumer areas. In the workplace, the union can also promote forums for the majority of workers who want to do a good job and see the employer prosper but feel frustrated when they see that reality falls far short of possibility. Contact with the membership and notions of service can be expanded with such programs that improve worklife.

Impact on Union Politics

Cooperation can be a mixed bag in terms of union politics. If members are not clear about what they are getting out of a cooperative program, or if the process is hidden, the union leadership can be open to charges of selling out or of being in bed with management. Further, dissident caucuses that are ideologically opposed to any cooperation will attempt to make any effort an issue.

Yet, if handled correctly, cooperative programs can be a decided plus. In fact, the turnover rate of union leaderships with good participation programs is far less than that in traditional adversarial settings. One reason is a perception by a broader segment of the membership that they are getting something out of the union's advocacy. In many programs, the union leadership learns new skills, which helps improve their performance. In many cases, the union is picking up new insight on how to plan and manage union affairs. Union officials are learning how to run meetings with less emphasis on ritual and Roberts Rule of Order and more by clear agendas and broader involvement and problem solving. This has helped in good programs to increase attendance at union meetings and to build participation.

Impact on the Union as an Organization

A cooperative project implies organizational change. Too often the sole focus is on the change in how the employer is managed. But if it is a joint process, then it also has its impact on and lessons for the union itself. Many cooperative projects serve to change the structure, problem-solving abilities, and communications capabilities of the employer. In the union, new structures may be needed to cope with added responsibilities. The union can use the problem-solving approaches generally used in a cooperative program to analyze the problems it faces. One trade unionist in Rhode Island set up a "quality circle" among the local labor council to determine answers to the political problems they were facing. More open communication and better listening can help the union perform its job better. Unions at all levels need to ask themselves the same question posed to employers, How can we do our job better? Further, the quality of work life for union leadership and staff also needs to be considered. Learning new approaches for improving organizational competence can only help.

The fundamental goals of the union remain the same as always in a cooperative program. The search for better working conditions and increased dignity on the job have always been union goals. The basic structure of elected representation also remains the same. However, there have been positive changes in the tone and content of the work unions do and communications among various levels within the union as a result of involvement.

Requirements for Labor Education

For unions engaged in cooperative efforts, traditional labor studies are even more necessary than for adversarial locals. Trade unionists should know their history to understand that cooperation often came after years of struggle. They need to understand labor laws and their applications to make sure that they are fully discharging their responsibilities. They need to know how to prepare for and conduct negotiations and to handle grievances to ensure that they are not leaving their flanks open to charges of negligence. They ought to understand the broader social agenda of the labor movement so that internal cooperation does not lead to insularity from larger issues in the economy and the society or indifference to the difficulties of others.

On the other hand, there are also new skills that need to be learned. Labor education should address the particular kind of negotiation and grievance administration in the cooperative environment. Labor history would take into account the history of union involvement in cooperation so that there is a sense of pride in previous union efforts and a clear perspective on the present. Problem-solving skills and the administration of joint union-management initiatives can be taught.

THE BENEFITS AND THE RISKS
OF COOPERATION FOR UNIONS

Rarely is any decision in the workplace unalloyed; there are good points and bad points in any situation. The precise mixture will vary from union to union and from location to location. The relative benefits and risks need to be weighed for any cooperative activity. We discuss below some of the critical risks and benefits. Yet simply listing the risks and benefits is not enough. Risks can be minimized and benefits maximized if thought is given to how to deal with them.

Starting with the initial premise that the union must maintain its clear identity as the representative of the workers, there are a series of possible pitfalls. If the union becomes an apologist for management or simply a prod for productivity, then it loses its authority as the workers' representative. This diminishes its effectiveness as a union and paradoxically makes it less useful to management. Involvement in joint activities ought to be no preamble to softness in negotiations over traditional collective bargaining matters such as wages and benefits. If the union allows communication to go directly to the membership without the union's involvement and acknowledgment of its role, then there is a danger of weakening union allegiance of the work force. Most people prefer cooperation to confrontation, and the union's being perceived as blocking positive activity can cause membership estrangement and resentment.

Some unionists are concerned about the diverse nature of the treatment of employees in participative programs, thereby possibly contradicting the principle and practice of shop rules. There may have been a long history of developing uniform rules to combat capriciousness in treatment or to encourage solidarity among workers in an industry. There are other pitfalls to watch for, including political splits, possible violations of the contract, job loss due to increased productivity, speedups, downgrading of jobs, or loss of comparability in an industry.

Clearly, many things can go wrong with a cooperative effort. If simple machines can go on the blink, how many more possibilities are there for problems in complicated human relationships testing out new ground? Yet each of the items mentioned has remedies and preventive steps that can be taken (these are discussed in Part Three).

Given that the union is able to fend off most of the possible difficulties, especially the internal politics, there are many benefits for the union. Some of these derive from the process directly through increased access to information and prenotification of changes in work arrangements and machinery. Hopefully, the additional input can help avoid management errors or decisions that would affect the membership negatively.

As discussed earlier, some of the benefits come from increased membership representation. In almost all programs, the amount of grievances goes down, sometimes dramatically. Members find that their concerns are being resolved more quickly and more fully. Another measure of member interest is attendance at union meetings. At present, most union meetings are chronically under-attended. In a number of cases, attendance at union meetings has gone up after instituting a participation program.

Of course there are a variety of other ways that a successful program better assists the membership. Work satisfaction may increase. The union may be able to address a broader range of personal concerns that extend beyond the economic. Membership education and skills levels are increased. Stress caused by poor supervision or unnecessary barriers to doing a good job may be reduced. Better communication with coworkers may result. The impact on stress and working conditions applies to union leadership as well as the rank and file. Too often, the union representative is caught in the middle of a grievance or faces the stress of having to represent problem employees and confront supervision. In all of these areas, improvement can be made.

The increased visibility of the union in a joint project helps its image both internally and externally. The membership sees the union taking the lead in innovation and advocating another dimension of human dignity in addition to compensation justice. A cooperative spirit aimed at improving customer service and quality can also win applause in the industry and the public.

A final set of benefits has to do with the broad impacts of cooperative programs that improve bottom-line performance. There may be more money that could go for higher wages and benefits, for modernization and expansion, or health and safety improvements, among the many possibilities. Increasing the pool of funds need not be through loss of jobs but rather by the expansion of the market and cutting nonpersonnel costs. The improved condition of the employer may result in saving jobs that would have been lost by falling into an uncompetitive position. Sometimes joint projects have resulted in more jobs.

HOW TO AVOID CO-OPTATION

Perhaps the biggest fear of a union in a cooperative program is co-optation. The union worries whether fancy management programs or slick consultants will be used to render the union toothless and impotent. There is a real distinction, however, between getting along and going along.

Most importantly, a union must keep in mind what its own interests are in the development and maintenance of a joint effort. A union should not be engaged in a program to "do management a favor" or because "we had no choice." A union should be involved in a cooperative effort because there are important objectives which it wants to meet through mutual activity. Too often, the union does not think through alternatives and negotiate more acceptable options to the management programs presented. If management is unwilling to engage in a give and take on the development of a joint program and its design, then it has no interest in a cooperative program.

Second, the program should be equal and joint. If the union is a junior partner in the program, it will generally be partner in blame and invisible in credit. With the union having little access to information about a program and separated from the levers of power over it, a program that starts off benign could become problematic. In some cases, union leadership lets a program go in but doesn't want to have anything to do with it. They reason that if the employer runs it, then they won't get blamed. Unfortunately, the hear no evil, see no evil, do no evil posture has the opposite effect. The membership demands to know why the union wasn't on top of the program and why it allowed it to happen in the first place. If the union has equal participation in all aspects of the program, then it can assert itself with confidence.

Third, the union must be knowledgeable about the alternatives for cooperation and the proper ways to design a joint initiative. Co-optation can come through ignorance. By allowing management to provide all of the information, do all of the design, and set the whole framework, the union has abdicated its responsibility. Some managers may need to learn how programs are done in a joint fashion—and the union can teach them.

Last, the union must be part of the evaluation of a program. An evaluation tells whether the program did what it was supposed to do and assesses its other impacts. Unless there is joint involvement in an honest evaluation, it may be hard to tell whether the union has been co-opted. The results should document a balance of benefits for the management and the employees. If there is little benefit to the employees, then the program needs to be changed to redress the balance.

Unions should keep in mind that good cooperative programs are ones that they have worked hard for and on, not ones where they have acquiesced to management. It is an extension of union advocacy, not a sellout.

WHAT IF THE DECISION IS NO?

Samuel Gompers presented the basic dictum of the labor movement almost a century ago—"more." The union's job is to obtain more for the membership than could be accomplished by workers acting alone. Of course this applies to benefits, wages, and time off, but Gompers also meant "more" to apply to the quality of life in society and the quality of work life. Workers want more democracy and say on the job. They want their work to be as positive an experience as possible. And they don't like it when their union seems to stand in the way.

When the union says no, it had better be because management refused to go along with a proposal that would have provided more say and more security in the relationship. In workplaces with bad labor-management relationships, many workers can be mobilized to oppose involvement. But this is only if the program is clearly a unilateral management program and can be shown to be not in their interests or if it is an employer ruse to undercut the union or manipulate employees. When the union is really opposed to any cooperative program, it better be able to stop it dead in its tracks. If this is not the case, then many workers will sign on to a positive program offered by the employer and there is little the union can do to stop it. This splits many in the work force from the union and creates tremendous problems.

The union may be forced to say no to particular proposals that do not include important safeguards or don't go far enough. When this is the case, the union, rather than being seen as opposed to change, involvement, and improvements in the workplace, is seen as the champion of real participation. The union's decision to say no should be reasoned and principled and the leadership should be confident that the overwhelming majority of the membership will stand together.

Yes or no, adversarial or cooperative, the union should be out to represent all of its membership in the best way possible. All unions use multiple strategies to advance the concerns of the membership. If real cooperation is possible, seek it, mold it, and use it.

ADDITIONAL RESOURCES

Bureau of Labor Management Relations and Cooperative Services. *Labor-Management Cooperation: Perspectives from the Labor Movement.* Washington, D.C.: U.S. Department of Labor, 1984.

Cohen-Rosenthal, Edward. "Should Unions Participate in Quality of Work Life," *QWL: The Canadian Scene* 4 (1981):7–12.

Donohue, Thomas R. "Labor Looks at Quality of Worklife Programs." Speech given at University of Massachusetts-Amherst, January 7, 1982, AFL-CIO Public Relations Department.

Kochan, Thomas A., Harry Katz, and Nancy Mower. *Worker Participation and American Unions: Threat or Opportunity.* Kalamazoo, Mich.: W. E. Upjohn Institute for Employment Research, 1984.

Kornbluh, Hy, ed. "Unions, Labor Education and Worker Participation Programs." *Labor Studies Journal* 8 (Winter 1984).

Nickelhoff, Andrew. *Extending Workplace Democracy: An Overview of Participatory Decisionmaking Plans for Unionists.* Ann Arbor: Labor Studies Center, University of Michigan, 1980.

Ontario Quality of Working Life Centre. "A Labour Perspective on QWL." *QWL Focus* 4 (Spring 1984).

3

The Management
Decision to Cooperate

WHY SHOULD MANAGEMENT COOPERATE WITH THE UNION?

Management has the responsibility for the success of the organization as a whole. In the private sector, management must make the company or operation as profitable as possible in order to fulfill its obligations to the stockholders. In the public sector, management must make the organization as effective as possible in order to fulfill the needs and expectations of the citizens and their legislative authorities. Management's partner in the workplace is the union representing the employees. This partnership can be effective or ineffective, positive or negative. Regardless of the quality of the partnership, the fact that the union is management's partner cannot be wished away. The character, health, and strength of the union-management partnership are major factors in the success of the organization.

Union-management cooperation is in everyone's—both employees and employers—interests. Union-management partners can cooperate for the mutual benefit and gains both will obtain. Problems shared by management and the employees can be successfully addressed and solved cooperatively. Responsible management uses every asset and avenue it can to maximize the success of the organization. When the union is willing to commit to the success of the enterprise by working cooperatively, then management ought to pursue this opportunity vigorously.

In reality, the basic question for management is, Why shouldn't management cooperate with the union? In the unionized workplace, this cooperation is built into the human dynamics of the organization. Regardless of the adversarial nature of the relationship or conflict that may develop, management and the union have to get along in order to work together. Once the union has been recognized, it will not fade away. Decertifications occur in a very small percentage of contracts, and fighting the union at every step is a costly proposition.

Establishing a cooperative framework recognizes reality and makes an asset out of the relationship. The collective bargaining relationship is the framework for cooperation and at the same time is a clear form of union-management cooperation.

Furthermore, union-management cooperation through its participatory forms is an extension of the management principle of delegating responsibility to lower levels in the organization. Such cooperation turns problems and solutions over to those who have to deal with them most directly, thus freeing managers to handle other problems and responsibilities. The real leading question for management about cooperation should be: How can it be done effectively?

Management should take the initiative in seeking union-management cooperation, thus affirming management's overall responsibility for leadership in the workplace. Furthermore, the improvements and gains that result will directly enhance not only organizational performance but also management's own quality of work life. In certain situations, some managers may feel that cooperating with the union doesn't mean exercising management leadership but rather giving in to "the other side." Cooperation does not require either management or the union to give in. Managers are not asked to betray their management team members. In fact, management serves management goals and objectives through successful cooperation, which in turn results in more effective, stronger management. Cooperation doesn't mean co-optation or changing sides; it means the two sides identifying and building upon common ground.

Flexibility is a new management imperative. Organizations must be able to respond to a rapid pace of change in virtually all areas. Maximizing flexibility is a strategy for managing the organization's response to change. Top management especially is concerned about the implications of the hierarchical management structure for the present and the future. In many organizations this hierarchy is more attentive to maintaining itself than functioning effectively. That hierarchical form may not be a good fit for the functions of management in a rapidly and continuously changing workplace and market. Management is seeking both new ways to manage generally and to manage organizational change specifically.

There have been some real changes in management itself over the last decade. To keep up with changes in the marketplace and changes in technology, management has been forced to move away from the old bureaucratic, status quo mentality into an entrepreneurial, change-oriented mentality. The search for management approaches that complement this new orientation has led to innovations within management, such as matrix management, vertical slice task forces, and a wide array of team-building strategies. These changes in management make it even more feasible for management to pursue union-management cooperation. In fact, these changes within management itself often stimulate management to examine its partnership with the union in a new light. Fostering union-management cooperation is the logical next step for management looking to an ever-changing but successful future.

WHAT ARE THE RISKS AND BENEFITS
OF COOPERATIVE EFFORTS?

Any worthwhile endeavor has risks and benefits built into it, and union-management cooperation is no exception. The challenge for management is to minimize the risks and maximize the benefits. Experience with union-management cooperation over the past 15 years demonstrates that real benefits result from the effort, but not without some significant risks.

Union-management cooperation efforts can fall short of their goals and objectives and can fail outright. If this happens, management probably can't continue to justify the investment it has already made in the effort. This then reflects badly on managerial performance. Since managers are judged by their results, concern about success is central. Management can minimize this risk by working with the union from the beginning to set realistic goals and objectives for the cooperative effort and clearly lay out a feasible design and plan. This risk can also be reduced by adopting a joint monitoring and evaluation process for assessing the progress of the cooperative effort. In this way, problems can be identified early and solved before they threaten the cooperative activities and their future. Furthermore, by using a joint process for staying on top of what is happening in the cooperative effort, management shares the responsibility for ensuring its success with the union.

Cooperation can upset the balance of power within management, within the union, or between management and the union. In all three of these cases, if the balance is stable and reasonably equitable when cooperation is undertaken, then the challenge is to structure the program so that it doesn't tip that balance. Conversely, if the balance is unstable and relatively inequitable from the start of cooperation, there is real potential for conflicts between both individuals and groups that may play out within the cooperative arena.

The key to minimizing this risk is to structure the cooperative effort carefully and to determine what implications the cooperative structure has for the various balances of power already in existence. Top management needs to be particularly sensitive to possible reactions of middle-level managers and first-line supervision. These people may feel that doing things cooperatively with the union reduces their own power. Structuring a clear, active role for mid-level managers and first-line supervision within the cooperative effort is the most effective strategy for preventing or minimizing the possiblity of a negative reaction from them. Cooperation can mean an increased ability to get things done and greater access to information. When that is the case, participation is empowering. As a result, both the organization and the cooperating parties become more powerful.

Last, sometimes the cooperative effort can disrupt parts of the organization's operations. When training is part of the cooperative effort, then participants will have to be freed up to attend. Further, many union-management cooperative efforts involve a variety of meetings that have to be fitted into pre-existing work schedules. At times, such meetings will disrupt operations or at least require creative scheduling and personnel assignments. Organizations that have experienced such disruptions have concluded that any negative impact of these disruptions was far outweighed by the positive benefits. Planning realistically makes the new union-management cooperative activities fit well into the management organization, the union organization, and the workplace as a whole. To be effective, union-management cooperation needs to be integrated into organizational goals, plans, structures, and operations.

Cooperation means change, and change needs to be managed. To prepare for cooperation, management must have a realistic sense of what is involved, the degree of difficulty, the connection between union-management cooperation and organizational change, the risks involved, and the strategies for eliminating or minimizing those risks. Then management will have confronted effectively the initial challenge of cooperating with the union.

The benefits to management of union-management cooperation are well described by the Federal Mediation and Conciliation Service as follows:

1. A forum to review budget considerations, complaints and other management concerns. This forum enables employees to see their role in problems that concern management and gain a better understanding of management's position on issues.
2. An opportunity for advance discussion of operations problems, planning and scheduling and other matters that have a potential impact on employee work schedules, overtime schedules, layoffs, recalls, temporary transfers or new job opportunities. Since new proposals unilaterally initiated by management without employee input are frequently resisted by employees, labor-management committees provide a forum for resolving such resistance before it arises.
3. An open channel of communication to establish rapport with the union. Day-to-day labor relations problems such as grievances are not discussed so as to avoid getting bogged down in small issues.
4. An opportunity to respond to the ideas, suggestions and complaints of employees. This demonstrates to the union and employees that management is sincerely interested in improving the workplace.
5. A means of communicating with employees through their own elected leader.[1]

Union-management cooperation in its many forms is a way to involve employees in decision making that affects their jobs and to provide an outlet for concern for the employer. In that way, it can motivate employees in the performance of their jobs. Motivating employees is a management goal around which there is often confusion and controversy. Usually management thinks it has to do something *to employees* to motivate them. Union-management cooperation provides a vehicle for working *with employees* in new ways. In turn, employees through participation become self-motivated. A 1979 Gallup poll conducted by the U.S. Chamber of Commerce found that "the overwhelming majority believe that if they are more involved in making decisions that affect their job, they would work harder and do better."[2]

Union-management cooperation can have a very positive impact on the collective bargaining process, on both contract negotiations and contract administration. Labor negotiations can be conducted more effectively because of better union-management relationships growing out of cooperation. Both management and the union improve their skills in problem solving, communications, planning, and group process through involvement in cooperative activities. They, in turn, apply these skills during contract negotiations. Day-to-day contract administration can become more problem-solving and problem-preventing oriented as a result of union-management cooperation in other areas. This saves management time and money by reducing time and energy spent in this area. Thus resources freed up from the more traditional contract negotiations and administration can be redirected into cooperative problem solving and problem prevention.

All of these benefits make management more effective and management's job easier. A better workplace can result from union-management cooperation. The benefits derived from cooperation result directly from specific problem solving and indirectly via improved relationships and attitudes, additional skills, smoother labor relations, and an enhanced operational environment.

WHAT ARE THE PAYOFFS OF COOPERATION TO MANAGEMENT?

Successful union-management cooperation results in significant immediate and long-term payoffs to management. The six most significant payoffs that relate directly to overall management goals and objectives are covered briefly below.

Higher Profitability

Improved profitability is one of the first major returns management realizes from union-management cooperation. Cooperation can help management to improve both the cost containment and the revenue generation sides of the profit picture. Historically, most joint problem-solving efforts initially have addressed cost containment issues. This is particularly true in cases where cooperation has been motivated by concerns for the economic health and survival of the organization. When the cooperative effort is spread to the shop floor level of the organization, problem solving is usually oriented to "working smarter, not harder." Involved employees focus on cutting waste, reducing bottlenecks, and making overall operations run more smoothly. All of these result in reduced costs. For management, having more "members of the team" focused on keeping costs in line is a real bonus.

Union-management cooperation leads to a variety of joint activities that address both cost containment and revenue generation. The end result is improved profitability, which means shared mutual gains for both parties as well.

That participation positively affects the bottom line is borne out by data from a survey conducted during 1983–84 and reported in *Personnel*. A random selection of 850 U.S. industrial companies was made from *Value Line Investors Survey* and *Moody's Industrials*. These companies were asked to complete a questionnaire describing the extent of participatory activities and the state of labor relations. The participatory measures drawn from the questionnaire data were then compared with the following financial measures: financial strength, stock price stability, price-growth persistence, earning predictability, sales per share, cash flow per share, earnings per share, average annual price/earnings ratio, average annual earnings yield, net profit, net profit margin, net worth, percentage earned total capital, and percentage earned net worth.

"Overall, the study clearly showed that the more participatory the firm, the higher the level of financial and behavioral success. Both the published financial ratings and the state of internal labor relations reported were more favorable for participatory firms."[3] The authors went on to discuss the implications for management:

> These results indicate that participatory management in the United States increases profitability to a significant extent—according to the Value Line financial indicators. Participatory management also helps create good industrial relations to some extent; this is reflected in some positive association between participation and the behavioral indicators. If these overall trends are typical, then it may be that a further competitive advantage can be achieved by intensifying participative efforts, both in participative and nonparticipative organizations.[4]

Union-management cooperation is a participatory management strategy that clearly improves profitability. If union-management cooperation achieved nothing else, this result alone should compel any management to consider a partnership with the union.

Improved Management Effectiveness

Another payoff to management from union-management cooperation is improved management effectiveness. This comes about in several ways. The cooperative programs generally attack organizational bottlenecks and problem areas as they try to improve operations. Also, the broader communications channels developed as part of the cooperative effort and the joint problem-solving process serve to enhance management effectiveness. Management can and does use these channels to keep employees at all levels better informed about the status of and challenges for the organization and to receive ideas for improvements. Effective management means obtaining the necessary resources and facilitating the completion of the work. Union-management cooperation opens additional avenues for pursuing these twin goals.

The joint union-management process provides additional technical assistance to and support for management in the running of the company or organization. Union officials and employees at all levels are more willing to share their valuable expertise with a cooperative management. The truism that the person doing the work generally knows how to do it best applies here. Through a cooperative effort, these people are more available to work with management to ensure an effective operation.

One of the key indicators of management effectiveness is quality. Quality improvement has often been a common goal of union-management cooperation in both the private and public sectors. Union members usually have important insights into how quality can be maintained. Systems such as statistical quality control and zero defects require the full cooperation of the work force. Quality can be a critical component in overall competitiveness and a source of pride in one's work.

In many programs, management acquires a set of new and/or strengthened skills that are useful not only to them in the cooperative effort but also in the exercise of their day-to-day management functions. These skills include those of planning, communications, group leadership, conducting meetings, problem solving, and conflict resolution. Some organizations assign their managers to the cooperative effort as part of their career development.

Managers with whom we have worked in union-management cooperative programs have reported that what they learn through the cooperative effort they have applied even more in their assigned management responsibilities. Something as simple as using a written agenda and a flip chart pad to facilitate regular staff meetings can be a significant contribution to managerial effectiveness. One manager said that adopting these two simple meeting management techniques changed his daily staff meetings from "morning beatings" into "morning meetings."

Today many managers feel assaulted on all sides by market pressures, a variety of demands from within their own organizations, and the accusation that management failure is at the root of any and all problems within American companies and organizations. Union-management cooperation is an avenue for enhancing management effectiveness that provides the individual manager with additional resources and broadened support to meet better his or her challenges.

Increased Organizational Flexibility

Another payoff to management is increased organizational flexibility. Managers and supervisors learn new ways to work together as they participate in the union-management cooperative effort. Probably the most important learning in this regard is that different levels and functions within management all have something valuable to contribute. One operations vice president expressed it to us this way, "I never thought personnel could contribute anything worthwhile to operations until we worked together on this [labor-management cooperative] program." The traditional isolation within management by function and/or level is often broken down in the process. New bases for real teamwork within management are established as a result of management working together in the cooperative effort. Management as a group becomes more flexible within its ranks.

Furthermore, increased organizational flexibility results when the cooperative effort experiments with different forms of structuring the work to be accomplished, such as vertical slice task forces, autonomous work groups, business or work teams, and the like. This increased organizational flexibility within management specifically and within the broader workplace generally allows management to adopt more innovative management approaches within all of its functions. These broaden the skill base and responses available to the employer to adjust to changes in service or product requirements, resource inputs to the work process, and technology.

Union-management cooperation can be the basis for a more flexible response to external market conditions. Probably the best recent example of this is the Saturn Project undertaken by General Motors in cooperation with the UAW. The goal of this endeavor is to create a new GM division that will make it competitive in the small and medium-sized car market. The plan for this project was developed over one year jointly by autoworkers, union officials, and salaried GM managers. By agreement, the Saturn Division includes such features as payment by salary for all workers, performance and attendance bonuses, decision making via a network of labor-management committees from the shop floor to the top management of the Saturn subsidiary, and much broader and more flexible job classifications for production and skilled workers. GM management's decade of experience with union-management cooperation provided both the stimulus and the foundation for this bold, new initiative in the auto industry.

Improved Working Environment for Management

Management can have an improved working environment as a result of union-management cooperation. Too often quality of work life improvements have focused solely on hourly employees. Supervisors and managers deserve and need such improvements as well. More positive working relationships with other managers and supervisors as well as union officials and rank and file employees grow out of cooperative efforts. Problems and challenges addressed by the cooperative effort can leave management freer to tackle problems solely within its realm. Managers at all levels can move away from being "Mr. Fix-its," "referees," or "policemen" to being coordinators and planners. These improvements can relieve management of some of the more significant sources of stress.

Further, the older, more traditional forms of managing have often led to a kind of "lone ranger" approach to the problems managers encounter. Such an isolated approach to managing can sometimes lead to management burnout, a variety of stress-related diseases such as heart disease and hypertension, and family and marital difficulties. Any manager with the "I can/have to do everything myself" attitude towards his or her work is a manager destined for personal and probably organizational difficulties as well. Union-management cooperation provides managers with additional problem-solving capacity and an improved working environment.

Managers active in a cooperative effort can be more pro-active in their management activities and less reactive. Such managers gain a greater sense of being in control even though they are sharing more responsibility. These managers are providing organizational leadership rather than just heroically fighting organizational brushfires. They can truly demonstrate their skill for management through the cooperative effort rather than just functioning as organizational caretakers.

Last, an improved union-management relationship usually results from the cooperative effort. This improvement can relieve or prevent many of the more traditional labor relations headaches and nightmares commonplace in confrontational workplaces. This is particularly noticeable to first-line supervision, who often feel as if they serve on the front lines of management. Improvement in the labor-management relationship plays out directly and quickly in the first-line supervisor/rank and file employee relationship. This impact of the cooperative effort significantly improves the quality of work life for first-line supervisors. Those supervisors involved in cooperative efforts almost unanimously report a shift in the attitudes and behavior of the people who work for them—a shift from sometimes working for but never working with the supervisor to working together in a spirit of real teamwork.

Enhanced Productivity

Enhanced productivity can result from successful union-management cooperation. Through joint problem solving, work procedures and processes can be made more efficient and employees involved in cooperative efforts themselves can become more productive. Many of the principles for fostering a successful productivity improvement effort are the same as those for fostering a successful union-management cooperation effort. These include involving employees in problem solving and decision making regarding their work and work environment; involving the union from the beginning of the effort; fostering more open communications, particularly regarding organizational goals, objectives, and performance; and providing training and education opportunities in support of personal growth and development.

Research supports the connection between employee participation and productivity improvement. In 1975, Suresh Srivastra and his associates surveyed more than 2,000 literature references on worker participation experiences in the United States to determine whether participative efforts improved productivity. Their survey included empirical studies, field studies, and correlational studies. Eighty percent of the field studies reported a positive impact on productivity from participation. The authors of this survey concluded that there was a pattern demonstrating a positive relationship between participation and productivity enhancement.[5] Another study conducted in 1977 by Raymond Katzell and his associates at New York University analyzed 103 worker participation experiments in the United States between 1971 and 1975. Again, more than 80 percent of the experiments resulted in favorable effects on one or more aspects of productivity.[6]

The employee involvement program at the Sharonville, Ohio, Ford Motor Company plant with the UAW provides an excellent example of productivity improvements resulting from union-management cooperation. In a typical manufacturing zone with all six production departments involved in the Employee Involvement (EI) effort, management reported a 22 percent improvement in direct labor efficiencies. To obtain this improvement only 2.5 percent of production time was diverted to EI activities.[7] Such improvement is not unusual for successful union-management efforts of this type. In general, the evidence supports a commonsense assertion that organizations are more productive when people are working together rather than battling and when their common focus is on organizational improvement.

Stronger Market Profile

The last return to management from union-management cooperation considered here is a stronger market profile. Often the cooperative effort addresses revenue generation as an area of common interest. Activities undertaken in this regard can include joint customer service programs, joint marketing efforts, and new business and product development. In the auto industry, both General Motors and Ford Motor Company have profiled their involvement in union-management cooperation in their print and electronic media advertising. General Motors did this in its ads describing "GM Is People." Ford Motor Company's ads stated "Quality Is Job One." In both cases, they are describing quality of working life/employee involvement programs and the positive results for potential car buyers from such programs.

Another example of building a stronger market profile is the use of joint marketing teams on Milwaukee Road Railroad. The use of such teams grows out of a systemwide labor-management cooperative effort that incorporates labor-management committees and quality circles throughout the property. A third example is a nationwide promotional campaign undertaken by the jointly trusteed International Masonry Institute designed to promote the use of brick and block by the construction industry.

In summary, union-management cooperation presents a real challenge to management—and a real opportunity. Union-management cooperation via collective bargaining is already built into the framework of the unionized workplace. While there are real risks to cooperation, these risks can be minimized or managed within the cooperative effort itself. There are far more significant benefits and payoffs to management in cooperation. At a minimum, these benefits and payoffs should stimulate management to consider carefully the advisability of cooperation with the union and seek to find the broadest possible areas of mutual concern for cooperation. Once committed to the effort, management should carefully and consistently pursue cooperation with its partner, the union.

ADDITIONAL RESOURCES

Burck, Charles G. "Working Smarter." *Fortune*, June 15, 1981 pp. 68–73.

Burton, Jr., Daniel F. and Sylvia Ann Hewlett. "Labor-Management Relations and Productivity: A Framework for Success." *National Productivity Review* (Spring 1985):185–194.

Katzell, Raymond A., and Daniel Yankelovich. *Work, Productivity and Job Satisfaction.* New York: Harcourt Brace Jovanovich, 1975.

"The New Industrial Relations." *Business Week*, May 11, 1981.

Ontario Quality of Working Life Centre. "Management in Transition." *QWL Focus* 3 (Summer 1983):2–29.

4

The Legacy of
Union-Management Cooperation

Union-management cooperation is almost as old as union-management conflict. Where initially there may have been struggle and conflict over union representation, the employer and union have always had limited choices—continued conflict or cooperation for mutual gain. Often, union-management cooperation is described as a sea shift in management culture and indicative of a new peaceful age in industrial relations. The historical record shows instead that there have been waves of increased union-management cooperation often associated with national and economic crises.

THE EARLY YEARS

The story of union-management cooperation in the modern era begins near the turn of the century. People concerned about the nature of labor and human relations in an industrial age sought various solutions to the problem. Some of the early unionists advocated cooperative syndicalism where the workers would cooperatively own and manage the enterprises themselves. In the last half of the 1800s, there was a spirited debate in the labor movement about whether to cooperate with the owners of capital or promote worker ownership. In the United States, the prevailing notion of business unionism supported traditional businesses and sought to improve wages, hours, and working conditions.

In other countries tremendous discussion centered on alternative methods for linking production and the producers via joint committees or councils. In Great Britain, the Whitley Report of 1917 called for the widest establishment of shop committees. Over the course of the next decade, councils and committees for industrial dispute resolution and employee participation spread in Germany, France, and elsewhere in Europe. Through the British colonial labor laws of 1924, works councils were farspread, including India. In Japan, the Conciliation

Society was founded in 1925 to promote employee representation and workplace familism.

Experimentation with workplace constitutionalism and representation also occurred in the United States where elaborate schemes were devised for joint participation. Filene's Department Store in Boston instituted in 1898 a Cooperative Association. The association was given the right to make or change any store rule subject to a veto by the owners. It took a two-thirds majority to override the owner's veto. In 1913, the Packard Piano Plant established a constitutional system with the workers electing a House of Representatives, the foreman electing a Senate, and the senior management making up the Cabinet. The two chambers enacted their recommendations, which were sent to the cabinet for approval!

Some changes in industrial governance rose out of a response to worker unrest. Following a bloody clash in 1914 at the Colorado Fuel and Iron Company controlled by John D. Rockefeller, Rockefeller retained W. L. Mackenzie-King, the former prime minister of Canada, to investigate the causes and propose solutions to the unrest. MacKenzie-King devised the Colorado Plan for representation of employee interests through Joint Committees of Industrial Cooperation and Conciliation. These were generally implemented in nonunion settings, but one of the principles was no discrimination for union membership.

SHOP COMMITTEES DURING WORLD WAR I

The shop committee approach is most clearly the ancestor of union-management cooperation and employee participation developments. A shop committee is "a form of organization for collective dealing by means of joint committees, composed of an equal number of representatives of both employees and the employer."[1] Soon after the United States entered World War I, the need for full production and domestic labor peace catapulted the theories of workplace cooperation into government action, and one of the key components was the shop committee. During the war years, 225 plans were established by the National War Labor Board (NWLB).

As a patriotic act, the American Federation of Labor (AF of L) endorsed the shop committee concept and urged union involvement. However, many of the committees were in nonunion settings and were set up to provide an alternative approach to dispute resolution and employee involvement. While some unions at the time were involved, the shop committees became anathema to many in organized labor because of this preventive use. Actually, union membership grew rapidly during this period, and many of the shop committees were in companies organized in the next two decades. William Leavitt Stoddard, administrator of the NWLB, supported the unequivocal right of employees to form unions. He addressed the juxtaposition by saying:

On the surface, therefore, the shop committee is neither a union nor a non-union scheme. It is primarily a method of organizing the employees of a given plant with the employers for the purpose of bringing about efficiency and better working conditions. The character of this organization is in several respects different than trade union organization. One important respect is that the organization is *dual* or *joint* and that it is based on the theory of cooperation rather than the theory of competition or conflict.[2]

EMPLOYEE REPRESENTATION PLANS OF THE 1920S AND 1930S

Immediately after the war, many employers abandoned their programs, but the shop committee and employee representation plans came back even stronger during the 1920s. The number of workers covered by shop committees climbed from 319,000 in 1919 to 1.5 million in 1924 in more than 814 firms, including Goodyear, International Harvester, Procter & Gamble, Commonwealth Edison, Armour, and Youngstown Sheet and Tool. Again, many of the companies introduced plans in order to stave off union organization.

The union movement responded with its own initiative by expanding on the positive aspects of previous experience. With recognition of collective bargaining with an independent trade union as a prerequisite, the AF of L at its 1926 convention declared: "Conflict and arbitrary management are poor production policies. Conference and cooperation lead to united work efforts. . . . Workers and management are reciprocally dependent. This is obviously a relationship which calls for cooperation that is to all intents and purposes a real partnership in a work undertaking."

A 1928 article in the *Monthly Labor Review* found examples of union-management cooperation on production issues in the following industries: railroads, printing trades, upholstery, carpet weaving, hats and caps, glass, clothing, street railways, hosiery, textiles, and construction.[3] The biggest success story of this period was found on the B&O Railroad. Cooperation later spread to many railroads in North America, and representatives from other countries came to study its success. The initiative for the B&O plan came from the International Association of Machinists. A later but similar program on the Canadian National was proposed by management. At first, the B&O project was started, in 1924, as an experiment in the Glenwood shops outside Pittsburgh. It proved so successful that joint shop committees were established thoughout the railroad and a system level committee established. This program lasted until the early 1960s.

As early as 1928, the Railway Employees Department of the AF of L reviewed the experience and found a dramatic reduction in grievances, greatly improved working conditions, more employee education and training, higher earnings for the employees, greater recognition of the union, more stable employment, and other benefits for the employees. The department summarized the lessons by saying:

that union-management co-operation is not a weapon. Instead it is a tool, a tool to be used by us jointly for mutual welfare.... The second big lesson to be learned from the performance of our cooperative policy to date is that our unions in particular and organized labor in general are capable of being as potent a force making for better industrial performance and so a richer life than any of the other factors composing our society today.... Our cooperative policy serves as a powerful antidote to the prejudice against unions held by so many people both in the ranks of unorganized workers and management.[4]

Daniel Willard, the president of the B&O said:

I am inclined to think that our labor policy was formerly influenced to no small extent by the ever present thought of the next war, or, in plainer words, of the next strike. Now we are trying at least to direct our labor policy to prevent war. We are consciously and earnestly trying to eliminate the causes which ultimately lead to war, in order that we may have peace. If it is necessary to have two sides in order to make war, it is equally necessary to have the co-operation of two sides in order to make peace.[5]

The first 15 years of the program resulted in more than 31,000 suggestions for improvement, of which almost 90 percent were accepted. The improved service and morale on the B&O allowed it to survive the depression in far better shape than its competitors.

The philosophy of Otto Beyer, the consulting engineer credited with designing the program, is particularly instructive. In a lecture at Harvard in 1928, he said:

I am not thinking of industrial plants whose personnel is made up of submissive, apathetic, timorous workers, or where the management is not troubled with "labor problems"; where in other words, it has its own sweet way. My conception is of a situation where labor and management are consciously, definitely and systematically working together for mutual benefit and public service. It goes beyond the mere peaceful settlement of wage questions and the orderly adjustment of grievances. It includes more than the protective relationship, often really nothing more than an armed truce, which frequently prevails under the conventional form of collective bargaining. I maintain that industrial relations are on a better basis when the employees individually and collectively, are quite definitely stimulated to help the management in the solution of its problems, and the employers take a similar attitude toward the labor force, each striving to improve the conduct of their industry and willing to share the gains which result. In other words, better industrial relations, in order to deserve the name, must make not only for peace, but also for progress—progress for the worker as well as for the employer and the consumer.[6]

LABOR'S INDUSTRIAL ENGINEERS

While some observers relate the development of cooperative programs in recent decades to the rejection of scientific management, the Taylorist school of workplace design must be placed in context. Taylor was contemptuous of traditional management hierarchy and arbitrary behavior. In 1914, Taylor outlined his position in an interview stating:

1. Scientific management is based upon the fundamental assumption of harmony of interests between employers and workers and seeks to establish complete and harmonious cooperation between them.
2. Scientific management attempts to substitute, in the relations between employers and workers, the government of fact and law for the rule of force and opinion. It substitutes exact knowledge for guesswork, and seeks to establish a code of natural laws equally binding upon employers and workmen.
3. Scientific management thus seeks to substitute in the shop discipline natural law in place of a code of discipline based upon the caprice and arbitrary power of men.[7]

Taylor himself had little use for unions that presumed to muddy the scientific accuracy of his designs. However, his heirs had a different perspective. During the mid-1920s, the Taylor Society advocated respect for collective bargaining and union participation in the setting of standards. In December 1925, William Green, the president of the American Federation of Labor, spoke in a widely reported address to the Taylor Society and the American Society of Mechanical Engineers where he drew "a close connection between union-management cooperation, labor's appeal for the elimination of waste and the philosophy of the Taylorites. . . . He opposed company unions, urged cooperation between workers and industrial engineers and advocated high wages and low production costs."[8] Favorable articles on the Taylor Society and scientific management regularly appeared in the *American Federationist* during the mid- to late 1920s. Green wrote in the official journal of the AF of L: "Through a reciprocal relationship, the common problems of industry can be solved, efficiency in service promoted, and economies in production introduced."[9] In 1927, at an AF of L–sponsored conference on the elimination of waste, Green observed that "industry is made profitable and the rewards of industrial efforts are increased in proportion to the cooperation established between employers, employees and management."[10] Thus leaders of the day saw industrial science and due process as strengthening each other. Union involvement brought greater commitment to the standards and more reliable data, and scientific management brought objectivity and order to the workplace.

Many labor organizations, especially those in the garment trades, brought industrial engineers onto their staffs to make sure that standards were fair and in many cases to consult with employers to improve their economic viability. In 1921, a landmark agreement was struck between the Cleveland area textile employers and the International Ladies Garment Workers Union (ILGWU) specifying joint involvement in the development of labor standards and union assistance in helping to improve the overall process of manufacture. Beginning in 1924, Amalgamated Clothing Worker Union staff were available to union plants that asked for assistance in cutting costs. The joint effort at Hart, Schaffner and Marx to lower the costs of production of men's suits served as a model for the industry.

During this period, the International Printing Pressmen and Assistants Union reviewed daily 500 newspapers from around the country. If there were defects in appearance or workmanship, the newspaper was notified by mail of the problem and ways to correct it. If the defect continued, an engineer was sent to visit the paper. The union also helped when new plants were being designed, including providing blueprints and in the installation and overhauling of machinery. All this was at no cost to the publisher. After initial reluctance, soon employers were calling the union for advice on improving production.

There were, and still are, a large number of other unions with staff industrial engineers to check standards and to assist in improving production and maintaining competitiveness. The joint research approach to cooperation and organizational improvement was widely employed from the 1920s for more than 30 years.

LABOR-MANAGEMENT COMMITTEES DURING WORLD WAR II

As the danger of facism rose in Europe and the Pacific, discussion of union-management cooperation and industrial democracy reached new heights. The Murray Plan put forward by Phillip Murray, the president of the Congress of Industrial Organizations (CIO), proposed to Congress joint union-management involvement from the shop floor to the industry level. While it was rejected by employers associations, the plan generated intense discussion. It was an early version of today's industrial policy debates.

In 1942, a classic work, *Dynamics of Industrial Democracy*, was published by Clint Golden and Harold Ruttenberg, two veterans of the Steel Workers Organizing Committee (SWOC), articulating a theory of cooperation that deeply involved workers and their unions in the production process. They asserted: "Workers have a passion for efficiency, detest needless waste, and love to work in an orderly shop, mill or mine where production flows smoothly. Where these conditions do not prevail, workers are full of ideas and practical suggestions on how they can be brought about, or, where they do prevail, how they can be improved."[11] Seeing a new age of industrial relations, Golden and Ruttenberg prophesized:

We believe that American industry is on the threshold of a new era in human relations—the greatest period in union-management relations. The turmoil and strife of the last decade have merely reflected the transitional character of the relations between workers and management. Out of this transitional period is emerging a new capacity on the part of those in industry, regardless of their different positions, in point of view of responsibility and authority to work together as a unit—literally with a singleness of purpose and action for the attainment of a common objective. . . . The increasing extension of democratic methods into industry will lead to fuller production and employment and toward increasing the stature, well-being, dignity and happiness of the individual worker.[12]

Though only for a short time, their prediction was correct. A new labor-management relationship emerged during the war years. With the escalation of World War II, President Franklin D. Roosevelt established the War Production Board (WPB) to help ensure maximum production. One of the major activities of the WPB was to promote the development of labor-management committees throughout American industry. These were endorsed by the AF of L, the CIO, the Chamber of Commerce, and the National Association of Manufacturers. In all, about 5,000 production committees were formed covering more than 7 million workers, including most of the large defense contractors. The kinds and targets of cooperation were various: suggestion systems, conservation of materials, transportation, absenteeism, care of tools and equipment, productivity, quality control, training. Each week the WPB distributed the *Labor-Management News* publicizing accomplishments and providing advice on how best to formulate committees.

In appraising the results, Clyde Dankert wrote: "Labor-management cooperation during the war period was unquestionably a success. It led to greater efficiency in industry and promoted the war effort in other ways. In addition, it afforded thousands of workers the opportunity of working 'with' management and not simply 'for' management, a non-economic gain of no small significance."[13]

This optimistic assessment was shared by *Business Week* as early as 1942 when the magazine forecasted:

Labor-management plant committees, dealing with production, efficiency, salvage and kindred problems, will almost surely survive the war. Not perhaps on as wide a scale as they have been established by the WPB promotion now, but in situations where they have worked well they won't be abandoned. They were coming anyway; the war just accelerated their introduction. Labor-management plant committees testify to the enlarging area of collective bargaining. More and more, business and industrial problems which have traditionally been regarded as purely management concerns are coming to be the subject matter for employer-employee discussions. There is nothing in sight which suggests that this trend will soon be reversed.[14]

The American Management Association published a guide for its membership on how to make the committees most effective. Ernest Dale, an economist for the American Management Association, surveyed the experience and came to these general conclusions:

> Employee cooperation to improve productivity is one approach to industrial peace. Since it results in cost reduction, it may be a means of reconciling the economic goals of labor and management by increasing the size of the total revenue available for distribution to employees, company executives, stockholders and consumers. Employee-management cooperation may also help in meeting non-economic aspirations. Such cooperation may aid in fulfilling employees' desire for participation in those areas of operation where they can make a contribution; it may provide a vehicle of information on matters of deep and immediate concern to workers; it may be a means of imparting a feeling of satisfaction and interest to employees *while at work*, a degree of satisfaction usually attained only by spending the weekly pay check *after work*. To management, employee cooperation can represent a transition from strife to constructive effort, a means of educating employees in the aims and the needs of the company thereby creating greater employee loyalty and better contract observance.[15]

THE CAUSES OF INDUSTRIAL PEACE AND THE 1950S

After the war, the labor-management climate worsened significantly. Without wartime pressures, and with the return of the servicemen to the work force (and the exit of Rosie the Riveters), tensions increased and strikes broke out. Management rights clauses and union security agreements became commonplace, demarcating separate lines of authority and recognition. At the same time, Americans abroad helping to rebuild war-torn economies instituted codetermination systems in Germany and built the foundation for Japanese consultation systems. At home, union-management cooperation was falling by the wayside.

After the war, several important studies were prepared that urged continuation of union-management cooperation and employee participation. In 1949, the Twentieth Century Fund convened a distinguished panel from management, government, labor, and universities whose report urged that labor and management should be "partners in production." The National Planning Association, a private organization, led by Clint Golden and Joseph Scanlon, pulled together an impressive group of industrial relations experts, including Clark Kerr, John Dunlop, Frederick Harbison, and Douglas McGregor. These investigations were conducted over a seven-year period and looked intensively at actual practice. The final list of conditions for industrial peace based on the association's review was as follows:

1. There is full acceptance by management of the collective bargaining process and of unionism as an institution.
2. The union fully accepts private ownership and operation of the industry; it recognizes the welfare of its members depends upon the successful operation of the business.
3. The union is strong, responsible and democratic.
4. The company stays out of the union's internal affairs; it does not seek to alienate the workers' allegiance to their union.
5. Mutual trust and confidence exist between the parties. There have been no serious ideological incompatibilities.
6. Neither party to bargaining has adopted a legalistic approach to the solution of problems in the relationship.
7. Negotiations are problem-centered—more time is spent on day-to-day problems than on defining abstract principles.
8. There is widespread union-management consultation and highly developed information sharing.
9. Grievances are settled promptly, in the local plant whenever possible. There is flexibility and informality within the procedure.[16]

Though there were examples of cooperation at all times during the 1950s, especially in the steel industry, union-management cooperation did not return to the earlier levels of the 1920s or 1940s.

SETTING THE STAGE FOR RENEWAL IN THE 1960S AND 1970S

Focus during the 1960s did not center on cooperative union-management relations but instead on general human relations theory. Douglas McGregor put forward the Theory X-Theory Y conception, which aimed managerial philosophy at a more inclusive and positive approach. The pioneering organizational development work of Kurt Lewin, Rensis Likert, Robert Blake, Jane Mouton, Richard Beckhard, and others developed action research models and new understanding of interpersonal and group dynamics that set the stage for today's cooperative interventions. In London, at the Tavistock Institute, Eric Trist, Fred Emery, Einar Thorsrud, A. K. Rice, Frank Heller, and others were working on the development of sociotechnical approaches to the quality of working life. These later evolved into a series of experiments in the 1970s in "quality of working life" in North America, Europe, and other parts of the world.

The 22-day wildcat strike in 1972 by a predominantly young work force at GM's Lordstown facility dramatically illustrated that the workplace was not immune to the strains of a society facing increasing challenge to authority and the status quo and a demand for expanded participation. For this reason, and because of the vision of Irving Bluestone, vice president of the UAW, the UAW demanded to be a part of GM's organizational development work that affected the union's members. During the 1970s, it was the GM/UAW accomplishments that provided leadership in the field. In retrospect, the 1973 agreement may have been the symbolic event that reopened an era of union-management cooperation. Also in 1973, a study was released by the U.S. Department of Health, Education, and Welfare titled *Work in America* generating intense discussion on worker alienation and the need for new forms of work organization. Joint experiments were tried in unionized workplaces in manufacturing, wood products, hospitals, and the public sector. These efforts generally provided important lessons, though most weren't long-term successes.

By the end of the 1970s there was tremendous growth of interest and activity. The overall difficult economic climate called for new responses, and union-management cooperation was once again a significant tool. The Japanese challenge sparked in unionized workplaces many joint approaches to quality circles. In government and the corporation, backroom deals and old boy networks were replaced by a concern for openness in the decision-making process and equal opportunity for all to participate. The cooperative strategy was rediscovered as a way to increase the viability of the unionized sector, competitiveness, and worker satisfaction.

LESSONS FROM THE HISTORICAL RECORD

Reviewing the historical record can be both illuminating and disturbing. Seeing essentially the same activities and principles being expressed in the past undercuts the notion that today's forms of cooperation and participation are really all that new. If workers have yearned for participation from the beginning of this century, then claims of a "new breed" of worker lose their punch. If previous efforts have taken aim at technological change, calls for urgency because of the latest technology seem somewhat old hat. Understanding that earlier prophets had talked about new ages in industrial relations and cultural shifts in management style ought to make us think twice about the validity of such claims today. On the other hand, it is comforting to know that consistent principles have been espoused for union-management cooperation for nearly a century. Still one worries about the present when so many of the programs of the past are now artifacts. What happened to them?

Cooperative programs aren't permanent. To the best of our knowledge, the longest running program is at the American Velvet Company in Stonington, Connecticut, with the Amalgamated Clothing and Textile Workers Union. Started in 1939, it is still going strong. Few have lasted that long. There seems to be a lifespan for cooperative programs. Structured programs last far longer than changes in personal relationship between the union and management leaders. At some point, the parties lose patience with cooperation and resort to confrontation, or the parties and environment change substantially. The cooperative programs frequently fail to keep pace with internal changes. Union-management cooperation is not an evolutionary or deductive process but invoked out of a particular logic of particular circumstances facing management and the union.

Macroeconomic forces play a major role in the longevity and incidence of cooperative programs. Cooperative union schemes were wiped out in the severe depression of the 1890s. The burst of programs during the First World War were hurt by the depression of 1921. The many programs established during the 1920s were decimated by the Great Depression. Large-scale industrial restructuring in the economy or changes in consumer behavior are generally unresponsive to union-mangement cooperation. Major changes in the work force and the end of national crises also seem to have a negative effect. After both world wars, cooperative programs fell by the wayside when the soldiers returned to the factories more used to conflict than cooperation and the sense of national emergency had passed.

Conversely, cooperation tends to increase when there are strong competitive pressures on the economy. When there is an excess of supply over demand, the partners are more motivated to work together. Pressured by outside forces, management looks to the union for help. Unions seek cooperation more when there is general acceptance by employers of their legitimate role and when they feel squeezed by unemployment and competition from nonunion shops. Cooperation has consistently made a positive impact on the performance of organizations but has not been strong enough to turn back tidal waves of economic change.

Larger social forces also have their impact. The correlation is no coincidence between the increased scale of participative programs and pressures for women's and minority rights and economic participation during the 1920s, World War II, and more recent decades. Political scandals like the Teapot Dome and Watergate affairs reduce confidence in closed approaches to decision making and increase interest in expanded participation.

Historically, there has been a contest between joint union-management programs and management-initiated avenues for participation. Employers seem perpetually to search for a mechanism that will make a union unnecessary. In the short term, many unionists have been apoplectic about the dangers of company versions when a longer vision reveals that company-dominated versions have not lasted. Many of the nonunion programs during World War I were found in companies that were later unionized, such as Westinghouse, Bethlehem Steel, and International Harvester. Company unions were eventually outlawed under the Wagner Act, and even at the Colorado Fuel Company, whose plan helped set off nonunion representation plans, its workers organized a union local in the 1940s. The highly touted employee representation plans in the steel industry provided the framework for the Steel Workers Organizing Committee (now the United Steelworkers of America). In the telephone industry, the Communications Workers of America rose out of an association of company unions that demanded greater independence. Unilateral management programs either folded for lack of consistent interest or inadvertently fueled unionization by showing that collective action was important in improving working conditions.

There is a long and proud history of union-management cooperation in the United States. Respected leaders of the AF of L and the CIO have indicated their support for union-management cooperation within the context of recognition of collective bargaining. American industry leaders have been joint partners in these endeavors for many decades. There is a homegrown and effective North American tradition and theoretical underpinning for cooperation. Admittedly, it has always been a minority or alternative plank to the adversarial conception of industrial relations but important nonetheless.

Most attempts to bring on union-management cooperation have been ahistorical. They have tended to review experience close to them in time and extrapolate a better and better industrial relations future. Their short-term vision leads to short-term commitment to the ongoing challenges of maintaining vital union-management cooperation. The real lesson of a longer view of history is that union-management cooperation has been a valuable tool in many industries and at many times. It alone cannot solve the economic and social problems that employers and unions face, but it can definitely make things better.

ADDITIONAL RESOURCES

Commons, John R. *Industrial Government.* New York: Macmillan, 1921.

Derber, Milton. *The American Idea of Industrial Democracy, 1865–1965.* Urbana: University of Illinois Press, 1970.

deSchweinitz, Dorothea. *Labor and Management in a Common Enterprise.* Cambridge, Mass.: Harvard University Press, 1949.

Golden, Clinton, and Virginia Parker, eds. *The Causes of Industrial Peace Under Collective Bargaining.* New York: Harper and Brothers, 1955.

Golden, Clinton, and Harold J. Ruttenberg. *The Dynamics of Industrial Democracy.* New York: Harper and Brothers, 1942.

Guzda, Henry P., "Industrial Democracy: Made in the U.S.A." *Monthly Labor Review* (May, 1984):26–33.

Jacoby, Sanford M., "Union-Management Cooperation in the United States: Lessons from the 1920's." *Industrial and Labor Relations Review,* Vol. 37, no. 1 (October, 1983): 18–33.

Murray, Phillip, and Morris L. Cooke. *Organized Labor and Production.* New York: Harper and Brothers, 1940.

Nichols, Osgood, et al. *Partners in Production: A Basis for Labor-Management Understanding.* New York: Twentieth Century Fund, 1949.

Stoddard, William Leavitt. *The Shop Committee: A Handbook for the Employer and the Employee.* New York: Macmillan, 1919.

5

American Industry Experience
with Union-Management Cooperation

INTRODUCTION

Union-management cooperation is widespread and growing in the United States today. In this chapter recent American experience in the private sector is described in manufacturing, building and construction, transportation, retail/wholesale, and communications. Activities occur at all levels—industry, company, and plant or worksite. A description of the public sector experience covers the various levels of government—federal, state, county, municipal, and township. Examples of union-management cooperation are found in every industry, but no industry except possibly auto is characterized by such efforts, and the percentage of employees involved is usually quite small. Area labor-management committees, which include a variety of companies, government units, and unions from a range of levels, are also growing.

The breadth of union-management cooperation throughout the United States is impressive. Nearly every area of the economy has some examples of these efforts. According to the 1983 U.S. Department of Labor *Resource Guide to Labor Management Cooperation*, 85 different national or International unions are involved in such programs. In both the public and private sectors at all levels around the country, all of the different approaches to union-management cooperation have been successfully applied. These include labor-management committees, quality circles, parallel organizational structures such as matrix management and task forces, sociotechnical redesign, autonomous work groups, and quality of working life programs. Furthermore, a wide range of innovative strategies for marketing, service, and product development has also been used in a variety of settings.

As our nation is characterized by diversity, so is our experience with union-management cooperation. Two truisms may be offered about this American experience. First, there is no one right approach for a particular kind of organization at a particular level. Success in various settings has been based on

47

experimentation by the parties involved, using various approaches or different versions of any approach. Second, success in union-management cooperation has come from tailoring the approach to the real-world setting and from creating innovative modifications, when needed, to make the approach better fit the environment. These truisms account for the wide diversity of successful labor-management cooperation efforts in our nation. The brief descriptions illustrate this wide range of current union-management activities. We focus on the successful efforts, but success is not universal or guaranteed. Others have failed or have been short-lived.

THE MANUFACTURING INDUSTRY

Union-management cooperative efforts exist in virtually all areas of manufacturing, involve all of the major manufacturing concerns and unions, and have taken many forms. The roles played by the management and unions also vary widely. Both management and the unions have initiated these efforts. Some began as unilateral or management-controlled efforts, then converted to cooperative union-management efforts. The union-management partnerships have varied from strong partner/weak partner relationships to those based on equal strength.

Most activities take place at the company or plant level. However, one example at the industry level is that of the Tailored Clothing Technology Corporation. Established in 1980, it united the Amalgamated Clothing and Textile Workers Union with the large men's clothing manufacturers. Its goal is to design new technology and manufacturing methods to make the industry more competitive, particularly with foreign manufacturers. In the clothing industry, labor-management cooperation has developed around technological advancements and foreign competition.

Heavy manufacturing, and the unions representing its workers, have been the overall leaders in union-management cooperation at the company and plant levels, with much of the pioneering effort being in the auto and steel industries. Probably the best known is the General Motors/United Auto Workers Quality of Work Life Program begun in 1973, a broad-based, open-ended cooperative effort established by Letter of Agreement. The program includes a National Quality of Work Life Committee, but local union officials and local management at the plant level have led in developing the program. It has taken many forms, including employee participation groups, business teams, quality circles, and vertical slice task forces. The success of this ongoing joint effort laid the foundation for the innovative cooperation on the Saturn Project. Through a series of union-management committees, the union and General Motors have been active partners in developing this GM division from its inception. Together the partners designed the technical systems, the human systems, and the production processes for Saturn.

Other industry precedents were established in the 1984 UAW/GM contract with the joint JOB Security Program and the New Business Ventures Development Group. The JOB Security Program makes the company and union partners in a $1 billion system for aiding workers displaced by new technology, outsourcing, or negotiated productivity improvements. The New Business Ventures Development Group makes them partners in a $100 million experiment in joint investment and job creation.

Elsewhere in the auto industry, unions and management have engaged in comparable programs such as the UAW/Ford Motor Company Employee Involvement Program, which has successfully fostered joint problem-solving groups and activities at the plant level throughout the entire company. The UAW/Chrysler Corporation Product Quality Improvement Program is another such effort. All of the major automakers attribute at least part of their recent market growth or comebacks to these joint cooperative efforts.

United Steelworkers of America and the companies within the basic steel industry have also pioneered in union-management cooperation, establishing a variety of labor-management committees in the 1970s. Beginning in 1980, Labor-Management Participation Teams at the plant level were formed in all of the major steel plants. The 1983 agreement converted the experiment begun in 1980 to standard operating procedure. As in the auto industry, the effort is a full, equal, and formal partnership of the union and management.

Within the rubber industry there have been comparable developments. These include the 40 year-old labor-management committee involving United Rubber Workers (URW) and Uniroyal, the 10-year-old labor-management committee involving URW and Kelly Springfield Tire Company, the modified Scanlon Plan between URW and Goodyear Tire-Radial Division, the joint quality circles program at Goshen Rubber Company and Firestone Tire and Rubber, and the Quality of Work Life Program between URW and General Motors Inland Division.

In paper manufacturing a representative example of plant level activity is the network of labor-management committees developed at two Westvaco Corporation locations in Luke, Maryland, and Covington, Virginia. In 1979, the United Paperworkers International Union (UPIU) and Westvaco established plantwide labor-management committees, later adding departmental and shift labor-management committees at both locations. Both efforts grew out of involvement with the Relations by Objectives (RBO) program used by the Federal Mediation and Conciliation Service to improve labor-management relationships. In 1984, Westvaco announced that it would be making major capital investments at both of these older mills in excess of $325 million. Westvaco cited the improved union-management relationship and the positive results of cooperation as factors in the expansions undertaken.

All the components of manufacturing have outstanding examples of union-management cooperation for mutual gain. Such approaches have demonstrated their applicability, whether in process, batch, or assembly operations. The success of these cooperative efforts in manufacturing rests on the maturity and strength of the union-management relationship prior to their undertaking, as well as the depth of common predicaments.

THE BUILDING AND CONSTRUCTION SECTOR

Union-management cooperation in building and construction has been concentrated at the regional or area level through multicraft labor-management councils or committees. There have also been national or industry level activities and job site union-management cooperative efforts, particularly in the safety and health area. Labor-management committees have been the most common approach at all levels, being the most adaptable to the complexities of the building and construction industry.

These complexities are most apparent at a job site. Multiple crafts, multiple unions, and multiple contractors and subcontractors work in different combinations at different times until the job is done. For this reason, job site union-management cooperative activities have been more limited than in manufacturing or similar "enclosed" work environments. At the same time the joint activities at the industry, regional, and area levels demonstrate how a range of unions and a range of employers, some of which are competitors, can cooperate to improve their specific operations and their industry as a whole.

Regional or area level multicraft labor-management committees or councils are spread across the country. Their primary goal is to promote unionized building and construction to the mutual benefit of all the partners, the building and construction trade unions and the contractors and subcontractors. In some cases, architects, engineers, suppliers, and customers are also partners in these cooperative efforts.

One of the most prominent cooperative efforts is PRIDE (Productivity and Responsibility Increases Development and Employment), established in the St. Louis metropolitan area in 1972. This effort is guided by a Memorandum of Understanding and a governing board with representatives of all of the partners, including architects, engineers, and suppliers. PRIDE pioneered the use of "lunch box meetings" at job sites to explain the movement and to solicit workers' suggestions for improvements. Through PRIDE, jurisdictional disputes have been virtually eliminated, several hundred work rule changes have been made, and productivity increases are estimated to be 10 to 15 percent. Many other joint building and construction councils and committees have modeled themselves on PRIDE and its successes.

A significant industry level cooperative effort began in 1981 when the International Union of Bricklayers and Allied Craftsmen (BAC) and the Mason Contractors Association of America (MCAA) established the International

Masonry Institute (IMI) to address mutual problems in a cooperative manner. The IMI is uniquely funded through local collective bargaining agreements. It is governed by a board of trustees with equal numbers of union and management representatives plus one impartial member. IMI's work and accomplishments have been in four areas:

1. Market Development Program: This program has stimulated increased use of stone, brick, and block through a series of targeted marketing campaigns, ranging from educational seminars for owners, managers, engineers, and architects to radio promotional spots to the public.
2. Apprenticeship and Training Program: A network of regional training centers has been established. Specialized skills training and more effective prejob training have also been delivered throughout the country.
3. Research and Development Program: This program focuses on R&D to benefit both contractors and craftsmen. They work together as a team in this area critical to the survival of both.
4. Labor/Management Relations Program: A very workable dispute settlement process is in use throughout the country as a result of this program. The program is now addressing a variety of QWL issues.

IMI is not only the broadest national program in the construction industry but also probably the broadest industry level program in the United States.

Another recent industry level cooperative effort is the Market Recovery Program for Union Construction undertaken by the Building and Construction Trades Department of the AFL-CIO and the National Construction Employers Council. The program is a nationwide effort to improve the competitiveness of the unionized construction industry, jointly sponsored by the 15 national unions affiliated with the AFL-CIO and the 13 employers associated with the council. A national agreement and a National Joint Labor-Management Committee provide the base for the program, which is carried out by local joint labor-management committees.

THE TRANSPORTATION INDUSTRY

Union-management cooperation efforts exist throughout the transportation industry at all levels—industry, system or property, and worksite or crew. Furthermore, such efforts are being pursued within all modes of transportation: railroads, trucking, highway operations, airlines, onboard ship operations, and mass transit. Most efforts are labor-management committees and, more recently, quality circles and broader QWL programs.

Two of the major efforts are on railroads, the Milwaukee Road Railroad Labor-Management Group (LMAG) and the CONRAIL Labor-Management Project. The Milwaukee Road Railroad LMAG grew out of a reorganization plan devised during bankruptcy proceedings. This plan called for wage diversion into stock ownership and for creation of the LMAG to build better union-management relationships and to increase productivity. Railroad management and the 13 local unions are the partners in the LMAG. As partners they have successfully undertaken development of local Labor-Management Action Groups throughout the property, middle-level Problem-Solving Teams, and shop floor quality circles. These quality circles were the first on a railroad anywhere in the world. LMAG also pioneered the use of union-management marketing teams to increase or initiate rail service and generate new revenues. The achievements of the LMAG contributed significantly to making Milwaukee Road a very desirable property in the recent bidding war for its purchase.

The CONRAIL Labor-Management Project is a systemwide program to promote railroad operating efficiency and productivity through labor-management cooperation, to provide efficient rail service, and to promote job stability and financial viability. Rail management and 18 labor unions are partners in this endeavor. A network of joint improvement committees in the various locations and divisions has been developed, as well as quality circles, in a range of work environments, including offices, railyards, shops, tracks, and trains. The CONRAIL project has contributed millions of dollars and incalculable teamwork, significantly guiding CONRAIL's financial turnaround and making CONRAIL the object of a bidding contest.

While both Milwaukee Road Railroad and CONRAIL are more extreme examples of the severe operational and organizational problems in the rail industry, they are representative of the problems and challenges facing much of U.S. transportation. Their successful use of union-management cooperation as a strategy for turning themselves around can serve as a model for other transportation companies. Also, they demonstrated that union-management cooperation must be adapted to the particular work environment. Transportation employees work in many different locales and often in small groups. This requires different approaches than those applicable in the more homogenous manufacturing settings. The involvement of all of the unions as a group directly with management as partners in one comprehensive program is especially significant. While the alternative of individual unions partnering separately with management may seem easier to establish and maintain, it makes for a weaker, less comprehensive program with reduced potential for significant results.

Union-management cooperation is firmly established in other modes of transportation as well. Airlines and airline unions have applied a wide range of cooperative approaches to their mutual benefit. Joint quality circle programs exist at Pan American, Hawaiian Airlines, Frontier, and Eastern Airlines.

At Eastern Airlines, quality circle programs are only part of the picture of labor-management cooperation. In 1983 Eastern Airlines and its unions Airline Pilots Association (ALPA), International Association of Machinists (IAM), and the Transport Workers Union (TWU) reached agreements giving employees 25 percent of the stock and seating four employee representatives on the board of directors. Also, the IAM and Eastern management are engaged in an extensive quality of work life program. Within this framework many QWL and productivity improvements have been made. The productivity improvements alone totaled more than $30 million in the first year.[1] A "contracting in" union-management committee was also established, and it determined that much work could be done more cheaply and cost effectively in house. A joint cost-cutting task force is in operation as well.

Republic Airlines and its six unions have a network of 150 union-management committees throughout the company, as well as a top-level Presidential Action Committee that makes recommendations for improvement to the company president.[2] USAIR and the IAM have union-management committees at the departmental level to focus on subcontracting issues.[3] United Airlines and the Association of Flight Attendants (AFA) conducted a quality of work life program in a framework of a top-level policy committee, station committees, and base or local project committees.[4] Pan American and Western Airlines have employee stock ownership plans (ESOPs) as well as other joint programs.

The National Joint Heavy and Highway Construction Committee coordinates problem solving at the industry level. Various state departments of transportation are involved in cooperative activities. Public transit systems across the nation have applied almost all of the various cooperative approaches with success.[5]

RETAIL/WHOLESALE OPERATIONS

Until this decade there have been few union-management cooperative activities in this industry at the worksite level. At the industry level the Joint Labor-Management Committee of the Retail Food Industry, established in 1974, involved the United Food and Commercial Workers (UFCW) and the International Brotherhood of Teamsters (IBT) on the union side and all of the major supermarket companies and the Food Marketing Institute on the management side. The primary focus of this committee has been on promoting communication to facilitate collective bargaining. No other comparable industrywide efforts exist within the industry at this time.

In the 1980s several significant union-management cooperative efforts were undertaken within particular companies. In the wholesale food sector, in 1980, the IBT Local 595 and Certified Grocers of California developed a joint productivity incentive plan. Certified Grocers is the largest wholesale food distributor in California, with more than 3,000 employees. This program developed the first negotiated work standards system in the wholesale food industry. The impact of the joint incentive plan has been great: productivity increases of 25 to 35 percent, decreased absenteeism, lower worker turnover, no layoffs, and no increases in on-the-job injuries. Based on its success, other companies have adopted variations of this plan.

In the retail food sector there have been two major union-management cooperative efforts, both with UFCW as the union partner. Beginning in 1982, UFCW and A&P agreed to reopen some of the A&P food stores in the Philadelphia areas as a new A&P subsidiary called Super Fresh Food Markets. This joint endeavor incorporated pay and benefits cuts and seniority system changes with a company-funded investment incentive fund for employees, a quality of work life program, and the right of first refusal to purchase former A&P outlets by employees. The result was the successful reopening of a number of A&P stores utilizing a QWL program to operate more effectively. Also, a number of former A&P stores have been purchased by employees to be operated as O&O Stores (Owned and Operated Stores). At a time in the industry when competition is at its greatest and the mortality rate among food stores is at its highest, these two accomplishments are all the more impressive. What made the difference in both situations was the strong union-management cooperation.

In 1983, the UFCW and the Pantry Pride food chain in southern Florida established a joint quality of work life program incorporating a number of unique features. Vertical slice task forces work on planning and address common industry problems, such as sanitation, cashier turnover, employee training, and absenteeism. A network of district labor-management committees and store problem-solving committees engage in problem solving throughout the organization. The Participatory Customer Service Program (PCSP) directly involves all employees in all stores in defining how to serve customers best within their own jobs and in fostering commitment to serving customers in those ways. These problem-solving activities have resulted in significant operational improvements. Customer service overall has greatly improved, as has overall employee job performance.

THE COMMUNICATIONS INDUSTRY

The 1980s have seen broad experimentation with union-management cooperation in this industry, often with unions as the initiators and leaders. The Newspaper Guild (TNG) pioneered this trend with the development of its 1972 bargaining goal entitled "employee voice." The goal was to use existing contractual avenues to give members more voice in the product and, alternatively, to establish joint committees to "discuss and make recommendations affecting all aspects of the operations of all Guild-represented departments." The Twin Cities Newspaper Guild achieved this goal in 1972, when it joined with the Minneapolis *Star and Tribune* Company in establishing the Worker Participation

Committee (WPC). The WPC has been the forum in which the orientation of the newspaper is analyzed and redefined, the impact and feasibility of technological change is addressed, and broader joint problem solving is fostered. Similar "Employee Voice" efforts have also been undertaken in other locations.

In telecommunications, the most extensive union-management cooperative effort began in 1980, involving the Communications Workers of America (CWA), the International Brotherhood of Electrical Workers (IBEW), and AT&T at the national level. Three national joint committees were established and were issued the principles to be followed in developing joint union-management activities at the local level. These joint efforts had spread virtually throughout the AT&T system prior to divestiture, and almost all survived the change. The 1984 negotiations also worked out joint strategies for dealing with the challenge of technological change.

Likewise, Common Interest Forums were established to bring together top management and union officials of the basic operating companies on a regular basis, to discuss and solve problems around changes in both the internal and external business environment. These forums focus on enhancing the competitive profile of the companies and improving employment security for all employees. As the business context and work environments have changed, so have the joint quality of work life efforts in telecommunications grown and changed. Much of their resiliency is attributable to the strength and commitment of both union and management partners at all levels.

It is important to note that in the communications industry, joint union-management efforts share certain characteristics: The efforts result from initiatives and goals established at the national or industry level; the unions have more often been the initiators in these joint efforts; and the joint activities are provided for and framed by the collective bargaining agreements in force. The results have been impressive and far-reaching.

THE PUBLIC SECTOR

Union-management cooperative activities have been increasing rapidly on all levels in the public sector. More union-management cooperative efforts were undertaken in the four years of 1980–83 than in the preceding ten years.[6] As in the private sector, many of these efforts are based on labor-management committees as the cooperative mechanism. Usually, when the effort begins, a labor-management committee is established at a fairly high level; later, subcommittees or labor-management committees at lower levels are established. There are some broad-based quality of work life efforts and quality circle programs as well. But it would seem that labor-management committees represent the cooperative mechanism most adaptable to the public sector environment.

Many different public sector organizations have undertaken such efforts. They include state, county, city, and township governments; particular departments or divisions within local, state, and the federal government; public school districts; transit authorities; public hospitals and other health care facilities; and state universities and colleges. Also some non-profit organizations have undertaken union-management cooperative efforts similar to those of local, state, and federal governments.

Two particularly successful and significant public sector union-management cooperative efforts are in New York: the City of New York Labor-Management Committee Program and the Joint Labor-Management Committee on the Work Environment and Productivity (CWEP) for the state of New York. The City of New York Labor-Management Committee Program began in 1978 with the citywide Productivity Council and QWL committees within the various city agencies. Project committees within each agency also dealt with specific tasks. The range of issues and problems tackled by this massive program covering 115,000 employees is formidable: productivity, service quality, production and equipment problems, training, career development, alternative work schedules, new technology, worksite improvements, and quality of work life issues.

The state Committee on the Work Environment and Productivity covers 103,000 employees. Beginning in 1979, it grew out of the Continuity of Employment Committee that focused on work force planning to reduce job cuts and displacement due to reduced budgets. It has a joint executive committee and two subcommittees, Continuity of Employment and Quality of Working Life and Productivity. Numerous other labor-management committees and subcommittees function on the agency and facility levels. The range of issues and problems addressed includes training, employee assistance, employee involvement, child care, sexual harassment, improved work environments, career development, and quality of work life.

A wide range of cooperative efforts have been implemented in many agencies at the federal level. Of particular note is the extensive employee involvement program between the U.S. Postal Service and the National Association of Letter Carriers.

While the public sector has not led the way in instituting union-management cooperative efforts, it has increasingly adopted joint cooperative approaches to deal with the complete range of issues and problems of the public workplace.

KEY LESSONS TO BE LEARNED

The primary lesson to be learned from this description of the diverse American experience with union-management cooperation is that it can be done in virtually any kind of work environment. Almost every cooperative approach has been successfully applied in practically every industry and work environment. Not every effort has worked, but with proper application every approach can work. The second lesson is that these successes are directly attributable to the solidity of the union-management partnership upon which they were built and the strength of the motivating forces. The particular technique or approach applied has been much less important than the specific joint partnership established. The final lesson is that cooperation is a building process, that it is not a quick fix, and that success evolves not overnight but over time.

ADDITIONAL RESOURCES

Barrett, Jerome T. *Labor-Management Cooperation in the Public Service: An Idea Whose Time Has Come.* Washington, D.C.: International Personnel Management Association, 1985.

Simmons, John, and William Mares. *Working Together: Employee Participation in Action.* New York: New York University Press, 1985.

U.S. Department of Labor. *The Operation of Area Labor-Management Committees.* Washington, D.C.: GPO, 1982.

———. *Resource Guide to Labor-Management Cooperation.* Washington, D.C.: GPO, 1983.

Zager, Robert, and Michael P. Rosow, eds. *The Innovative Organization.* New York: Pergamon Press, 1982.

6

The International Dimensions
of Union-Management Cooperation

Union-management cooperation and employee participation are global phenomena. Evidence of cooperation and the desire for more cooperation is not limited to any one country or any one region of the world. Highly developed forms of joint activity are found in countries with high degrees of unionization such as Sweden, West Germany, Japan, Israel, and Singapore. There is a strong correlation between the degree and strength of unionization and the level of employee participation in decision making. Countries with low levels of unionization or very weak unions generally do not have extensive model programs for employee involvement. This chapter provides a very brief overview of the experience outside of North America.

The fact that cooperative programs exist throughout the world illustrates that, cultural characteristics provide the flavor of participation but not the motivation. Often much national chauvinism is attached to participative approaches. While it is true that cooperation and participation do need to be adapted to national and local characteristics, the desire to be involved and the common sense of seeking common ground knows no national or racial boundaries. There is a universal desire on the part of workers and their unions to be part of the process and a wide-ranging interest by employers to seek more effective management through joint efforts.

In international parlance, cooperation is often associated with the activities of production or consumer cooperatives. As such, some view "cooperation" as possible only when there is ownership and management by employees. Therefore, some would quibble with the term cooperation describing their joint labor-management activity. But if our definition of cooperation as pursuing at least one objective is applied, cooperating they are, though they may see themselves as having generally very different fundamental objectives.

UNION-MANAGEMENT COOPERATION IN JAPAN

The Japanese "economic miracle" has focused attention on the labor relations dimension of the Japanese economic game plan. The areas with the highest productivity and economic impact in Japan are the large export-related industries. In Japan, 90 percent of workers in these large companies are members of trade unions. The trade union movement has been an active part of the Japanese productivity drive in the postwar period.

Some of the mythology of the Japanese situation needs to be immediately and clearly laid to rest. While the union movement in Japan is organized on a company basis, most local unions are aligned into two major federations, SOHYO and DOMEI, as well as several smaller ones and some industrial groupings. As much as in most other countries, these federations and associations forcefully advocate for their membership. In some cases, such as the auto industry, there is a very close relationship, and in others, such as the public railway system, there are highly adversarial relationships. In a survey conducted by the Asian Productivity Organization of Japanese workers, 46.9 percent classified labor-management relations as confrontational or class antagonistic.[1] Japanese unions and workers are not docile puppets. Most American unions also negotiate contracts with individual employers and are very concerned about their companies. Except for building trades craftspersons and a few other trades, there is a strong attachment to a particular employer. The much greater mobility of workers in American industry than in Japan weakens overall enterprise affiliation of American workers. Since there is less turnover in unionized work operations, one could presume the attachment to the enterprise is probably closer to the Japanese among unionized workers in America than among nonunion employees. It is true that there is noticeably greater attachment to the employer in Japan, but this has little to do with the kind of unions in each country.

Second, Japanese society is not removed from conflict. There are many conflicts and tensions inside Japan, politically, economically, and socially. There are often prescribed means for resolving conflicts, but the notion of Japan as an island of harmony is erroneous. The Japanese success comes not from unique cultural characteristics. If that were the case, then there would be equally high productivity and harmony in manufacturing compared with service and government employment. This is far from the situation. Further, high quality and productivity have become characteristics of Japanese industry only in the last few decades. The improved performance in certain sectors and in recent times comes from improved managerial practices and supportive government policy.

Nor is the reason for Japanese success "happy workers." While many Japanese work hard and enjoy their work, many are dissatisfied. The Indianapolis/Tokyo Work Commitment Survey conducted in 1982 found that 81 percent of American workers expressed satisfaction with their jobs compared with 53 percent of Japanese workers.[2] The reasons for this finding are difficult to determine, but probably have to do with the lack of mobility and job options for Japanese workers.

The key to Japanese successes does not lie in pop sociology. Rather it has to do with the power of concerted action in certain sectors. In addition, the bonus system and the lifetime employment guarantees provide very concrete incentives for involvement and mutual gain. A Japanese worker can make 30 to 60 percent of his or her annual income through the bonus system—a great incentive to improve profitability and overall economic performance. Further, for the 40 to 60 percent of the national work force that are in large companies with lifetime employment and are full-time, permanent workers, this security also increases long-term commitment and minimizes fears about participation. Hence participation is built not on Eastern mysticism but on the pillars of union affiliation, job security, and gain sharing along with astute management practices.

There are several systems of participation in Japan. The success of the quality control circle (QCC) movement has been widely publicized and emulated in other countries. While union members do participate, in Japan the union is rarely actively involved in QCC establishment or administration. Some companies have experimented with sociotechnical redesign of work and other "small group activities." The union is consulted on these developments but does not take an active role. After World War II, joint management committees of equal membership were established in some companies. Joint approval was required on issues like capital expenditures, corporate borrowing, investment, plant opening and closure, hiring and firing, work hours, and appointment and compensation of directors and auditors. Many contracts included a clause that business and managerial decisions be referred to the joint management committee. The numbers of these kind of arrangements have declined significantly since the 1950s.

Less well publicized, though presently the most important for union-management cooperation, is the joint consultation system (*roshi kyogisei*) where the union and management meet to consult on the direction of the enterprise. Beginning in the mid-1950s, these spread under the sponsorship of the Japan Productivity Center. Robert Cole, one of the foremost authorities on Japanese cooperation, reports,

> The number of firms with formal joint consultation systems has continued to grow. The 1980 survey of 434 firms sampled in the private sector reports that 98.6 per cent of the firms had *company level* joint consultation systems (with little variance by firm size). Sixty four per cent had *plant level* joint consultation systems, ranging from 37 percent of those firms with under 300 employees to 94.3 per cent of those firms with 10,000 or more employees. Finally, 16.6% had *workshop level* joint consultation machinery, ranging from 7% of those with under 300 employees to 34% of those firms with 10,000 or more employees.[3]

According to H. Okamoto, the activities of the joint consultation system vary widely:

> The extent of trade union involvement in decisions through the joint consultative committee varies with the items under discussion. The rights involved in the process are normally specified by collective agreement. First, matters of working conditions involving the concrete application of basic agreements on wages, hours and ergonomic conditions, wage structures and fringe benefits terms, are subject to joint discussion or prior-to-decision negotiations. If a decision is reached, it becomes part of a formal agreement or *de facto* a binding promise. If agreement is not reached, the union can refer the matter to collective bargaining.[4]

In addition, policies and programs on safety and welfare are discussed and the union has a veto. Joint consultation is also used on personnel matters such as recruitment, selection, placement, transfer, education and training, and job analysis and job evaluation. According to Okamoto:

> Questions concerning manning rules, ergonomic conditions, mass lay-offs, periodic or large scale transfer, discipline and discharge come within the scope of joint decision or prior to decision negotiation. Fourth, matters concerning production, including production planning, scheduling of equipment and machinery, measurement of productivity and rules of the suggestion system, tend to fall into the category of joint understanding-oriented consultation in that management preserves the right to make decisions but again looks for suggestions and understanding from the union.[5]

The joint consultation system also informs the union on such business issues as long-range investment, financial updates, community relations, environmental concerns, and the overseas activities of the company.

In Japan, union-management cooperation is institutionalized very widely and undertakes important tasks. At the shop floor level, union members work closely with management through quality circles, JK groups, and other small group activities to improve organizational performance. At higher levels of the enterprise, the joint consultation and joint management provide mechanisms for common deliberation and action. At the regional level, recent years have seen the growth of joint consultation linked to regional issues. At the national level there is also consultation of all parties. For example, under the Ministry of International Trade and Industry (MITI), responsible for planning the Japanese industrial strategy, the trade unions are represented, provide their input, and help constitute the consensus of action. Japanese management and unions work hard and consistently at finding areas of common ground.

UNION-MANAGEMENT COOPERATION IN WEST GERMANY

Joint worker-management forums are commonplace in West Germany. The highest level of union-management cooperation is the system of codetermination (*mitbestimmung*). There are actually two forms of codetermination in Germany. One was developed in the coal, iron, and steel industries immediately following World War II. In those industries, capital and labor each select half of the directors of the enterprise and jointly agree on a neutral chairperson who only votes in the case of a tie. The system was put in place by Allied forces as a way to prevent the pro-Hitler ownership of those industries from returning to power.

In 1952, the Works Constitution Act was passed providing for one-third of the supervisory board seats to be worker representatives in companies with more than 500 employees. After a long battle, this was amended in 1976 so that the supervisory board of the enterprise has ten shareholder representatives, seven representatives of the work force, including at least one executive, one white-collar worker, and one blue-collar worker, and three trade union representatives. This applies to the 700 enterprises with more than 2,000 employees. Each side was dissatisfied with the results. The employers took the law to court, claiming it usurped property rights, and the unions complained bitterly that parity was undermined.

The codetermination laws have curious political dimensions. On one level, they are designed to curb corporate power and advance worker interests. Committed unionists rally for the expansion of power for workers, and employers caution against confusion of interests and restrictions on flexibility. In practice, the mechanisms serve to integrate the work force better and provide greater input to management decision making.

With their roots in the Weimar Republic, the works councils today are vital organs for joint decision and activity. Works councils are established by law in all enterprises with five or more permanent employees. According to the International Labour Office,

> the rights and obligations of works councils cover areas which are subdivided into social matters (e.g. operation of the enterprise, conduct of employees, hours of work, leave arrangements, prevention of accidents, welfare services, workers' housing, remuneration methods, job and bonus rights), the organization of jobs and the working environment, staff and personnel policy, vocational training, individual staff movements (recruitment, promotion, transfer, dismissal) and economic and financial matters. While with regard to social and staff questions and the organization of jobs, works councils have far-reaching co-determination rights (which means that in case of a disagreement between management and the works council, a neutral arbitration committee decides) on financial and economic matters their rights are essentially limited to information and consultation. Whatever the detailed legal provisions, which have

been filled in and interpreted by a host of court decisions, the over-all objective is close co-operation between works council and management.[6]

The employer must consult with this body regarding plans affecting investment, technology, work processes, and employment. In companies with more than 100 employees, a financial committee, under the jurisdiction of the works council, reviews financial data regarding the firm.

The works councils generally do well. However, representative democracy endemically cannot deal with the full range of constituent concerns, and shop floor workers often show a lack of knowledge of and satisfaction with their representatives. There is also a tendency for a new layer of bureaucracy. Some managers remain concerned about the additional steps required and the limitations on management authority. Some trade unionists are concerned about the overidentification with company interests instead of class identity.

A third system of joint concern in Germany is the "humanization of work" drive. Funded for a number of years by the federal government, the program catalyzed employers and unions to look at the nature of the work process and the technical requirements to ensure a better fit between the worker and the job. Much of the work focused on technical ergonomic concerns. Some looked at the work organization itself and examined new forms of shop floor and office level organization. One innovative part of the program was the funding on union staff of experts on the humanization of work to advise the national organization and local affiliates.

In Germany, worker participation is an extensive part of the fabric of industrial life. While intense debate occurs over in which direction to go in the future, there is little controversy over the application of joint structures.

UNION-MANAGEMENT COOPERATION IN SCANDINAVIA

The Scandinavian countries provide important models for cooperation and worker participation. In Sweden, Norway, and Denmark, a social-democratic philosophy sought the extension of political democracy to economic democracy. Yet over the years, joint approaches have become standard operating procedure, and the current situation looks to ways to extend the accomplishments. Labor is seeking still more economic democracy, and management has shown increasing interest in worksite reforms.

Board level representation is found throughout Scandinavia. In Sweden, under the Codetermination Act of 1972 and strengthened in 1976, workers through their trade unions are entitled to seats on the boards of directors of firms employing more than 100 employees. The union representatives are barred by law from participating in decisions that affect labor negotiations or disputes. In Norway, for most undertakings larger than 200 employees, the board of directors has one-third representation of employees. For smaller firms, worker representation is optional. A survey in 1975 reported that in enterprises between 50 and 200 employees, 54 percent had board level worker representation. "According to another survey carried out at the same time, more than half of the heads of Norwegian companies thought that the worker members of boards made a useful contribution to meetings, while 48 percent thought it neither positive or negative and only 1 percent thought it negative. Among the respondents, 78 percent thought that the workers' representatives had shown as much concern for the profitability of the undertaking as the other members of the board."[7]

The representatives are selected by the company assembly, which has one-third representation from the work force. The company assembly makes final decisions on investments. Denmark also has one-third worker representation on the boards of firms with more than 50 employees.

Works councils are very active in Norway and Denmark but were superseded by other mechanisms in Sweden after 1976. In Denmark, "collaboration committees" are required in all firms with more than 50 employees and recommended for smaller firms. These bodies review personnel policy, organization of work, safety, and general operational issues. In Norway, "cooperation councils" are applied in firms with more than 100 employees and may be merged with mandated working environment councils. The Norwegian councils must be consulted before any changes are made in production plans, methods, health and safety, vocational training, and personnel issues. Investment plans must also be reviewed. There are appeals boards to arbitrate disagreements between management and the committees in both countries. In order to make the committees as effective as possible, national centers provide technical assistance and support.

Work environment and job redesign represent other key areas of common interest. Efforts have been made in all three countries. Of particular note is the Volvo/Kalmar plant, where joint union-management efforts center on job redesign and the development of autonomous work teams. The president of Volvo, Pehr Gyllenhammar, said:

> At Kalmar, the objective is to organize automobile production in such a way that employees can find meaning and satisfaction in their work. This is a factory that, without any sacrifice of efficiency or financial results, will give employees the opportunity to work in groups, to communicate freely, to shift among work assignments, to vary their pace, to identify themselves with the product, to be conscious of responsibility for quality, and to influence their own work environment. When a product is manufactured by workers who find their work meaningful, it will inevitably be a product of high quality.[8]

Norway has been fertile ground for experimentation in new forms of work organization. The Work Research Institute has made important contributions to the theory and practice of participation, especially in the maritime area.

In discussing cooperative job redesign projects in Norway, Tor Aspengren, president of the Norwegian Federation of Trade Unions, has said:

> Through the experiments which have been made under the auspices of the Co-operation Project recognition has been achieved for the fact that there exist positive alternatives to the traditional principles of management and the traditional forms of enterprise organization and work administration. It would hardly be possible to develop a standard model which would suit every situation, as the conditions of our working life are too different and multi-farious. But with positive will to look for new and better principles of work organization, there will be few places where the work situation cannot be improved ... From the trade union movement we have often directed hard and justified criticism against the traditional forms of enterprise organization. We therefore also see it as a part of our responsibility to take part in the co-operation necessary to develop a new and better enterprise organization.[9]

In Norway, the develoment of joint approaches to technological change is notable. Beginning in 1975, union officials were designated at the worksite level as "data" or "technology stewards" who are involved in technological change at every step of the process. They provide a clear avenue for union involvement and codecision on technological change issues and a means for ensuring that work force and ergonomic effects are seriously considered.

The Scandinavian design for worker participation takes the widest imaginable approach. In each category, they provide examples of innovation and accomplishment. Worksite redesign and work life concerns have been extensively analyzed and approached. At the enterprise level, representative bodies are used to generate a dialogue on how organizations should be managed. Economic democracy and employee ownership have been a widespread fact through extensive cooperatively owned enterprises and part of intense national debate in the private sector. At the core of the Scandinavian systems are motivations for a humane society that take into account the needs of workers and the society at large.

UNION-MANAGEMENT COOPERATION IN OTHER ADVANCED INDUSTRIAL COUNTRIES

Mechanisms for joint involvement are found in many parts of the industrial world. In Europe, works councils are in place in France, Belgium, Holland, Luxembourg, Austria, and Italy. The French "comites d'enterprise" have been weak bodies for discussion, though the Mitterand government has considered ways to meet its goals of decentralization and modernizing industry through strengthening joint initiatives. In Switzerland, worker representatives actively participate on workers committees or personnel committees. Austria is characterized by cooperative activity at all levels from national economic policy to the shop floor. This collaboration has been credited with long-term stable economic growth and a high standard of living. Australia and New Zealand have seen increasing experimentation with quality of working life and joint consultative bodies. Promotion of industrial democracy is the national policy in Australia. The New Zealand Industrial Relations Act of 1973 set up the mechanisms for voluntary works councils.

A wide variety of experiments in quality of work life have been conducted throughout the industrialized world. Many of these have been coordinated through regional centers, such as the European Institute for the Improvement of Living and Working Conditions centered in Dublin, and national programs in France, the United Kingdom, Australia, and Holland. The Tavistock Institute in London is an independent center for the development of new approaches to work.

UNION-MANAGEMENT COOPERATION IN THE THIRD WORLD

Union-management cooperation is not limited to advanced industrial countries; nor is it confined to countries with certain education levels, GDP growth, or industrial structures. Given the difficulty of the task, cooperation is important in the Third World. Most such countries are capital-poor and overflowing with people. Strategies that build cooperation and joint effort among the population are very sensible. However, in many cases, the union movement is too weak to be of real influence or assistance. Too often, corruption and bureaucracy undermine effectiveness. Yet a review of legislation in many countries in Africa, Asia, and the Americas shows that cooperative mechanisms are often established as a means for development, peaceful industrial relations, and improved organizational performance. Still, the reality is usually far from the promise and the machinery works poorly, if at all.[10]

UNION-MANAGEMENT COOPERATION IN INDIA

India is one of the most interesting laboratories of union-management issues. Experiments in union-management cooperation go back many years. Works councils were started in the mid-1920s and early 1930s in India under British colonial labor laws. The Gandhian trade union tradition promotes assertive trade unionism and industrial change through nonviolence, dialogue, and participation. In 1947, the Industrial Disputes Act required employers of more than 100 employees to set up a works committee with equal representation. Their charge was "to promote measures for securing and preserving unity and good relationship between the employers and the workmen." In 1955, one of the keystone experiments in sociotechnical theory was conducted by A. K. Rice in the Ahmedabad textile factories. In 1956, there was a push for Joint Management Councils. The Industrial Policy Resolution declared, "In a socialist democracy, labor is a partner in the common task of development and should participate in it with enthusiasm. There should be joint consultation and workers and technicians should wherever possible, be associated progressively in management."[11] In 1977, at the initiative of Prime Minister Indira Gandhi the Indian constitution was amended to include: "The State shall take steps, by suitable legislation or in any other way to secure the participation of workers in the management of undertakings, establishments or other organizations engaged in any industry."

Indian unions are generally very supportive of partipative management, yet are sharply divided on the method for selecting representation. The president of the Indian National Trade Union Congress, the largest federation, wrote:

> The main thrust behind the principle of labour participation in management would be to give everyone in the organization and undertaking a sense of unfettered involvement in it, and a means to identify himself with the work.... Participative process has several dimensions. It can be at the corporate levels, or it may be in the form, of a consultative process and finally as a system of determining co-targets of production at the shop-floor level. The beginning phase of participative process in a democratic set-up is really a consultative process. It must promote and evolve on a lasting basis with tangible benefits to the workers and society at large. Such participation will alone bring about democratization of the process of management and ensure appropriate motivation for raising the levels of productivity and improving the performance of the enterprise.... It is time that we make a bold move in giving concrete image to the objective of participative management to usher in a new culture of community cooperative interests rather than the age old conflict between labour and management.[12]

The Tata Iron and Steel Company (TISCO) is the best example of participative management in Indian industry. Since the founding of the enterprise in 1903, TISCO has exhibited progressive industrial and community relations. In 1912, it began providing information to workers on management activities; in 1944, joint involvement in grievance handling was initiated; and in 1956, a joint union-management participative machinery started with interlocking levels of joint governance. Joint Departmental Councils are at the bottom, Joint Works Councils at the middle level, and at the top is the Joint Consultative Council of Management. At the major operational levels are also joint town and medical councils that address health, education, and town management. Between 1957 and 1972, more than 14,000 suggestions were processed with a more than 70 percent acceptance rate. Almost half of the suggestions were operationally oriented and 17 percent centered on safety matters. The company says:

The idea that workers are appendages to machines or mere "hands" engaged in production has become outmoded. It is now recognized that they are human beings seeking fulfillment in the three dimensional world of feeling, thinking and acting. The principle has come to be accepted that both management and employees should have the opportunity to influence and contribute to the thinking and functioning of industry. This spirit of cooperation and of working together in the fulfillment of a common purpose is necessary to ensure harmonious industrial relations—as distinct from mere peaceful industrial relations—and a healthy growth of industry.[13]

There are many examples of worker participation and union-management cooperation in India. Some have been successful, some have failed, and many hang in limbo. Examples of successful programs include activities in a post office, an electrical power plant, a forge plant, an income tax department, and other locations. All resulted in increased productivity, better work organization, and income. In developing countries like India, the hardest part is getting the initial agreement from management and the union to proceed. After that, maintaining the new social technology can be as problematic as maintenance of mechanical technology in developing countries. The problem in India is not that union-management cooperation has been unable to solve important problems; rather it is the magnitude of problems and workplaces that need to be addressed.

UNION-MANAGEMENT COOPERATION IN ISRAEL

In extremely important ways, the Israeli economy, society, and industrial structure are based on union involvement. The Israeli labor federation, the Histadrut, owns a huge chunk of the economy. More than 19 percent of the industrial domestic product and 23 percent of the employment is in Histadrut-owned firms. Solel Boneh, a cooperatively owned construction firm, builds more than 25 percent of the construction in Israel. The entire passenger transportation system is part of the labor-managed economy, as are the second largest bank, Bank Hapoalim (Bank of the Workers), and the major health care delivery system. Trade unionists sit on the boards of directors of labor-owned firms and also on those of privately held firms whose employees are members of the union. The labor movement has a department of productivity and industrial democracy that provides training to trade unionists. Begun in the 1940s, even before Israel became a state, there are now more than 650 Joint Productivity Councils covering more than 300,000 workers largely focused on incentive systems. These councils have been credited by the Histadrut with a real increase in productivity of more than 50 percent since their introduction. Beginning in 1956, plant councils and joint management boards were formed in Histadrut industries to promote wider input into decisions.[14]

The kibbutz is a well-known form of Israeli cooperation. Ownership and decision making are shared by all members of the kibbutz. While a small percentage of the Israeli population lives on kibbutzim, their influence is felt throughout the economy in agriculture, tourism, and manufacturing. Most of the kibbutzim are affiliated with Histadrut. In recent years, there have been very interesting experiments in work redesign carried on in the kibbutz industries to improve performance and satisfaction and to mesh better the technical nature of jobs with the general values of the kibbutz cooperative.

The pressures on the economy caused by international tensions make cooperation essential but difficult to realize in the face of incredible inflation. Without the cooperative mechanisms, however, the economy would probably disintegrate. Israel provides a model for union involvement in the development process and concern for overall economic performance. Representatives from many developing countries come to Tel Aviv to study at the International Institute for Development, Cooperation and Labor Studies.

OVERVIEW OF EXPERIENCE IN OTHER PARTS OF THE WORLD

In Yugoslavia, the workers in a company own its shares, vote on management and the board of directors, and take part in improving the operations of the organization. This system also applies to public sector organizations.

> The "supreme authority" in each enterprise is the entire workforce, which votes by referendum on crucial issues such as merging with other firms, relocating plants and distributing the income. From month-to-month, according to the self-management laws, the workers formulate policies including the price of products, production and financial plans and workplace policies through their elected worker's councils.[15]

The workers councils select the management of the firm. The trade unions negotiate collective agreements with the firm and facilitate the self-management process through education and encouragement of constructive involvement of workers.

In the Basque country of Spain, the Mondragon cooperatives have shown that common ownership and good business sense can go hand in hand. Funded out of their cooperatively owned bank, Caja Laboral Popular with more than 200,000 members, new enterprises are researched to determine economic viability. The cooperative entrepreneurs are provided extensive training and capital support. All employees become part owners of the business. There are more than 80 cooperatives with 17,000 employees. They include the largest producers of refrigerators in Spain, machine tools, and other durable and consumer goods. Trade unions are a strong part of the setup, though mainly as a link to broader political concerns.

In Tanzania, for more than 15 years a self-management approach, *ujjama*, has been used to help build the country. Worker committees are established in every business with more than a few union employees. The union federation, NUTA, is tightly linked to the government. The councils in the workplaces are charged with the responsibility to look into and advise on wage policy, marketing, planning, productivity, worker education, budget, and quality and quantity of production. In addition, on the board of directors 40 percent are worker and management representatives and 60 percent from the community. The International Labor Office sponsored quality of working life experiments in Tanzania and half of the sites developed successful programs that increased performance, income, attendance, and working conditions.

Starting in 1966, in Venezuela, worker representatives nominated by the trade unions were placed on the boards of directors of public enterprises and economic development bodies. Under Allende, Chile created vast structures for worker participation but they were abandoned by the military regime. Peru has experimented with cooperative enterprises with mixed results.

In Eastern bloc countries, the issues of worker participation have been deliberated as well. In most cases, they are linked to the trade union organization. Since there is no free independent trade unionism in Communist countries, the cooperation between the two partners is somewhat suspect. However, forums such as the standing production conferences in the Soviet Union, economic committees in Bulgaria, and participation meetings in Hungary do provide some input. In Czechoslovakia, the trade union committee is given the powers of codecision in certain management decisions. In Poland, workers councils were formed in 1956 after worker unrest. However, their lack of effectiveness in fostering effective participation was revealed during the worker uprisings of 1980.

Many examples could be cited from Sri Lanka to Nepal, Algeria, and Zambia. China and Singapore could be highlighted. Our aim here is solely to describe the range of approaches, not to provide a complete catalog. Not all of these approaches work out, but efforts are being made. A global recognition of the necessity and possibility of cooperation has yet to be matched by effectiveness in application. As discussed earlier, when macroeconomic conditions are very bad, cooperation can aid in solving but not eliminate the basic economic malaise.

There is a revealing spread of viewpoints based on economic/political ideology. Under capitalism, some managers and unions seek to maximize profitability through joint action to ensure greater mutual prosperity. Others reject any collaboration with the other party as giving up their rights of self-determination. In democratic socialist economies, worker and union participation is put forward by some as a basic human right and a means for common improvement, while others reject cooperation on the grounds that it is too oriented toward a particular industry's performance and not sufficiently focused on broader industrial or class interests. In developing and nonaligned countries with interest in cooperative development, worker participation is viewed as an alternative to reliance on capitalist or Communist development and a way to enlist the energies of the population. Others reject it in favor of large-scale macroeconomic reform and infrastructure development and may fear creating alternative power centers in key industries. In the Communist world, worker participation is viewed in some quarters as irrelevant in the "proletarian" state and by others as a major way to organize production.

The range of application and rejection stretches across political ideology. Either this says that worker participation has no ideology or the range of issues it addresses is broader than the categories commonly provided. The Solidarity movement in Poland was fundamentally about this issue of worker participation and illustrates the paradox. Solidarinocz, the Polish independent union, had as a central demand worker self-management. The insurgence in Poland had little to do with antisocialism but tapped a widespread disaffection with the process and outcomes of the Polish workers' experience. Similarly, when the workers in Lordstown had their wildcat strike, it was not as some would paint it a revolt against capitalism. Workplaces in the East and West are remarkably, and unfortunately, similar in terms of work organization, top-down control, and technology. The demand for better quality of work life and more worker participation is a global response to the problems of work organization.

The diversity of activity at the international level provides important insights for any development. It confirms that there are many ways to structure effective participation and cooperation. It shows that culture can be used to help enhance the cooperative enterprise. It illustrates that government can play a positive catalytic role in encouraging cooperation. It demonstrates that the fundamental issues cross political boundaries and attack the central questions of how modern organizations should be structured in any society and how workers and their unions can be seriously involved.

ADDITIONAL RESOURCES

American Center for the Quality of Work Life. *Industrial Democracy in Europe: A 1977 Survey.* Washington, D.C., 1978.

Asian Productivity Organization. *Labor-Management Consultation Mechanism: Survey and Symposium Report.* 2 vol. Tokyo, 1984.

Friedrich-Ebert-Siftung. *Industrial Democracy in Asia.* Bangkok, Thailand, 1980.

International Labour Office. *Workers Participation in Decisions Within Undertakings.* Geneva, 1981.

Roberts, Benjamin C. *Towards Industrial Democracy: Europe, Japan and the United States.* Montclair, N.J.: Allanheld, Osmun, 1979.

Stokes, Bruce. *Worker Participation: Productivity and Quality of Working Life.* Worldwatch Paper no. 25. Washington, D.C., December 1978.

Windmuller, John P., ed. "Industrial Democracy in International Perspective." *The Annals* 431 (May 1977).

II

Guide to Approaches for Union-Management Cooperation

7

Reorienting the Roots:
Collective Bargaining and Grievance
Procedures as Problem-Solving Tools

PERSPECTIVES ON COLLECTIVE BARGAINING

Collective bargaining is the primary mechanism in North America whereby union-management cooperation is sanctioned and quality of work life is improved. The central fact about bargaining is that both parties reach an agreement they can live with. The contract sets out mutual obligations and understandings. It often provides the language that sets into motion the other more elaborate forms of union-management cooperation discussed in this section. While the cooperation can range from truculent to reluctant, from cautious to extensive, this mutual agreement provides the common ground of the relationship. Since wages, hours, and working conditions help determine the quality of one's working life, all collective bargaining agreements are QWL documents.[1] The particulars may vary, but the objectives of the contract to improve the lot of the worker and to help order human resources management are constant. Despite those common features, collective bargaining approaches can run the gamut from harshly adversarial to strategic joint problem solving.

There is an alternative to the dominant win-lose collective bargaining negotiations. A sensible analysis shows that consistent and long-term adversarial bargaining is self-defeating. If management consistently "wins" in negotiation by limiting wage and benefit levels, it will make it more difficult to attract and retain employees who will do better at other locations. The federal sector has recently been an example of this shortsighted thinking by capping the pay of federal employees or holding it well below inflation. Many capable employees left public service to find more rewarding positions in the private sector. Further, if employees feel that they have been had, then they react with poor service, low productivity, and inferior quality. Short-term, contract-to-contract labor relations is as effective a management strategy as dividend-to-dividend financial planning. It can show splashy immediate results but may erode the long-term viability and growth potential of the employer.

For labor, the spoils of victory can also be short-lived. Winning compensation package gains that far outstrip those in the industry can lead to competitive disadvantages, thereby inhibiting long-term income and spurring job loss. Work rule agreements that reduce flexibility and productivity can provide short-term protection and long-term problems in adjusting to change and competitive posture. The alternative for both parties is seeking win-win solutions that increase value while addressing distributional issues.

Realistically, most collective bargaining won't follow the prescriptions outlined in this chapter. Most bargaining is distributional—in other words, how the pie will be divided. Compensation, investment, and returns to shareholders all make legitimate claims. The balance among them needs to be addressed and the solutions are often difficult. This chapter does not discuss traditional distributional bargaining over wages and hours. Nor is arbitration or mediation covered, which are generally viewed as the total range of industrial peacemaking tools. Many texts address the preparation for and conduct of traditional adversarial collective bargaining, dispute resolution, and contract administration. We are not going to discuss intimidation, feints, trade-offs, good guy–bad guys ploys, histrionics, and other games people play in negotiations. In many cases, they are the necessary and appropriate strategies to use. Usually, the traditional approach can be better implemented using more professional techniques. We, instead, prefer to center on more creative ways to improve the basic bargaining relationship and to adopt negotiating strategies that are anticipatory and problem solving. Our concern here is not better technique in bargaining but a new perspective on the bargaining process.

The place to begin the search for cooperative possibilities is the collective bargaining relationship. This section starts by looking at negotiations, contract administration, and hiring and separations as the basics of any relationship. Chapter 8 identifies many specific ways that labor-management committees can be used. Chapter 9 takes a fresh look at organization structures, and Chapter 10 considers very broad-ranging and advanced forms of cooperation aimed at growth. Unions and management can consider any one or combination of these alternative approaches to cooperation. The possibilities for cooperation are shown in Table 7-1 by level in the organization.

IS UNION-MANAGEMENT COOPERATION A PROCESS OR A PROGRAM?

Before outlining alternatives, we want to address head-on the most common question of whether cooperation needs to be expressed in programmatic initiatives.

TABLE 7-1
Union-Management Cooperative Approaches by Level

Top-Level Cooperative Strategies

Strategic collective bargaining
Integrative collective bargaining
Labor-management committees
Parallel structures
Union-management task forces
Sociotechnical redesign
QWL programs
Joint marketing efforts
New product development
Board level labor representation
Joint investment decision making
Profit sharing
Employee stock ownership

Middle-Level Cooperative Strategies

Problem-solving grievance handling
Joint new hire and orientation sessions
Joint preretirement and layoff sessions
Labor-management committees
Employee assistance programs
Union-management task forces
Sociotechnical redesign
QWL programs
Customer service programs
Joint marketing efforts
Joint new facilities planning
Productivity gain-sharing programs

Shop Floor or Office Level Cooperative Strategies

Quality circles
Joint job redesign
Flextime
Autonomous work groups
Participatory customer service programs
Pay for performance
Pay for knowledge

When it comes time to translate union-management cooperation from theory into practice, many difficult choices are presented. To some, union-management cooperation is a state of mind where the principals in the relationship have trust and respect for each other, characterized by an ability to talk to each other. Some fear to concretize that relationship into a specific set of activities, worrying that it will ruin the magic of the relationship. Others stay away from establishing programs, saying that programs have a beginning and an end and theirs has no endpoint. Some proponents of cooperation have shied away from formal programs and measuring results since it is the "process" that is important to them.

Frankly, we couldn't disagree more. Certainly, we value good interpersonal relationships and general feelings of goodwill between management and the union. But those parties who stop at an attitudinal interpretation of cooperation are at best squandering the possibilities to turn their common commitment into specific outcomes that will be of mutual gain. At worst, they are papering over differences that will ultimately erode the facade of cooperation over time. We suggest that union-management cooperation has to take concrete form in terms of activities and programs, not because we advocate any particular approach but because action is the arena for cooperation, not passive acceptance. David Nadler and Edward Lawler, in reviewing the broad conception of joint QWL activities, concur when they note: "It is not enough to say that we are now going to manage in a QWL manner. There must be tangible, specific, and observable actions aimed at changing the way work is done."[2] They assert that "probably the most critical factor determining the success, viability and long term impact of QWL efforts is the structure of the participative processes that are created."[3] Union-management cooperation is best served when well conceived and well managed.

HOW TO MOVE FROM A CONFLICTUAL TO A COOPERATIVE FRAMEWORK

Some union-management relationships are generally characterized as conflictual. In this case, some of the methods in this section may be helpful. Very good work has been done on how to move the relationship from warfare to being open to joint cooperative activities. The Relations by Objectives (RBO) program of the Federal Mediation and Conciliation Service provides a direct model of how to use the collective bargaining relationship as a springboard to joint labor-management committees and other cooperative activities.

Developed in 1975 and first used with the Georgia Pacific Corporation and the United Paperworkers International Union, the FMCS has initiated more than 100 Relations by Objectives (RBO) programs to help overcome union-management difficulties arising out of very difficult negotiations or after bitter strikes. These have also been implemented in Canada with great success. It is one tool available to preventive mediation to help avoid continuing problems in the collective bargaining relationship. According to the FMCS, RBO

> is utilized in those situations where the labor-management relationship has deteriorated to an unacceptable level and the leadership at the top becomes committed to rescuing it. It is basically a conflict resolution process in which the RBO group, generally comprised of representatives of all levels of management and the union, is guided through their own intensive analysis of their present hostile relationship, the setting of mutually acceptable objectives to improve that relationship, and the planning of action steps and a timetable to meet those objectives. [Internal memo]

The RBO process has seven steps, initiated in a three- to four-day intensive session of 12 to 14 hours per day with 20 to 40 people. The first step is each group analyzing separately the relationship with an emphasis on what participants believe the union and management each should do to improve the relationship. In fact, most of the discussion centers on operational issues at the organization. The second step is a joint meeting where these lists are shared, clarified, and discussed. The parties are often surprised by the degree of overlap. This leads into the third step, which is to agree on a single list of goals for improvement at their location. The group breaks down into smaller union-management teams to discuss action steps on the goals identified. They then report back to their union and management groups about what they discussed and the proposals they wish to put forward. The final step is to come together to review the action steps and agree on a course of action. The joint initiative that emerges from this process is maintained in an ongoing way based on an action plan and a joint committee resulting from the session. Sometimes the mediator assists with follow-up and may chair the joint committee.

The strength of the RBO approach is not only its recognition of the industrial relations issues but also its focus on developing concrete alternatives. Management and union negotiators feel comfortable working with mediators who are well versed on the collective bargaining relationship. The FMCS has been very pleased with the success of the RBO program and points to both improvements in the labor-management relationship as well as the operations of the companies involved. John Popular, who developed the initial program for FMCS, points to the impressive results that have emerged from this process in terms of better communication between the union and management, reduced grievances, and strong operational improvements. He says: "As a catalyst for improving attitudes at all levels, RBO is the starting point for long-range cooperative efforts to enhance employee participation and improve productivity and quality."[4]

For more intense conflict, a more psychologically oriented process might be followed. Readers are cautioned that this should be undertaken only with highly competent facilitation. The National Training Laboratories pioneered intergroup laboratories on conflict resolution. Based on this experience, Robert Blake and Jane Mouton tested a conflict resolution model that addresses the differences between labor and management and helps set the tone for cooperation. The basis for their approach is

> rooted in behavioral science theory about intergroup relations. It seeks to treat symptoms of intergroup pathology in a way that is analogous to the medical treatment of illness. The orientation is based on recognizing union and management disputes as symptoms of pathology in the problemsolving area, diagnosing the causes that produce the symptoms and treating the causes directly, rather than dealing with symptoms only.[5]

This conceptual approach is the basis for the union-management intergroup laboratory that seeks to expose root problems in the relationship.

The basis for such a laboratory is an acknowledgment that

> the union-management situation, in particular, is very prone to becoming an intensely hostile, win-lose relationship; although its general purpose should be a problemsolving one. During these next two days, what we [the management, union and consultants] wish to explore are problems that are blocking the relationship—to identify them, and if possible to plan constructive steps for their elimination.[6]

The focus is on understanding the character and nature of the relationship, not resolving concrete issues. Blake and Mouton prescribe an approach that moves the participants through development of self-images and images of the other party, sharing and discussing these perceptions and their implications, diagnosing their present relationship, consolidating understanding on key issues and points of friction, and winding up with plans for the next steps in the resolution of the problem areas identified.

This kind of intense analysis and application of intergroup conflict management may be necessary for deeply rooted and intensely personal conflict between the union and management. Almost 20 years later, Blake and Mouton came up with a version that is in many ways a synthesis of the two approaches described above.[7] In a four-day session, the parties accordion back and forth between separate and joint sessions. They start with describing the characteristics of a sound relationship, then describe their actual relationship, examine the gap between the two, and develop specific plans about how to move more toward the ideal relationship. At each stage, the parties formulate their thoughts in separate sessions, present them to the whole group for clarification and discussion, and where appropriate, develop joint statements.

JOINT STRATEGIC APPROACHES TO COLLECTIVE BARGAINING

There are basically two approaches to cooperative bargaining: strategic and problem solving. The strategic approach looks to the future as the relevant period when the agreement will be applied, and the problem-solving approach looks to resolve the difficulties that have occurred in the past. The broadest framework is the strategic possibility. It creates a community of interest so vital to healthy cooperative relationships. Its advantage over the problem-solving approach is its more positive emphasis and ability to formulate more comprehensive and anticipatory agreements as opposed to the more traditional form of collective bargaining, which is incremental and reactive to particular demands placed on the table. However, problem-solving approaches allow the parties to choose a manageable number of commonly perceived difficulties to work on with each other or to back into broader problem areas more delicately.

To enter this type of bargaining, the parties have to make a long-term commitment to each other. They become, in fact, partners in production. It is representative of Harbison and Coleman's highest form of relationship, union-management cooperation. By doing so the parties accept two fundamental overall strategic objectives: (1) the long-term success of the employer either as a business or as a government agency and (2) the permanent presence of the union as an agent for the employees to maintain employment and improve working conditions. A strategic approach to collective bargaining may be a complement to other strategic decision making by management and the union or may be a catalyst for that kind of decision making overall. This approach would seem to have great potential in the public sector where civil servants make a long-term commitment to public service in their agencies but usually cannot directly bargain wages, benefits, and hours. Too often rather than opening up the space for exploring common commitment, public sector bargaining gets mired in the pettiest of issues.

The first step in joint approaches to strategic analysis does not start with the establishment of specific goals. It starts with a joint scan of the environment. Environmental analysis of future political, economic, and social trends is very important. The union and management should also review projections of market (including the competition), product cycles, financial resources, natural and other input resources, technology, and human resources. This may mean constructing a series of probable scenarios. Next a hard look is taken at the current positions of management and the union to examine opportunities and the need for change. This means applying an old idea in industrial relations of joint study teams preparatory to the actual bargaining sessions.

The union and management need to generate a list of joint strategic objectives. These might include quality of product and service, wage and benefit stability, employment security, wise use of new technology, market and product diversification and expansion, and other, similar areas that may be of common interest. At this stage, the effort is to consider an overall definition of their common enterprise based on the previous analysis. These need to be further specified into concrete objectives and functional strategies for the operations of the work organization, the nature of the collective bargaining relationship, and the development of employees. Many of these will not be realizable within the term of one labor agreement. But at some point an agreement that moves in the direction of the strategic common concerns needs to be reached. The criteria for evaluation of collective bargaining proposals become primarily their relationship to long-term strategic objectives and not short-term satisfaction of present demands. The partners need to develop a concrete plan for how to implement their objectives and engage in ongoing monitoring to check that the plans are being followed, if the objectives are being met, and if the objectives require rethinking.

Clearly, this kind of bargaining is not possible in most settings where the major problem is getting beyond animosities in the relationship that block simple understanding. However, it may be a way to leapfrog over a focus on the negativeness of the relationship to frame the issues in broader, more positive terms. The literature on strategic planning does not address this form of strategic management and needs to be reoriented to the joint union-management approach.

INTEGRATIVE COLLECTIVE BARGAINING

In 1965, Richard Walton and Robert McKersie outlined a model of collective bargaining that analyzed not the topics of the bargaining setting but its process. These divided roughly into two basic kinds of bargaining. The first is most familiar: "The joint decision process for resolving conflicts of interest is distributive bargaining. The term itself refers to the activity of dividing limited resources. It occurs in situations in which one party wins what the other party loses."[8] It is distributional bargaining where a fixed sum needs to be divided up in such matters as wages, benefits, profits, and hours.

But all collective bargaining is not win-lose. Each labor-management negotiation also consists of a considerable amount of integrative bargaining. Integrative bargaining is of two types: "In the first, one (or more) possible resolution(s) of the agenda item by itself offers both parties a gain in absolute terms over their respective positions in the status quo; for such a resolution neither party experiences any loss."[9] The second is when the parties are trying to find the "maximum mutual utility function"—the best possible alternative even though it might be the least worst or not have a similar value to both sides. When bargaining issues are posed as problems, then there is integrative potential for their solution. When issues need to be adjudicated the best that can be done is to arrive at a compromise. Concerns such as absenteeism, job security, management flexibility, job classifications, productivity, safety, job satisfaction, benefit cost containment, overtime, and other issues can be battlegrounds when posed as distributive dilemmas and opportunities for joint resolution when an integrative framework is employed.

There are three steps to the integrative bargaining problem-solving model:

"Step 1 involves a maximum exchange of information about the problems perceived by each party in order that these problems be clearly identified and defined in their essentials."[10] Initially, the parties need to identify a topic as having integrative potential. In the process of learning about and discussing the issue, the problem will be more clearly clarified or may even be redefined by the parties. Specificity is much better than expounding on general principles. This represents the problem identification and data collection phase.

The second step "assumes alternative courses of action (potential solutions) are not immediately apparent but rather have to be discovered or invented. It also assumes that the full consequences of a course of action are again not obvious; instead they have to be inferred from an analysis of all the facts available."[11] The parties generate the maximum number and range of alternative solutions to the problem. The third step involves assessing the various alternatives to see which best serves the interests of both parties. Some options may be better for certain parties than others. The most comfortable balance of benefits has to be found in order to be able to move ahead with that alternative.

In order to engage in integrative bargaining, the parties must be willing to explore openly for alternatives to commonly agreed-upon problems. It is best if those involved in the process have access to information that could help the understanding of the problems and assessment of alternative solutions. Based on an empirical study, Lane Tracy and Richard Peterson identified the key elements for successful integrative bargaining:

> Problem solving is more likely to succeed when both sides explore subjects informally and non-committally during the regular bargaining session and when both take a farsighted view. From the union point of view problem solving is also aided by both sides discussing their feelings about a problem and the cause of it, as well as by management's ability to state issues clearly and specifically. Management negotiators further relate success in problem solving to exploration of subjects outside of the regular bargaining sessions and to an absence of criticism from the union negotiators.[12]

For example, statements made while brainstorming in integrative bargaining cannot be used as weapons as part of distributive bargaining, and the freedom to test alternatives without negative consequences is important. Walton and McKersie are clear that while a minimum level of trust and openness is needed, there does not have to be a totally harmonious setting for integrative bargaining to work well.

During the 1950s, in the steel industry, an interesting application of integrative bargaining sprung up in joint study teams that met prior to negotiations to examine particular issues of common concern. The Human Relations Commission in the steel industry provided a model for joint study efforts. The ground rules going into the sessions were "freedom to advance an idea without committing one's self to accept it in the last analysis, ability to change position frequently, and freedom to make a proposal without consulting the parent organization.''[13] Other joint study teams were set up on such issues as training, subcontracting, wage incentives, medical care, and sabbatical leaves.

Usually bargaining contains a mix of distributional and integrative functions. Knowing when to be in which mode is not always easy since the styles are very different and often contradictory. One can start by roping off some areas of mutal concern for testing the integrative model. These can gradually expand to find more areas of common concern. One can engage in hard distributive bargaining and still use clear integrative bargaining approaches. There may even be times when integrative solutions can be surfaced while trying to sort out intractable distributive issues.

FRAMING THE BARGAINING SETTING AS A MUTUAL WIN UNDERTAKING

Fundamentally, the collective bargaining setting is a problem-solving exercise. Each party comes to the table with a set of problems it wants to resolve. On management's side these could be overall compensation costs, flexibility in operation, absenteeism, and a host of other issues. The union brings to the table how to keep up with rising living costs, job security, career mobility, fair treatment in the workplace, and a series of other concerns. In traditional bargaining, these get placed on the table in terms of proposals and counterproposals. A fair compromise is attempted, but both parties are seeking to distribute the benefits closer to their bottom lines.

Integrative bargaining as described in the previous section is a way to engage in problem solving where the focus is on the problem at hand, not the specific proposals. A good example of this is found in the 1982 bargaining between Ford and the UAW. Ernest Savoie, director of the Ford Labor Relations Planning and Employment Office, reports:

> When the negotiators came to the 1982 table, they came in a problem resolution mode and they came with a demonstrated, highly visible set of successful local experiences [Employee Involvement Programs]. The value of this was more and more evident as the negotiations progressed. There was full, upfront problem exploration without the posturing that is sometimes a part of more traditional bargaining.[14]

The agreement resulted in an integrated web of approaches, including improved employee involvement language, "Mutual Growth Forums," an extensive joint employee development and training program, pilot projects for lifetime job security, profit sharing, and assistance to displaced workers.

The precise manner to conduct win-win negotiations is concisely and clearly outlined by Roger Fisher and William Ury from the Harvard Negotiation Project.[15]

They identify four basic principles for general negotiations that seem equally applicable to the union-management setting. These are described briefly below.

1. *"Separate the people from the problem."* In collective bargaining negotiations, the bargainers are agents for interests beyond themselves. The manager has an obligation to maintain the most flexibility for management and to cap the cost of an agreement. The union committee has an obligation to its membership to obtain the best possible deal in terms of overall compensation, job security, and working conditions. When either bargainer personalizes the positions, agreement is much harder to reach. The issues become personal honor and not problem resolution. On the other hand, bargainers are people first and deserve to be treated with dignity and respect. In collective bargaining, the two parties need to deal with each other beyond the negotiation of the agreement. It is therefore important to pay attention to maintaining a long-term, positive union-management relationship by separating the specific issues of disagreement from personal antagonism.

Fisher and Ury identify certain key behaviors that help best manage the relationship between the parties in negotiations. These include imagining yourself in the other's shoe, not blaming the other side for your problems, discussing each other's perceptions, and phrasing your proposals consistently with your counterpart's values. By both parties participating actively in the exploratory process, greater commitment to arriving at workable solutions can be developed. The parties should also exercise good communication skills. The key to a mature and problem-solving union-management relationship is to recognize that at times the other side needs to let off steam and actions are not always consistent. There are going to be times when the relationship will be frustrating, caused by mood swings or being boxed in by the situation. Sometimes commitments will not be followed by everyone on the other team. The parties need to roll with the punches and keep focused on solving the problems at hand and maintaining ongoing understanding.

2. *"Focus on interests, not positions."* Each side comes to the bargaining table with legitimate interests. In most cases, there are multiple interests and all will not have an equal weighting. Some may be in common and some may not. Almost never is there total opposition of interests. The parties should openly acknowledge the interests of the other side. The best place to start is to identify common areas of interest. In some other situations, the interests may be very different but complementary, such as increased productivity and increased wages. This builds the framework for agreement.

Negotiators should be sensitive to the reality of the other party's interests. In essence, this is self-interest, because unless the other side's interests can be addressed there can be no agreement to proceed with meeting one's own interests. This is particularly true in the union-management relationship where the parties are so reciprocally dependent. While past practice and a history of conflict and disappointment can create concerns in the bargaining relationship, the major emphasis should be on the future and what can be done; the past is a record that cannot be altered. There are learnings from the past, but getting stuck there does no one any good.

3. *"Invent options for mutual gain."* Fisher and Ury identify four areas that inhibit generation of other options: "(1) premature judgment; (2) searching for the single answer; (3) the assumption of a fixed pie; and (4) thinking that 'solving their problem is their problem.'"[16] The parties need to apply creativity when looking at difficult problems to arrive at a variety of alternative solutions. Rarely is there a simple single either/or choice.

When brainstorming alternative solutions to the problem doesn't come up with answers, try to reframe the issue by putting it into a different context or making hypothetical modifications in basic assumptions. While reframing may not always help solve the immediate problem, it may stimulate the creative juices necessary to break conceptual deadlocks on the original problem definition. Sometimes it helps to break the problem up into its constituent causes or parts and try solving the parts of the problem.

Helping to solve a problem for the other side may open up room for that side to solve one of your problems. For example, the statement that an employer cannot pay comparable industry wages poses not a position but a problem. Alternatives can focus on cost cutting, marketing, better management, or other issues to see if solutions are available. The same might be true for work rules. A work rule is a way to address a particular problem the work force experiences. There may be many ways to address the problem other than the specific approach placed on the table.

4. *"Insist on using objective criteria."* When negotiations become based on the relative muscle of the union and management, then problem solving has broken down. One side may win, but there can be substantial indirect costs. Before agreeing to specific proposals there must be some agreement on the common criteria for acceptance. These may include standards of cost, fairness, reciprocity, professional standards, prevailing rates and conditions, scientific measurements, precedents, equity, legality, effectiveness, efficiency, verifiability, and/or other mutually agreeable measuring rods. Fisher and Ury suggest that the parties "(1) frame each issue as a joint search for objective criteria; (2) reason and be open to reason as to which standards are most appropriate and how they should be applied; and (3) never yield to pressure, only principle."[17] By arguing on merit and common criteria, the parties can be assured that they are talking the same language and that they jointly are evaluating the proposals that emerge in a common framework of analysis.

Employing this method of negotiation, the parties can meet their basic individual interests by giving full rein to joint exploration of acceptable alternatives. The union and management retain the right to assert their interests and to withhold agreement until they feel they are sufficiently met. This method helps protect the long-term relationship while opening up options for the resolution of issues faced by both sides. In this way, the negotiation session is not just a test of will or slicing the loaf in half through compromise but a search for better solutions that will maximally benefit all concerned.

GRIEVANCE HANDLING AS A MANAGEMENT DIAGNOSTIC TOOL

In traditional contract administration and grievance handling, each side has a wins/losses tote board. Often lost in the counting are the merits of the grievances. Grievances are not an opportunity for the employer to assert that management is right all the time, nor is it the forum for the union to take it out on the employer. Rather, the grievance procedure provides an ongoing setting to give definition to the contract and an avenue for continuous clarification and discussion of the mutual relationship.

Right or wrong, grievances are telling statements on an organization. The grievance procedure can, with proper record keeping and imagination, test the heartbeat of an organization and provide clues for improvement. The most important part of the grievance process is to understand why a grievance is filed and to diagnose the patterns of the grievances to determine what the organization as a whole should do. In some cases, a party may be technically correct, but the grievance is a sympton of a deeper problem. Rather than hide from the issues, the union and management should face and address them.

Arthur Sloane and Fred Witney, in a basic text on labor relations, point out:

> Depending on the attitude of the company and the union, the grievance procedure can also be used for functions other than the settlement of complaints arising under the labor agreement. Many parties, for example, use the grievance machinery to prevent grievances from arising as well as to dispose of employee, union and employer complaints. Major grievances are viewed here as symptomatic of underlying problems, and attempt are jointly made to dispose of these problems to prevent their future recurrence. In other cases, the parties may utilize the scheduled grievance meeting time, after the grievance itself has been dealt with, to explore ways of improving their general relationship and also as an avenue of bilateral communication on matters of interest to both institutions."[18]

Grievances can relate to any one or a combination of the following factors:[19]

1. *Interpersonal communications:* Many grievances are a result of the lack of effective communications between the supervisor and the employee. They represent a breakdown in talking where the grievance procedure and discipline becomes a substitute

for discussion between the parties. In many cases, the situation has already deteriorated to where the parties think that talking to each other is a waste of time. This may be a symptom of a breakdown in trust between the parties.

2. *Factual communication:* The grievances may represent a misunderstanding of the factual basis of the contract or company procedures. In some instances this may be a genuine difference in interpretation. In other cases, it may be that the factual basis of the contract was not explained well enough.

3. *Discrimination:* Perceived or actual discrimination in the workplace on the basis of sex, race, religion, national origin, or physical handicap can lead to the filing of grievances. A sense of fairness underlies many grievances, and concerns about inequities in decisions may surface as discrimination in the traditional sense or broader sense of inequitable treatment.

4. *Employee problems:* In many cases that deal with absenteeism, tardiness, or erratic behavior, the employee may have a serious problem that is generated outside the workplace. These can relate to alcohol and drug abuse, marital problems, and/or depression. There also may be other health-related problems that affect performance. These can spill over into the workplace. The problem is located in the employee.

5. *Management problems:* Some grievances relate to work flow, work pace, production standards, job descriptions, tools, and the structure of work. This category is not always as obvious as it seems. Poor structuring of work can cause stress, and this can result in grievances that appear more personal in nature. In reality, health and safety grievances relate to the operation of the enterprise.

6. *Union problems:* Grievances can result as a function of internal union politics. They can be grandstanding by individuals seeking election or a way to embarrass another faction within the union. This kind of grievance should provide the impetus for serious thought and effort at conflict resolution and expanded participation within the union.

7. *Mobility:* Grievances related to seniority, promotion, training, performance appraisals, transfer, and job assignments all surround the concerns about mobility. The positive face of this is the issue of career advancement and income potential and the negative is concern about the nature of future assignments.

8. *Income:* Disputes over wages, incentive payments, differentials, overtime, benefits payments, and other matters regarding financial payments relate to overall income concerns.

9. *Time:* Time is also another major area for grievance, and these include vacation, overtime, excused time, scheduling, lateness, absenteeism, and similar issues.

10. *Job security:* This topic covers the frequently grieved matters of suspension, dismissal, and other disciplinary matters.

11. *Work environment:* This category deals with the amenities of work, such as parking, the cafeteria, bathrooms, and other services and functions that are not a direct part of the work process.

Some grievances may fall into more than one category. Looking at which category they fall into may help to identify areas where overall action is needed to deal with the underlying causes. Each party should divide them out as it sees fit. A comparison of both parties' listings will be revealing of the degree of difference or common judgment. The grievance process provides a way to adjudicate differences. If there is a difference of opinion on the basic categories that cannot be resolved, then this difference should be respected and the traditional course of adversarial contract administration take its course. If there are areas upon review of the pattern of grievances where both parties see a need for action, this can provide the basis for joint discussion, problem resolution, action planning and activity. Each party is also open to use its judgment of the situation to attempt solutions to deal with the basic causes of the grievance. By doing this quarterly, the parties can monitor the developments in the organization and highlight emerging problem areas or underline areas of improvement. Engaging in this joint process will help reduce the irritants and underlying conditions that increase the number of grievances and open up communications between the parties.

The wise perspective of the American Society for Personnel Administration's handbook on grievances states:

> A grievance is one of the products of an employee-supervisor relationship. The existence of a grievance does not necessarily mean that the relationship has broken down. Actually the grievance may mean the relationship is healthy. An employee expression of dissatisfaction through the grievance procedure may be more beneficial to the organization than if he bears his grievance silently for a long time... No action should be taken in the area of prevention of grievances until a complete analysis of the organization's problems is made.... Grievances are a product of the behavioral structure of the organization, and a formula for their prevention must be developed within that behavioral structure."[20]

GRIEVANCE HANDLING AS A JOINT PROBLEM-SOLVING SESSION

For particular grievances the issues are who is right and who is wrong. Charges have been filed and they must be decided. We do not address the due process issues of grievance handling; these are covered in most texts on labor and industrial relations. When addressing variations on the normal theme, the parties have to protect due process and fair and full representation.

In addition to reviewing the general patterns of grievances, each individual grievance can first be approached as a problem-solving challenge. Good problem solving involves a cycle of problem identification, data collection, data analysis, development of alternative solutions, development of a plan for the best alternative, and the evaluation of the results. Any particular grievance can also follow this process. By phrasing issues as a common problem, the claim can be addressed in terms of looking for effective solutions, not who wins.

A key point is adequate definition of the problem. The item first stated may not in fact be the major problem. Referred to as "iceberg grievances," the particular claim may obscure the fundamental disagreement. It helps if both parties can attempt also to view the situation or incident from the perspective of the other party. The step most critical to effective win-win grievance processing is the development of alternative solutions. The remedies suggested by the two parties in the initial petition may not be the only ones; there may be more integrative solutions. To complete the process as a final step, the situation should be evaluated to ensure that it does not recur.

Many, if not most, grievances can be dealt with effectively through adopting a systematic analysis of their occurrence and a problem-solving approach to resolution of particular grievances. This can improve organizational performance, enhance employee satisfaction, and save substantial time and money. Rather than a bane on the existence of organizations, grievances can be important warning signals and reminders of the need for organizational change.

CONDUCTING JOINT NEW HIRE ORIENTATION SESSIONS

One way to demonstrate cooperative behavior and to increase awareness is to conduct joint new hire orientation sessions. These orientations will differ based on the nature of the union and the employer. They can be conducted for employees who work for many employers such as building tradespersons and for those who work for one employer.

In workplaces where union membership is a condition of employment after an initial trial period, it is a show of good faith to include the union as part of the orientation session to explain the history, role, and structure of the union, how the dues dollars are used, and how the new employees can get involved in or use the union. The contract and the grievance procedures should be explained. It is particularly important to let new employees know how they can put forward proposals for bargaining, ratify the contract, and file grievances if necessary. In organizations without a union or agency shop provision, there is nothing preventing the employer from inviting the union to make this presentation. Doing so can go a long way in creating a good relationship with the union. It demonstrates convincingly that the employer wants to find ways to work together and will not attempt to sabotage the union's relationship with the membership.

Without exercising censorship, it is best if the two parties are aware of the presentation to be made by the other side. This avoids worries, uncomfortable situations, and open conflict. It is still better if the new hire orientation is used as an opportunity for cooperation and both the union and management work up an outline of what new employees should know and conduct the session jointly. Probably a joint presentation will be more complete, balanced, and moderate than separately held explanations. If the union and management are working together on joint initiatives, the orientation session is a good time to let the new employees know that there are areas of common concern that the two parties are addressing.

The union that has contracts with many employers such as in the building trades or the performing arts can provide the locus for this introduction. It can invite a range of employers to come together to present information to new members and employees about their practices. The union can provide an introduction to the benefits that the membership receives, how they relate to the various employers, their rights under the contract, and ways to participate in the union.

CONDUCTING JOINT MEETINGS FOR PRERETIREMENT AND LAYOFFS

The flip side of providing joint activities in terms of hiring and orientation has to do with joint activities for separations other than for discipline. The most positive of these has to do with preretirement activities. After an employee's long period of service and membership in the union, the partners can help ease his or her way into retirement. One of the best ways this can be done is to institute a voluntary cutback in hours worked when retirement age is reached. This allows a gradual transition to retirement without the shock of sudden separation from coworkers and routines maintained over many years.

Increasingly essential in our society is adequate preretirement education about financial planning, health issues, legal concerns, consumer education, additional employment after retirement, volunteer work, leisure activities, continuing education opportunities, and other critical issues. This is an opportunity to describe fully the pension benefits that the employees will be receiving from the employer or the union. The union can inform retirees about ways that they can stay active with the union through the increasing number of retirees clubs. Properly approached, retirement from one job can be the entry to another set of engaging activities; ignored, it can be traumatic. The time to consider retirement issues is not immediately prior to retirement, but at least five to ten years earlier so that adequate planning can take place. These programs can be jointly sponsored, designed, and even presented by the union and management working together.

More difficult is working through the times when there is separation from the employer due to long-term layoff or plant closures. While each party should do everything it can to regularize work to avoid layoffs and to ensure the survival of the organization, this is not always possible. In Canada, there has been model joint activity including the government to help ease transitions to new jobs and to deal with the difficulties that can arise from layoffs.[21] In the case of layoff, the employees need to hear clearly what the situation is, what rights to recall they will have, how to apply for unemployment benefits, what social services are available in the area, and other information that will help them cope realistically and as well as possible during the layoff. When there is a plant closure, the union and management have a responsibility to those who have lost their jobs to help them with all of the above information as well as employment counseling and health care information.[22] In some cases, the employees may be eligible for Trade Adjustment Assistance, which can help with retraining and relocation. The union may want to establish an ongoing support group for workers dealing with the pain of unemployment and the frustrations of looking for new work and trying to support themselves and their families. The union and management need to marshal the resources available in the locality to be of help. In the United States, the local Private Industry Council (PIC), composed of employers and unions, may be able to put together a program that can help out. In Canada, federal and provincial authorities can help.

CONCLUSION

The collective bargaining relationship provides the basis for cooperation. Sour and negative relationships can be turned around by examining what went wrong and what could go right. Contract negotiations can be approached cooperatively either as an exercise on strategic planning or for joint problem solving. Similarly, contract administration, especially the grievance procedure, can be used to diagnose overall problems in the workplace and the relationship as well as for specific problem solving. Finally, the basic hiring and separation issues can provide an opportunity for demonstrating cooperation. The collective bargaining relationship and the contract can also be the basis for other mechanisms of cooperation (described in the following chapters). Collective bargaining has always been a dynamic arrangement for dialogue and commitment between management and the union. Its creative possibilities can be the foundation for a wide range of approaches for cooperation.

ADDITIONAL RESOURCES

Bomers, Gerard B. J., and Richard B. Peterson. *Conflict Management and Industrial Relations.* Boston: Kluwer-Nijhoff, 1982.

Dunlop, John T. *Dispute Resolution: Negotiation and Consensus Building.* Dover, Mass.: Auburn House, 1984.

Fisher, Roger, and William Ury. *Getting to Yes: Negotiating Agreement Without Giving In.* New York: Penguin, 1983.

Jandt, Fred E., with Paul Gillette. *Win-Win Negotiating: Turning Conflict into Agreement.* New York: John Wiley, 1985.

Paine, Frank T., and Carl R. Anderson. *Strategic Management.* New York: Dryden Press, 1983.

Walton, Richard, and Robert E. McKersie. *A Behavioral Theory of Labor Negotiations.* New York: McGraw-Hill, 1965.

8

Building Linking Structures:
Labor-Management Committees

INTRODUCTION

In terms of specific mechanisms for union-management cooperation, far and away the most common form is the labor-management committee. Joint committees serve as a bridge between collective bargaining and joint problem solving. A labor-management committee is composed of representatives of management and the union who meet to deal with a mutually agreed-upon topic. Sometimes these committees are called for in the contract and probably as often they are not. They may be general committees whose purpose is to maintain open communications between the union and management, or they can be oriented toward specific topics such as health and safety. There is probably no issue that has not been the subject of a labor-management committee somewhere.

In general, labor-management committees are rather safe appendages to existing structures that can be used for communication and problem solving. In a few cases, labor-management committees have decision-making authority. In appraising why committees are so common in the United States, two professors of management observe: "First, labor-management committees offer a less radical, more gradual departure from traditional American patterns of industrial relations in that they leave intact the separate perspectives, interests and capabilities of both management and organized labor. Second, the mechanics of labor-management committees are already available and have been utilized successfully for many years."[1]

Labor-management committees have a long history. The shop committees of the early part of the century were among the earliest versions. In the United States, more than 20,000 general labor-management committees were established during World War II. In the postwar period, advocates promoted joint production committees. Starting with World War II, the Canadians also experienced large-scale use of joint committees, and intermittently the Canadian government promoted labor-management committees as a voluntary approach to joint consultation and workplace improvement.

Labor-management committees come into existence in several ways. In many circumstances, they arise out of the collective bargaining arena where an issue is clearly of common interest and affects matters of an ongoing nature during the duration of the contract. Committees also emerge from collective bargaining as a way out of issues that were not resolved during the bargaining sessions but were not strikable issues. Hence a committee is empowered to deal with the issue after the acceptance of the contract. Some "committees" are proposed as window dressing for issues that no one got to on the table but a constituency requires a show of some action on the item. Labor-management committees can also be proposed and constituted at any time by either party suggesting that they be formed. Sometimes joint committees evolve by adding representatives of the other party to an existing unilaterally established committee.

Labor-management committees are also created at the area and industry levels. Area labor-management committees have been formed successfully in many parts of the United States to forge a partnership for economic development in a city, county or state among multiple employers and unions. They often have ties to the local government. In some cases, they work with local employers and unions to develop labor-management committees on-site. In several industries, such as retail food, men's clothing, and masonry, national level industry committees have been promoted to help with modernization and to assist the smooth conduct of labor relations. While both of these are valuable and interesting approaches for union-management cooperation, this chapter focuses more on the particular employer-union relationship.

To be honest, labor-management committees have a mixed record of accomplishment. They can be excellent and provide a real forum for common analysis and decision making. In practice, many of these committees never meet their potential, and too frequently committees agreed to in contracts never actually meet on a regular basis. They often wither away when the person most interested in the topic leaves or becomes concerned with other issues. Members of labor-management committees rarely receive training on how to manage a committee or how to engage in joint problem solving, and sometimes the results show this lack of skill base. Resources are not often allocated specifically for the work of the committee and they must scavenge off other parts of the organization to meet their needs.

The effectiveness of a committee varies according to the caliber and level of the people involved, the resources and training available to the committee, and the attachment the organizations involved place on the topics addressed by the committee. Labor-management committees would do well to take a realistic look at themselves and determine ways to improve their overall effectiveness.

GENERAL PURPOSE LABOR-MANAGEMENT COMMITTEES

As a starting point for union-management cooperation, some organizations during the term of the contract have set regular meetings between management and the union for the purpose of ongoing general communication. Meeting as little as twice a year and as frequently as once a month, an agenda is prepared that is largely informational. Management informs the union of operational results of the period since they last met and what major initiatives are planned for the future. The union shares information and concerns of a general nature that it has learned from the membership. There is some discussion of the issues presented but little in the way of in-depth or ongoing problem solving. Open communication is a building block of any successful cooperative effort and these meetings serve a valuable function in terms of providing an avenue for discussion. These information-sharing meetings are good ideas even as part of more extensive joint efforts.

Some organizations have adapted the labor-management committee concept to the quality of work life approach. When all of the employees in a work area cannot be on a team or problem-solving group, representatives are used as a form of general labor-management committee. In the RBO program discussed in Chapter 7, a general committee operates at the top and there may be several layers of labor-management committees at the departmental or divisional level for the purposes of general communication and problem solving. Some advocates of labor-management committees have added problem-solving responsibilities to the general informational labor-management committee.[2] Most QWL programs are governed by a labor-management committee and some of the lower level problem-solving groups are in fact labor-management committees.

The Federal Mediation and Conciliation Service provides "Ten Summary Points for an Effective Labor-Management Committee" that are very applicable to most labor-management committees:[3]

1. Both parties share mutual interests in the long-term survival and success of the enterprise and the community, even though they may have conflicting goals in other matters.
2. Both sides want to make the labor-management committee work and have realistic expectations of what it can accomplish. Participation in regular sessions symbolizes this commitment, which is known throughout the organization.
3. Labor members of the joint committee are believed and trusted by the rank and file; management members have sufficient status and authority.
4. Maximum voluntary participation is encouraged; employees, including supervisors, are kept informed and involved in matters considered by the labor-management committee and have opportunities to express their views on its recommendations.
5. The joint committees do not take up matters that infringe on the rights of either party as established under the collective bargaining agreement or the grievance procedure.

6. Job security is recognized as basic to the program's success.
7. The parties have a mature, open relationship. Each is willing to listen to the other side. Both agree to concentrate on finding answers to problems at hand and discovering opportunities for collaboration.
8. The joint committees are promptly informed about the status of their recommendations. If they are not, the committees will lose interest and stop operating.
9. Numerous channels of communication are encouraged and an atmosphere of mutual respect prevails. However, communications must be accompanied by substantive recommendations.
10. New ideas are encouraged, and their value weighed objectively. Concrete problems of interest to both management and labor must be pursued by the committee if it is to continue to function productively.

HEALTH AND SAFETY COMMITTEES

Joint health and safety committees are the most common and most important forms of labor-management committees. According to a nationwide study by the University of Michigan, 75.8 percent of workers believe that on health and safety they should have complete or a lot of say.[4] This is higher than in any other category. In 1974–75 at least a third of all collective bargaining contracts contained language calling for health and safety committees covering more than 3.2 million workers and 41 percent of all employees in the surveyed group.[5] Many more committees exist, though they are not specifically mentioned in the agreement. Since that time, there has been continued growth in the joint health and safety arena due to increased awareness of the possibilities of joint action and the promotion of joint approaches by OSHA under the Carter and Reagan administrations. In fact, there may be well over 100,000 joint health and safety committees in the United States alone. Despite the good work done by many of these committees, the structure's potential has barely been utilized. A minimal number of joint committees receive training on health and safety matters or how to operate effectively as a committee.

Kevin Sweeney, in discussing safety and health committees, observes:

> Cooperative labor management committees generate a body of very precise information that had been previously unavailable. Consequently, management is in a better position to see health and safety as a real cost factor. Such information provides a greater incentive to engage in proactive problem-solving and forecasting. From the perspective of labor, the committee's most immediate benefit is labor's involvement in the decisions that affect the welfare of every employee. Those on the job are afforded a mechanism for contributing to the solution of problems and the improvement of their work environment. Their jobs will become safer, less stressful, easier to perform and more rewarding.[6]

There are a wide variety of activities that a joint committee can undertake. These include periodic inspections, red-tagging of dangerous areas, safety and health education, hazard screening, analysis of accidents, and publicity and communication activities. The committee may review and analyze employer records to determine areas of common problems and conduct regular safety audits to identify difficult areas that need more in-depth problem solving. Prevention techniques can include review of new machinery from a health and safety perspective as well as identifying the potential health hazards of chemicals being introduced into the work area. The committee needs to be knowledgeable of federal and state regulations on health and safety and receive ongoing, thorough training on health and safety issues.

In a study of joint committees in New York State, Thomas Kochan, Lee Dyer, and David Lipsky identified critical problems in making joint committees work.[7] One problem was maintaining continuity over the long term; the programs tended to wither away and lose effectiveness over time. The researchers identified the key to countering this as continued rank and file involvement in the committee's actions. Another major problem was "buffering the committee from the collective bargaining process." Describing successful programs, Sweeney says:

> What does a truly empowered committee look like? It has a clearly defined mandate from top management and union leadership. More than likely key decision-makers will serve on the committee. It has the influence to persuade production managers to stop work when a safety hazard has been detected. It has a budget so that it need not be dependent on other departments whose resources are already being stretched. Its presence and activities are widely publicized throughout the organization through a variety of communications mechanisms such as newsletters, safety reps and incentive programs. It has a track record for quick response to employee complaints. Its members are highly visible as they perform regular plant audits and elicit employee input. It has the information it needs to be able to determine how much its efforts are producing results.[8]

Health and safety committees are an important joint initiative. They are relevant to almost any kind of work environment whether that be manufacturing, transportation, building and construction, or offices. They can mesh well with management safety and health efforts carried on independently in accordance with managerial responsibility and liability in this area. They can also complement union health and safety committees that may coexist. Reducing accidents and health hazards in the workplace is an important joint goal. Joint health and safety committees are not a substitute for adequate government regulation of health and safety since monitoring is necessary to avoid inadequacies of internal programs or collusion to avoid inspections. Joint efforts sincerely approached can reduce the need for inspections and government intervention through improved safety and health results of tangible benefit to employers and employees.

APPRENTICESHIP AND TRAINING COMMITTEES

Perhaps the second most common and most taken for granted kind of joint union-management committee is for apprenticeship and journeyperson upgrading. In 1978, more than 500,000 people were enrolled in joint apprenticeship programs in the United States. These committees are found especially in the construction and building trades. However, joint apprenticeship programs are also found in many other parts of the private sector and in the public sector as well.

The mutual interest in apprenticeship is clear to see. The employer needs to have assurances of well-trained competent craftspersons or skilled trades. The union builds its claim for better wages based on higher skill levels in its ranks. The employer and the union bring to the committee real-world experience on what is actually needed on the job. The committees should also take a concerted look at the future to make sure that graduates of the apprenticeship programs will have the skills they need to compete in the five to ten years after their completion. Members of these committees should ensure that apprentices have the general background on the industry and the union and the real competencies needed for high-quality work in their craft. The committee itself may also require additional training on the latest developments in its field and how to guide instructional programs.

But initial apprenticeship alone is not sufficient. Change is constant in terms of new procedures, tools, machinery, materials, regulations, and other matters that affect employees after they are indentured. A joint committee can inventory current skills, recent changes, and future needs to establish an effective ongoing continuing education program. They can establish a training record for journeypersons tracking their continuing education and new areas of specialized competency. By cooperating on a regional basis, committees can provide skills in highly specialized areas not supportable on the local level. For example, the Bricklayers and Allied Crafts union established regional programs for marble workers, for whom there is no great demand in any single area.

Ongoing employee training and retraining is not restricted to the traditional industries where apprenticeships are common. Additional skills are essential for modern employment. Employees who do not receive continuing education are like funds not put in the bank, the value of the initial reserves goes down over time. Each and every job requires a set of initial skills and ongoing skills development to maintain and expand the capabilities of employees. Joint training committees can be used in any environment to help in the identification of training needs as well as to assist in the design, delivery, and evaluation of training. Doing this in a joint manner can enhance the effectiveness of internal training conducted by any employer and augment the skills and employability of the employees. Joint training committees, while not common in manufacturing, the public sector, and service industries, are greatly needed to provide for comprehensiveness and responsiveness for ongoing learning.

In recent years, there has been an expansion of external education and educational opportunity through negotiated tuition assistance programs affecting millions of workers. The use of these negotiated funds has been discouraging, with hundreds of millions of dollars of entitlements untapped. Typically less than 5 percent of the eligible work force takes advantage of the opportunity, and those who have the least education are least likely to participate. Joint action by the union and management can encourage employees to further their education. The National Institute for Work and Learning points out: "In recent years employers and unions have found innovative ways to build skill development, career development, and succession planning programs combining both in-house training and employee-initiated learning using tuition assistance. . . . Joint responsibilities is a key concept in effective use of tuition assistance plans."[9]

In the last few years, there has been an exciting development in joint union-management education and training initiatives in the auto industry and similar activity in the telecommunications and steel industries. The CWA and the telephone companies negotiated in 1983 joint Training Advisory Boards designed to develop, promote, evaluate, and modify personal and career development training and relocation training for laid-off employees. In 1982, the UAW negotiated with Ford and General Motors a fund that is now based on a dime-an-hour contribution (50 cents for each overtime hour) to help pay for training and retraining current and laid off employees. These are administered jointly at the national level but each local plant has a Joint Skill Development and Training Committee which is responsible for the local funds and activities.

The Ford-UAW program has also been particularly active. In addition to a wide range of services for dislocated workers, active workers are involved in an extensive range of programs including life/education planning, basic skills enhancement, prepaid tuition aid in any subject, onsite educational activities, counseling programs, retirement planning, and non-credit personal development programs. The national program staff drawn from both management and the union assists the 85 local committees who develop and screen proposals. The program is explicitly designed to be complementary to other joint UAW-Ford programs such as health and safety educational needs. According to directors of the joint program: "The Employee Development and Training Program is one of the more extensive joint efforts underway between Ford and the UAW. Because of these joint efforts . . ., UAW-represented Ford-hourly workers have more opportunities than ever before to become involved in decisions affecting their work; their job satisfaction has grown; they are upgrading their skills; and they have the chance to undertake a wide variety of projects of their own choosing. In addition, because of the joint actions of Ford and the UAW, Ford product quality has improved, operating styles are changing, information is widely shared, and the working environments in Ford plants have generally improved."[10]

EMPLOYEE ASSISTANCE COMMITTEES

Every workplace should consider a joint employee assistance program. One of the fastest growing new employee–oriented programs in the 1980s, Employee Assistance Programs (EAPs) make a lot of sense for both management and labor. At the minimum, employee assistance programs provide a way to help troubled employees, especially those with alcoholism and substance abuse problems. When more broadly considered, EAPs can provide help in an extensive variety of areas, including family counseling, financial advice, stress management, legal assistance, weight loss, and smoking control. In addition, EAPs can also focus on preventive wellness efforts, including diet, exercise, and lifestyle issues.

The initial impetus for most programs has to do with substance abuse. Alcoholism and drug abuse adversely affect the workplace in many very important ways. They lead to increased absenteeism, turnover, discipline, poor quality, lower productivity, and a host of other problems. They increase tensions between supervisors and employees and among employees themselves. Abusers provide dilemmas for the union, which has a legal and moral obligation to defend them against charges, though the underlying problem may be related to substance abuse. These problems can affect any kind of employee at any level. By joining together, the union and management have greater resources and credibility in dealing compassionately and effectively with the broadest range of employees.

On one hand, the workplace has an obligation to deal forthrightly with the consequences of abuser behavior and to insist that standards be maintained. However, the human dimension must also be taken into account as well as the investment that the employer has already made in the employee. Every effort should be made to provide the assistance troubled employees need to deal appropriately with their problems. This can range from sponsoring workshops to counseling and support groups in the work area to enrollment in detoxification and withdrawal programs. By working sensitively and sensibly with the issues, real progress can be made. Ignoring the problem or handling it wrongly can lead to greater workplace disruptions and increased human tragedy.

Labor-management committees in the employee assistance area have some very important demands. They need to be especially well planned and organized.[11] For some employees, EAPs provide a lifeline, and the program should be as strong as possible. In most programs, internal employees trained to be sensitive to employee problems are used to generate referrals to specialists (usually external) in the various areas addressed by the EAP. Often these include detoxification centers, community mental health programs, legal clinics, and physicians. These resources should be as accessible, community-based, and cost-effective as possible. The control over the program should remain inside the work organization with the committee and its joint coordinators. While advice from professionals should be taken seriously, turning the program over to the "professionals" would in most cases be harmful to the program's credibility and effectiveness.

In addition, the committee should provide training to management and union leadership at all levels to alert them to how to make a referral (or utilize the services themselves). The most important level, however, is building teamwork between the first-line supervisor and the shop steward on how to recognize and appropriately handle problems in the work area.

Confidentiality is also an essential element of a successful EAP program. It must be ironclad, or few if any will participate in the program. Though the individual employee's identity needs to be kept confidential, the union-management committee will want to monitor the program carefully to make sure that it is adequately addressing the full range of needs in the workplace, that provider agencies are being effective and responsive, and that all levels of employees are being reached.

Employee assistance programs are important efforts to improve the quality of work life.[12] Most QWL advocates believe that redesign of work will reduce alienation and hence personal trauma or that new structures will empower those who have been locked out. Theoretically, the improved environment will lead to personal health. Frankly, the real world is less utopian and there remains the need in the best of workplaces to help individuals better cope with their personal problems and the tensions of the larger world. On the other hand, EAPs should not be apologists for poor work environments, and information about recurring "personal" issues in the workplace may provide important clues for needed organizational change, health hazards, or other ways the structure exacerbates personal difficulties. As part of an overall effort at organizational change, EAPs can provide an important complement to the effort. Standing alone, EAPs can be an important first step in union-management cooperation and a vital service to many employees.

ENERGY AND RESOURCE CONSERVATION COMMITTEES

Energy and natural resources fuel the production process and represent a natural place for the union and management to work together on cost reduction and productivity. The energy and resource issue is a triple win-win-win issue at the local level. If energy and resources are saved, then the process is less costly to manage; there are more resources available for other items (including compensation); the country benefits by less reliance on external energy sources; and the global ecosystem suffers from less disruption and depletion of resources. In addition, reduced resource pressure increases geopolitical and economic stability.

Fascinated by the possibilities in this area, we conducted extensive research in conjunction with the University of Michigan comparing the experience in the United States and Japan of employee participation and union-management cooperation in resource conveservation.[13] The research found that higher conservation savings was clearly linked to greater participation. The strongest relationship was when there were energy conservation committees and an employee involvement program. It further found that there was no area of technical improvement, natural or energy resource, or organizational improvement where employees did not have some input on conservation.

The findings would probably apply to any technically oriented joint effort. Conservation committees would probably be more effective when the following suggestions are followed:[14]

1. If appropriate, have both establishment level and corporate or agency level energy conservation committees.
2. Aim for high levels of coordination between ECCs (Energy Conservation Committees), other establishment conservation activities, and the employee involvement program(s).
3. Create well-defined and established broad authority of the ECC "to plan on a regular basis," "to monitor and evaluate programs," "to make final decisions," and "to implement on a regular basis."
4. Deliberately determine the composition and size of the committee based on its authority, making sure to have necessary functions or departments represented, necessary levels of management represented, and a large enough committee to have all the relevant representatives.
5. Acquire and make available resources to the ECC's work, including a budget as well as engineering, computer, and research and development assistance. Training is helpful for the committee in both energy conservation techniques and social process (for example, meeting facilitation and management).
6. The ECC should choose a wide array of activities to involve other employees in its work. Activities should include monitoring and evaluating conservation programs and considering both new technologies and machinery as well as new work processes or designs.

The Japanese workers have been involved in conservation more extensively and over a longer period of time. They continue to report significant savings via employee involvement, which demonstrates that conservation is an ongoing challenge and can harvest long-term yields. Due to the length and breadth of their experience they tend to have more involvement with cogeneration, alternative fuels, and other more frontier areas of conservation. Union members took part in two-thirds of the committees. In the United States, there have been a few interesting cooperative ventures. In one public sector case, the Maryland Department of Health and Mental Hygiene included the union in an innovative effort targeted at conservation inside the state institutions as well as in the homes of employees and patients.[15] The Sheet Metal Workers Union is working with contractors to promote, install, and guarantee solar energy equipment in commercial, government, and residential property.

Unions and management can cooperate fully in efforts to deal with both technical and organizational measures to improve resource use. The importance of resource use to the overall economy of the nation and of enterprises and agencies merits focused committees aimed at conservation. In many situations, technical (engineering or machine-based) solutions represent the extent of the conservation strategies considered. Such technical solutions require human cooperation to identify, implement, and then use that technology effectively. Industrial and energy engineers can be very helpful in providing technical insight, but workers have an intimate knowledge of their work processes and environment that can identify resource problems and possibilities. Committees should consider ways to train employees to conduct basic energy and resource audits in their work areas and monitor use patterns. The overall aim of a cooperative conservation effort is to use human and organizational energy and resourcefulness to save natural resources and energy. Resources and energy may not be the largest part of an overall budget, but it is an essential one to manage wisely and efficiently.

NEW TECHNOLOGY COMMITTEES

New technology holds the possibility of being a topic of great conflict or of great cooperation, and sometimes a mixture of both. Not cooperating on new technology may create a lose-lose situation. Management will have reduced utilization of the new equipment or approach and generally have had to trade costly provisions around manning, timing, and wages to win union acceptance. The union may be forced to negotiate concessions from a worst case scenario with little room or time to maneuver and settle for the least loss to the membership.

Few in labor are of the Luddite variety, and the serious difficulties of introducing new technology is an issue addressed by unions throughout the world[16] and throughout their history. Unions often have great attachment to technology, for this provides a basis for their memberships' skill and craft. Productivity improvements and market possibilities opened by new technology can provide the basis for an increased standard of living and greater job security. A study of union response to technological change found that union objections primarily had to do with the lack of planning for the consequences of change rather than with the particular technology.[17] For management, technology is a critical component in a competitive mix.

The process of working together on technological change is, quite frankly, unrelated to a particular technology. Whether it is new computerization, fiber optics, VDT terminals, scanners, numerically controlled machinery, robotics, biotechnical advances, or any other technological advancement, the specific technology is important solely in terms of the training needs of a joint committee and the related recommendations that emerge from the common effort. The areas for involvement and the process for joint problem solving remain largely unchanged.

When the parties work together on technological change, the beginning point is not after the new machinery is installed. The two parties must be plugged in together at the very beginning. This starts when the basic objectives for the new technology are being formed. It must be remembered that technology is a tool toward some end, and those ends are determined by people. The particular machinery or process is generally neutral; how it is used is critical. Common agreement is possible when the discussion centers on how to reduce hazards and accidents, improve feedback to the operator, how to improve quality, make more sensible work flow, reduce stress, and other benefits. But strong disagreements can emerge around such issues as reductions in employment, overall pay and skill requirements, increased health and safety risks, and additional external monitoring. If the new technology prompts major job changes, then the consequences need to be addressed early in terms of retraining, reassignment, or the growth approaches described in Chapter 10.

After the objectives have been determined comes joint involvement in the design of the new technology. There are usually several design options of any new technology that meet basic objectives. Ergonomic concerns about the fit between people and machinery are relevant in the design stage. Just as cost, technical feasibility, and a series of other operational issues are weighed as part of making design decisions, so must there be an early awareness of the potential impact of design decisions on employment, relocation, health and safety, bargaining unit changes, skills, income, job qualifications, career advancement, job control, job pressures, and job satisfaction. Rarely is any decision without pluses and minuses, but the human resources and industrial relations consequences of technology design decisions are best surfaced upfront and early. The question is always the mix. Knowing that there was serious joint effort to seek the most mutually beneficial mix can moderate later concerns.

In a third area, a number of employers have begun to involve labor in meeting with vendors to ensure a good fit between operator needs, and performance and vendor specifications. Very often, costly modifications have to be made in the workplace to compensate for design omissions. In major purchases, some companies have sent joint union-management teams to examine other applications of the machinery or to visit the manufacturer.

Another area for cooperation is the implementation of the new technology. Unfortunately, it is only at this stage that many employers recognize the need for input from the work force, especially if the first effort to put it in place didn't work well. Implementation implies not only the physical startup and adaptation of the particular technology to the rest of the mechanical and operational process but also the development and delivery of training for the new machinery's operators.

The final area we discuss is joint involvement in the evaluation of the technology against the initial objectives. The work force provides an important source of information about how effective the technological change has been and what, if any, other implications resulting from the changes need to be considered. The evaluation should measure the impact on both operational effectiveness and quality of work life. Richard Walton provides an overview of the possibilities in joint efforts in this area:

> The potential benefits of labor-management planning and problem solving in relation to new work technology include the better utilization of basic technology because of attention to economic and social effects; stronger labor and management institutions; and greater employee voice. In addition, the mutuality/participation system is expected to be *more inventive* in developing new solutions to both old and new problems; *more adaptive* to changing conditions; and more productive of a *higher level of commitment* to solutions on the part of employees, unions and management.[18]

JOINT COMMUNITY FUND DRIVES

Listed last because of the limited nature of the engagement is undertaking joint fund drives for community service. This is an important kind of joint initiative anywhere. However, when labor and management cannot agree on internal joint projects, working to help those most in need in the community presents a forum for experimenting with joint initiatives. The labor movement and employers have been active in their support for the United Way, the Red Cross, and other charitable organizations.

The United Way recognizes that the best campaigns inside of a workplace are those where the union and management are cooperating. They jointly take leadership roles in explaining to employees the local recipient agencies of the United Way and the ways that they help. One of the very early efforts highlighted by the United Way was in 1967 at the Chevrolet Shell Division of General Motors with the UAW.[19] It was found by common effort, support, and explanation that the average contribution per employee increased more than 250 percent from the former unilateral solicitations. Joint meetings were held with employees to explain the United Way Campaign and publicity and communications were handled jointly. Management enthusiasm and encouragement help create a climate of giving; the union official can point to the close relationship between union community service programs and United Way agencies.

Fund drives are one way to work together on community service among a wide range of other alternatives to work together to improve the community. Both parties could jointly adopt a school and provide a balanced perspective on the labor-management relationship. They can aid in blood donations, food banks, shelter for the poor, care for the elderly, cleanup of environmental eyesores, provide big brother and big sister programs, and a host of other options. What is needed is the will to work together in service to the broader community. This is especially important in towns where certain unionized industries are dominant.

For the company it proves good corporate citizenship; for the union it enhances its community image in addition to the direct services or funds that are provided.

CONCLUSION

Labor-management committees come in almost any size and description and deal with almost any topic. General labor-management committees provide more open-ended forums for the exchange of information or, if desired, for joint problem solving. The adaptability of labor-management committees, however, should not be a precursor to lax implementation. Well-run labor-management committees can have strong impacts on organizational performance and industrial relations. They need to pay attention to understanding well the particular content of their concerns and the process of accomplishing their objectives through the committee.

Committees can address general communication and problems inside their organization and/or help in the larger community. When working inside, the range of issues can stretch from specific committees on workplace problems such as absenteeism, fire safety, job design, and contract bidding to any other issue. The possibilities span the production process from resource use to quality to technology introduction and use. They can contribute directly to the welfare of employees while having strong organizational impacts via employee assistance programs, education and training initiatives, and health and safety efforts. The particular application of labor-management committees rests in the imagination of the partners and their common will to use a common forum effectively.

9

Developing New Organizational Structures: Quality Circles to Sociotechnical Redesign

TRADITIONAL STRUCTURES: THEIR STRENGTHS AND WEAKNESSES

At some point for the designers of workplaces, form followed function. Yet the functions they were created for vexingly refuse to stand pat. To serve better a changing external environment and shifting demands inside an organization, new forms of work organization need to evolve. Unions and management often find themselves in situations where the traditional structure cannot respond to, or may be the cause of, significant problems. This chapter discusses a variety of possible work arrangements. We hold that no form of organizational structure is a given. Instead, the internal parties need to exercise choice and judgment in their construction and maintenance.

The attachment managers and unionists have to particular forms of organizational structure is amazing. The structure provides mooring against the winds of organizational change and a safe harbor from a stormy external environment. Managers receive status from where they are positioned inside the organizational structure. It tells them who to report to and for whom they are responsible. By referring to the current structure, most managers can triangulate where they have come from and where they could go. Organizational structure creates boundaries where others parallel or below cannot cross without permission. Paradoxically, many managers tend to view structural adjustment below them as the way to confront change and above them as a way to alter power. It becomes an all-purpose magic wand even when the real issues are performance and the quality of relationships. The most dreaded part of any managerial change at the top is reorganization. Often this solves one set of problems while creating another perplexing set. And the transition can inhibit productivity while unsettling the lives of employees. Managers first need to distinguish between situations that call for structural change and those that don't. It is easy to mandate a new alignment but more difficult to make it work in practice.

We have been surprised also at the tenacity with which unions hold on to the current organizational framework. If one brought together unionists from a variety of organizational structures, each would argue vehemently about the merits of his or her basic structure while criticizing its application. Frankly, often the most positive point about a current system is that it is the devil people know. Over the years, they have been able to figure out what could go wrong and how to work it or avoid it to their best advantage. These learnings become institutionalized in work rules, past practice findings, contractual job classifications, bidding rights, and other forms of accommodation. However, these practices are based in fact on accepting the prior management's assumptions on how work can be organized. These assumptions may not have been accurate, may not have been examined in light of other alternatives, and the impact on the membership may have been negative. Thus many unions will resist team-oriented work settings not because they are "bad" but because it upsets the uneasy balance established with more routinized and assembly line operations. Earlier battles were fought by unionists when segmented work approaches were introduced by management. This observation about unions across the board should lead individual unions to be less reactive to management's initiative and more proactive in proposing organizational styles appropriate to their work environment and better accommodating the needs of the membership.

Resistance to new organizational approaches illustrates not only the obvious, that people resist change in any organization, but also several other powerful organizational truths. Organization of work codifies power in work organizations and provides the medium through which relationships are built and maintained. When work organization is changed, managers are rightly concerned about where they will end up, the erosion of their influence, and the impact on their career paths. Unions are concerned that change will bring abuses of the power of the organization and erode solidarity and connection among the membership. These are legitimate concerns. In a cooperative union-management relationship, these concerns are public and are addressed head-on and the mechanisms for their resolution are multiple. It is the power of organizational structure that can energize joint efforts at organizational change or stymie them if ignored.

A traditional approach to work organization may indeed be the most appropriate form. But the excuse that it is traditional is not enough. It must be *currently* appropriate. Management and unions need to view the range of alternatives in work organization from top-down hierarchy, to parallel structures, to egalitarian redesign, to bottom-up organizational styles. Decision makers need to choose those that are most appropriate or the mix of those that best serve various functions. These approaches need to be woven together in a coherent fashion.

Any form of organization needs to address the following questions: Does this form of work organization best address our market conditions and customers (in the public sector, "customers" are the people and groups served by the agency)? Does the work organization promote maximal efficiency in the use of resources? Does the organizational style ensure high-quality standards and organizational effectiveness? Does available technology impose contours for the work organization? How can individual development of the employees as well as workplace community and teamwork in the firm be best incorporated? This chapter explores some of the possibilities in work force organization ranging from minimal add-ons such as quality circles to radical sociotechnical revisions.

QUALITY CIRCLES

Quality circles have become very popular in the United States. As late as 1979, only a few companies were experimenting with quality circles, but by 1983 the International Association of Quality Circles estimated more than 135,000 circles at more than 8,000 locations in the United States. There has continued to be substantial growth in the field since then. While initially found in manufacturing, quality circles have spread to all kinds of workplaces, including the public sector and service jobs.

A quality circle (QC) is a worksite problem-solving group. Teams of five to fifteen employees from a common work area have responsibility for analyzing problems in their work area and proposing solutions to the next level of management. Members of the circles are provided specific training on problem identification, problem analysis, and solution development in order to analyze problems that affect them. Usually the groups meet once a week for an hour under the direct supervision of the first-line supervisor. Facilitators are trained to assist the various circles, and the program is often overseen by a senior level steering committee. In joint union-management programs, the steering committee, usually with equal representation from both parties, directs the program.

As constructed, quality circles do not challenge managerial authority and responsibility but provide a valuable extra tool to managers astute enough to welcome it. The devotion of about 3 percent of the workweek to reflection and action on improving the other 97 percent of the time is a minimal essential for sound management. Nor does a quality circle change the structure of work organization. Many involvement programs are called quality circles even though they do not operate at the shopfloor or office level. A basic tenant of quality circles is that they encompass a common work area. Many work settings do not have enough people who are related by task or even by location to be able to form a traditional quality circle. While problem-solving groups may be formed in those areas, they represent a distinct variation on employee participation. On the other hand, there are programs that go by other names, such as employee involvement (EI) groups and employee participation groups (EPG), which are in reality quality circles.

The idea for quality circles came to flower in Japan, but there are major differences between the Japanese and the American versions of quality control circles. The highly successful Japanese experience rose out of the teachings of Edward Deming and Joseph Juran, both quality control experts. The Japanese were motivated by the necessity for quality improvement in the export industries. Under the leadership of the Japanese Union of Scientists and Engineers, training on the techniques of quality control was given to first-line supervision, and then to other employees via quality control circles that primarily dealt with quality and productivity issues. The American versions have a distinct organizational development slant and place far less emphasis on quality control issues. Quality of work life concerns and attention to the group process are stressed. Most Japanese circles meet on their own time, whereas American versions generally meet during paid working hours.

Unions are split regarding quality circles. Since most applications of quality circles are unilaterally operated by management or are management-dominated, some unions have rejected the label and/or the practice. They are concerned that circles will deal with collective bargaining issues and divert solutions to problems away from the union winning via the contract or grievance procedure. Some view QCs as too narrow in scope because they do not deal with broader organizational policy. They worry about how to keep tabs on what is happening within the circles with limited resources available to the union. Some unions see quality circles as union-busting techniques or speedup gimmicks—and in fact they have been used in this manner in some locations. The United Electrical Workers, an independent union, resolved that, "UE continue to oppose 'quality circles' and other phony participation schemes devised by management." Several other unions, such as the International Association of Machinists and the American Postal Workers Union, have taken a hard line nationally against any involvement.

However, many more unions (and some locals with national opposition) have become involved in successful joint quality circles programs.[1] In these versions, the union is an equal partner.[2] It has equal numbers on the steering committee, equal numbers of facilitators, and sometimes co-leads the circles. On Conrail and the Milwaukee Road railroads, there are examples where very successful circles have had all union members as the quality circle members, a union member as a leader (as part of a supervisors union), and a union facilitator. One such circle came up with a return of $750,000 on its first project!

As an example of a more positive position, the International Union of Electrical Workers, affiliated with the AFL-CIO, adopted the following position:

1. The IUE go on record in support of the concept of quality circles and encourage union participation where the union feels such participation is in the best interests

of its membership and where it is determined and assured that management has made an equal commitment to the mutual goal of such a program.

2. Where quality circles are considered, that the Union insist that it be a part of the planning, development, implementation and evaluation process.

3. Local unions should make certain that Quality Circles do not in any way infringe on the collective bargaining process or on matters and conditions covered by the collective bargaining agreement. . . .[3]

Owen Bieber, president of the United Auto Workers, notes that while the quality circle "does not solve all problems and it does not change the grim non-inspiring nature of many factory and office jobs . . . it does make things better." He goes on to conclude: "It is quite apparent that properly constituted, quality circles is a methodology by which unions can greatly enhance the furtherance of worker democracy at the worker's place of employment."[4]

Quality circles can harness the positive problem-solving potential of shop floor or office level employees and often does lead to impressive gains in performance and productivity. The combination of specific training and the use of small group dynamics results in an exceedingly powerful tool. This approach is best suited to changing terms and conditions of work and not to broad organizational change or major policy decisions. Some advocates of quality circles have taken on an evangelical air. While quality circles can be a valuable way to develop shop floor problem solving, they are hardly a total response to cooperation, participation, or organizational change—but then again neither is any other particular strategy.

PARALLEL ORGANIZATIONAL STRUCTURES

Another approach to organizational change that doesn't replace the traditional system is the development of parallel organizational structures. This approach is different from the "informal organization" since it is an explicit and planned part of the organizational fabric. Teams are established from various parts of the organization to address current and future institutional challenges. It is management with the aid of a complement of broadly and creatively engaged task forces.

Sometimes organization charts get in the way of organizational effectiveness. What earlier were functional divisions of authority and responsibility too often become ossified into rigid boundaries that may not meet the current and future needs of the organization. According to Barry Stein and Rosabeth Moss Kanter,

> The parallel structure thus provides a means for managing change and providing flexibility and responsiveness. It is a source of opportunity and power above and beyond the (limited) sources that exist in the bureaucratic

structure, and one that, in particular is important for people in positions least characterized by those properties. It is thus a structural mechanism for building high quality of work life and environmental responsiveness *permanently* into an otherwise bureaucratic organization.[5]

Dale Zand describes the "collateral organization" in similar terms and views the overlaid structure as the one best suited to deal with diffuse problems and circumstances since they are capable of higher quality, faster, and more creative solutions.[6] The collateral organization provides organizational choice to those managing change as to the appropriate forum for resolving pressing issues.

What makes parallel structures work is their provision of a forum for the combination of perspective. Perspective in an organization is often defined by position in the hierarchy. Yet a diversity of perspectives is often needed to solve cross-disciplinary and cross-departmental challenges. The parallel approach implies that all people in an organization can contribute regardless of job title and that they can meet as equals in the parallel setting. At the same time it acknowledges differences in authority in the traditional sphere and does not seek to replace the traditional hierarchy. The outputs of the parallel system are inputs to the formal organization, and a test of its success is the degree of acceptance inside the traditional structure. The traditional hierarchy provides for the maintenance of the system and fulfills the functions of control and continuity. Stein and Kanter state: "The main task of the parallel organization is the continued reexamination of routines, exploration of new options and the development of new tools, procedures and approaches. It seeks to institutionalize change."[7]

Another, similar approach to organizational change has to do with creating permanent fluidity in the structure through the development of matrix management. Where the parallel organization provides structures for flexibly dealing with selective *issues* in an organization, a matrix provides an overall flexible structural framework to deal primarily with *task management*. In traditional management structures, each employee has one boss to whom he or she reports. In a matrix structure, each employee has more than one. Usually the number is two, a functional supervisor and a task/product/program group supervisor. Matrix management can range from essentially a set of parallel structures overlaid on the traditional system to advanced matrix organization where most of the organization is configured in a matrix model.

Matrix management was born in the aerospace industry during the 1950s and has been successfully introduced into a wide range of organizations. It typically affects only the top part of the organizational hierarchy, and employees at lower levels may not even be aware of its existence. Matrix organizations work best when there are more than one critical function in an organization needing integration, when the organization deals with complex and interdependent tasks, and when the organization is large enough to have a variety of functional subspecialties that could be assigned to matrix teams, thus affording an economy of scale.

The most important features of the matrix are the requirements for team-work and planning among different functions in an organization. Teamwork provides new energy and imagination and reduces delays in transition between functional specialties. Planning requires greater clarity on what is to be done by whom and when. There is sometimes confusion that team management means an anarchistic approach to management. In fact, team approaches require greater planning and understanding because less is taken for granted by virtue of position.

Though highly unusual, there is no reason why the union cannot be included as a partner in parallel structures, though its role has not been clearly defined in the literature and practice on this approach. Since the union is centrally connected to issues of power, opportunity, and perspective in an organization, it should have intimate connections with the construction and implementation of parallel arrangements. The union provides perspectives that would be very valuable for these deliberations. It can be involved either in equal activities like the union-management task forces (described below) or as a member of matrix and parallel teams. Very few organizations have a matrix approach for the total organization and therefore include bargaining unit members in the matrix configuration. For the union, operating in a matrix environment can be difficult because of dual or shifting lines of authority. Agreement may need to be reached with several centers of authority. In situations where bargaining unit members are involved in the matrix, this has an impact on job descriptions, wages, career paths, and transfer issues.

UNION-MANAGEMENT TASK FORCES

Union-management task forces differ in nature from the labor-management committees discussed in the previous chapter. Where a labor-management committee has an ongoing life related to its subject area, task forces mesh with the principles of matrix and parallel organizational structures by their impermanence and attachment to innovation and function. A union-management task force is a flexible structure designed to meet jointly perceived changing needs. While task forces can be used in organizations that adopt the matrix style of management, they can also be part of other ongoing union-management cooperative activities.

Task forces chaired jointly by representatives of the union and management can draw broadly from throughout the organization to help solve problems facing more than one unit of the organization, plan for impending changes, and consider new opportunities. Task forces work best when the ongoing union-management group recognizes that it could use additional expertise or perspectives on an issue or when it is considering a topic affecting a broad cross section of the work force. The task force itself should be constituted of union and management decision makers. They should determine its mission, time frame, resources, and membership. The length of time a task force exists and how long it meets vary depending on the scope of the task or the pressure for results, but the parameters are set ahead of time. The decision maker to whom the task force reports is also determined based on the mission and composition of the group. All of this should be specified in advance.[8]

Three types of union-management task forces seem most appropriate: problem solving, planning, and ad hoc. The *problem solving task force* is rather straightforward. It addresses issues of broad concern in the organization and seeks to come up with solutions to the problems encountered. One task force at a location we worked with took on the question of employee turnover and surveyed previous employees to find out their reasons for leaving. It then went on to devise solutions to the major problem areas it could address. Another looked at sanitation problems and constructed appropriate charts to help clean up the problem areas.

A *planning task force* examines upcoming events or changes. These future challenges can provide the basis for a joint task force. This inclusive planning can help normally scheduled changes or new initiatives be better accepted and integrated with the work force. Another type of planning task force can look at new ideas or opportunities that the organization might undertake. Most organizations are rife with ideas for new opportunities but there is precious little opportunity to develop them. Too often, joint union-management activities just react to the negative or problem side of their situation. This version of task forces seeks to be anticipatory and explore the affirmative.

Both problem-solving and planning task forces require some training to solve problems and plan opportunities better. But some issues or topics simply do not require in-depth analysis. It may be an issue of communication with a particular group of employees or only call for a session or two to address the issue. The third category is then *ad hoc task forces*, short-term cooperative efforts. This category should not be overused because it is the more in-depth approaches that have the deeper impact on the organization.

A task force is a means for inclusion of employees from various levels of the organization. Sometimes the fact that people are brought together is more important than the specific outcomes. They feel included and empowered. Task forces provide flexibility to the union and management partners. They can magnify the possibilities for problem solving, planning, and communication since a union-management committee can handle more activities through chairing several joint task forces than if they all worked together on all of the projects.

SOCIOTECHNICAL REDESIGN

Sociotechnical approaches to analyzing work impel management and the union to look deeply at how work is conducted and offer a reorientation from traditional workplaces. At one level, sociotechnical systems (STS) make obvious a rather simple statement, that in the design of work the social system and the technical system should be considered in tandem. Very often, people are forced to adapt to the rigidities of machinery and technical requirements in ways deleterious to their work lives and to the performance of their organization. On the other hand, the human relations schools of management have placed an over-reliance on the individual worker. The sociotechnical approach attempts to work with the synergy of the two sets of concerns. T. G. Cummings defines the two central principles of STS analysis:

> The first is the joint operation of two independent but correlative systems: a social system composed of human beings who are the required actors in the performance of work and a technological system made up of the tools, techniques and methods of doing that are employed in task accomplishment.... The second concept is that a sociotechnical system continually interacts with an environment which both influences and is influenced by the work system.[9]

The sociotechnical approach is heavily influenced by the concepts of joint optimization and open systems theory. Roles change dramatically when work is looked at as an open system rather than a closed system. In closed systems, managers spend most of their time attempting to counter entropy—or the disintegration of order into chaos—by controlling and pushing the various members of the system, that is, employees and other departments. In an open system, the manager's primary role is interacting with the boundary between the external environment, that is, customers and resources, and aiding the internal structure. The manager draws energy from the surrounding system and helps reorder it inside the work system to produce the desired outcomes. The union also shifts from combatting control to co-concern for boundaries.

Albert Cherns, a leading authority on sociotechnical systems, provides nine principles of design. To paraphrase, these are as follows:[10]

1. "The process of design must be compatible with its objectives." This means that if the final result is meant to be inclusive, then all of the major parties should have input into its construction.
2. "Minimal critical specification ... the negative simply states that no more should be specified than is absolutely necessary; the positive requires that we identify what is essential." The STS approach provides latitude for decision making to those who have to do the job.

3. "Variances, if they cannot be eliminated, must be controlled as near to their point of origin as possible." The analysis of "variance," which is any unprogrammed event, is a key activity in sociotechnical design. Doing this reduces the overall incidence of problems as well as the time and communications steps required to control situations requiring decisions.

4. "The principle of multifunctionality" allows diverse responses to changes in the environment. Treated like a simple machine, work organization gets stuck when the situation doesn't exactly fit predefined categories. When organically created, the organization is adaptive and creative in responding to the new demands of the environment. This principle leads to the common emphasis in sociotechnical design of multiskilling.

5. Boundaries between groups should be as contiguous as possible in terms of technology, territory, and time. Managerial responsibility should be the management of the boundary conditions and serving as a "resource" to the work team.

6. "Information systems should be designed to provide information *in the first place* to the point where action on the basis of it will be needed." Instead of filtering information to the shop floor through higher levels of management, information should be directly supplied. This empowers the place where information is provided, reduces the time needed for communication, and cuts back on distortions in communications caused by passage through multiple layers.

7. "The systems of social support should be designed so as to reinforce the behaviors the organization's structure is designed to elicit." Payment methods, hiring and firing, training, grievance administration, work measurement, performance appraisal, promotion, vacation policy, hours of work, and other personnel policies should all be congruent in terms of basic values and be mutually supportive of the operational system.

8. "An objective of work organization should be to provide a high quality of work." These have been expressed in terms of meshing with human desires and values, including autonomy and discretion, opportunity for continuous learning, optimal variety, opportunity to exchange help and respect, meaningful contribution, and a meaningful future.[11]

9. "Design is a reiterative process. The closure of options opens new ones." In short, the process is spiral and therefore there is no definite point of completion but only a rejoining of the process at another level.

Cherns addresses the role of the union in the process: "Can they [unions] be partners in design? This is a role that seldom has been offered to, and even more rarely accepted by, unions. It is not a role for which they have prepared themselves. Yet without them the viability of the design is in some doubt. And the design of a social support system implies designing the functions of the shop steward if not the union official. Our first principle, compatibility, requires that the unions be brought into the design if that is at all possible."[12]

A joint work redesign team is frequently used in sociotechnical efforts. The union and management can cooperate on establishing the best fit between the organization, the work team, the individual employee, and the technology. Usually an organization design task force is established. In small locations, all workers, union stewards, and supervisors can be involved on the task force. If the site is large, then representatives will need to be selected from the union, management, and employees.[13]

The major steps in a sociotechnical redesign effort are as follows: In the initial scan, the design team members are asked to "identify influential factors in the environment; to specify the organization's major inputs and outputs; to characterize the organization's major historical, social and physical features; to define the enterprise's mission or business objective; and to articulate the organization's philosophy for management of its members."[14]

Second is an analysis of the technical subsystem that looks at the variances in the organization that occur in converting the inputs into the work system into outputs. The design team goes on "to build a profile of the many factors in the conversion process that must be controlled through the organization's tools and procedures; to specify each step of the conversion process; to group these into unit operations; to detail what might go awry in the conversion process, that is, to identify variances; to match variances with unit operations; to pinpoint variances upstream that could interfere with steps downstream; to decide which variances need most emphasis; and to determine what information and responsibilities are required to control each key variance."[15]

The next step is to analyze the social subsystem, including a review of "the division of labor, mechanisms of coordination, and degree of fulfillment of psychological job requirements in the organization."[16] The fourth step is the integration of the previous activities into proposals for the organization covering the mission, organizational philosophy, major inputs and major outputs, a description of work group organization, and needs for improved technical approaches to better control variances. The aim is to find the best fit between the technical and social systems. However, given the principle of minimal critical specification, the final design should be as lean as possible.

Since sociotechnical systems generally involve job redesign, we cover it here, though this can be done independently of the more complete STS approach. The major ways jobs can be changed are job simplification, job enlargement, job rotation, and job enrichment. *Job simplification*, as its name implies, streamlines, or reduces the number of component tasks of jobs to make them easier to perform. *Job enlargement* and *job enrichment* do exactly the opposite. These entail the concepts of horizontal or vertical loading of the job. Horizontal loading, or job enlargement, increases the range of tasks that an employee performs in terms of number and variety. Vertical loading, or job enrichment, adds more dimension and responsibility to a particular task, including planning and input on policy regarding the job. *Job rotation* provides a way to alternate what tasks an employee accomplishes, though the nature of the task is not changed. All of these changes have implications for collective bargaining.

Job redesign efforts should pay attention to the critical variables of skill, variety, autonomy, feedback, and significance. According to experts in the field, the quality of work life improves as these measures increase.[17] The less repetitive the tasks, the more the worker has a sense of working on a "whole" product; and the more the task is important to the overall production of the product or delivery of the service, the more meaningful an employee's work experience and the more motivated the worker will be. The more independence one has, the greater the sense of responsibility at work. The more timely and helpful the feedback from coworkers, supervisors, and machinery, the better communication and responsiveness there will be. These combine to create greater job satisfaction and higher quality of workmanship.

AUTONOMOUS WORK GROUPS

Autonomous work groups represent an application of sociotechnical systems at the shop floor level. They serve to create an adaptable approach to work by forming small teams of employees who take responsibility for all of the functions in their work area, including concerns normally handled by supervisors and some managers. These groups plan and carry out the distribution of work tasks, the pace of production, training of coworkers, scheduling, quality control, maintenance, and other activities necessary to work performance. They become a system unto themselves, subject only to outcome criteria or resource constraints imposed from outside of their team. Sometimes this approach to work organization is called "work teams," "self-managing teams," or "composite work groups." An autonomous work group is defined as one where the group members select their own group leadership. When management selects the leader of the team, it is referred to as a semiautonomous work group.

Since a fundamental of the autonomous work group is multiskilling, ongoing training is critical. Each member of the group is trained in all of the functions involved in the work unit. This means that competencies and learning requirements need to be carefully and fully defined. As new skills are learned and the competencies demonstrated, wages are generally increased. All fully trained members are paid the top of the scale. Although this broad training can be time consuming and expensive, the investment in human resources is necessary for the flexibility desired in the autonomous work group. It also provides the basis for the flow of information and experience necessary to formulate better improvements in workplace operations. Although everyone can perform all or most of the functions, the group decides on the specific allocation of tasks. Members of the team take turns at different jobs, including being team leader.

Substantial labor relations problems may be caused by this form of work organization. While a great deal of the experience with this form has been in nonunion settings, such as the General Foods Topeka plant,[18] there have been successful introductions of autonomous work teams in unionized settings in North America, Europe, and Japan. Clearly, the multiskilling has an impact on job classifications and compresses them into one or very few categories. It also requires negotiation over the rates of pay, the specific competencies to be considered, career paths, and other matters of traditional union concern. Seniority rights in bidding between groups are often required by unions. When other criteria cannot be agreed to by the teams, then seniority should be an ultimate basis for decisions on the allocation of tasks. In nonunion locations, often hiring and discipline is a task of the group. Sometimes, it also can initiate termination proceedings. In unionized locations, the individual member still needs the right to grieve to enforce the contract, but who to grieve against becomes muddled when the team is making the decisions. In hiring, firing, and discipline, while management may consult with the group, the decision and responsibility has to be clearly in the hands of management.

The autonomous work group is difficult to implement: It requires considerable thought on what it takes to operate effectively; it requires consistent attention to the group functioning of the teams; it requires reorientation of senior level management to be able to work with the group; and it requires the union to learn new skills and new ways of operating. Many managers have difficulty with the concept. On one hand, it involves an unusual level of trust in and delegation of responsibility to workers. To many managers, the person "best" for the job should be doing it most of the time, not rotating it among others who may be less able. Further, the notion of training workers in all functions runs counter to the prevailing practice of just training employees in the skills they need to know and use frequently. Employees with reserve skills represent unused potential (or idle capital in human capital theory). The underlying principles of autonomous work groups run exactly counter to the scientific management school used by most industrial engineers and the philosophy taught to most managers.

The basic concept behind autonomous work groups is an effort to overcome the alienation of workers caused by the increasing segmentation of work into smaller and smaller bits. The group process gives the individual employee a chance to look at the entire process from start to finish. It also provides a social support network that most traditional workplaces miss. While this provides its promise, there is a danger of the overuse of group pressure. In one General Motors location, young work team members decided that they did not want any older workers in their group. A peer group can at times be more vindictive and coercive than the worst supervisor. This points to the need to ensure that majority rule doesn't impinge on minority rights, especially those related to equal opportunity. Further, the group has to be aware of the dangers of group tyranny.

Autonomous work groups have been used successfully around the world. Among the most famous are those at Volvo and Saab in Sweden in connection with the Swedish Metalworkers Union. They have been used successfully on ships as well as in other locations in Norway. Some of the earliest experiments were conducted in the mines in England under the direction of the Tavistock Institute. Among the first European companies to use autonomous work groups was

Phillips Industries in the Netherlands, where groups were used to assemble television receivers. In the United States, they have been used extensively in the paper and petrochemical industries. In addition, they are increasingly being introduced in the automotive industry, as at the General Motors Delco-Remy plant in Georgia. During the 1970s an attempt was made to apply this concept at the Rushton Mining Corporation in Johnstown, Pennsylvania. While the operational results and health and safety benefits were very good, the effort failed to overcome internal union political problems and it collapsed.

In general, the greatest benefit from autonomous work groups has been increased flexibility and skills/levels. Productivity gains as measured by output per personhour have not always come in the wake of their introduction. However, substantial bottom-line improvements are made by reducing absenteeism, cutting turnover and replacement costs, and improving the speed of implementing changes. Generally, workers like being part of these groups and develop strong attachments to them. The end result is a far more integrated operational and social approach to shop floor level work organization.

QUALITY OF WORKING LIFE (QWL) PROGRAMS

Quality of work life (QWL) is sometimes used generically to describe union-management cooperation or workplace participation generally. An example of this use is the definition put forward by the American Society for Training and Development, which described QWL as: "A process for work organizations which enables its members at all levels to actively participate in shaping the organization's environment, methods and outcomes. This value based process is aimed at the twin goals of enhanced effectiveness for the organization and improved quality of life at work for employees."

There is wide disagreement on the particular definition of QWL.[19] Some would argue that it is any one of the other approaches described in this part. To some, QWL connotes industrial democracy and new power relationships in the enterprise. To others (and they were some of the earliest proponents of the phrase), it is another way to describe sociotechnical activities. And to still others, it focuses on ergonomic concerns and strictly quality of work life issues without touching productivity or organizational performance. However, there is a more specific application of the term used here. QWL programs have the characteristics of being multitiered efforts at organizational change that may use a variety of specific techniques to accomplish its broad objectives. The QWL program provides an umbrella for generating, sanctioning, and maintaining these efforts. The dominant characteristics of QWL are its open-ended agenda and broad application.

In terms of the union-management relationship, QWL programs usually result from an agreement among the top leadership on both sides. Almost all explicitly avoid collective bargaining issues and the grievance procedure. In unionized work organizations, the term QWL signals a reorienting of the union-management relationship toward a more cooperative approach. Most QWL programs tend to focus on operational issues. An exception is the New York State QWL program, where other quality of working life issues, such as day care, employee assistance, and flextime, are also addressed.

The QWL approach can be attractive because it invites greater cooperation, flexibility, and information sharing. A massive QWL effort is in place in the telephone industry between AT&T and its spin-off companies and the Communications Workers of America and the International Brotherhood of Electrical Workers. We worked with Pantry Pride, Inc., and the United Food and Commercial Workers to develop a QWL program with labor-management committees, union-management task forces, store level problem-solving groups, and a departmental customer service program all integrated into one program. Many other unions and managements have employed their own approaches.

The major North American example is the 1973 agreement between General Motors and the United Auto Workers to engage in a joint QWL process. They have employed top-level labor-management committees, autonomous work groups, business teams and shop floor employee participation groups among other techniques. For example, the Buick division broadly experimented with a wide variety of approaches. In general they have been very successful in improving performance:[20]

> The plant is organized into six business teams, each consisting of the necessary production activities and support elements: engineering, scheduling, material handling, quality control, maintenance and accounting. The system has made support employees an integral part of the plant's operations. The quality control circle concept, which has flourished in Japan and is being introduced by a growing number of firms in this country, has been incorporated into the business-team structure.[21]

The union and management have worked on a large number of issues, from new plant design to product bidding to greater employee involvement.

A decade ago, one of the major issues within the rubric of quality of working life were alternative working time arrangements. Today, the debate is largely over whether new working time patterns should be considered. Some QWL programs have looked at flextime as a way to improve performance and the quality of working life. Flextime allows an employee to come and leave within a band of time so long as a certain number of hours of work is performed. For employees, this better adjusts to personal schedules, traffic patterns, and family commitments. It gives the employee a greater sense of control over his or her life. For the employer, flextime reduces greatly the amount of discipline about tardiness and increases productivity since employees tend to show up when they are most needed.

Flextime is very difficult to implement in assembly line manufacturing, but it is well suited to most service industries and custom and batch production facilities. In the federal sector and in many state and local governments, flextime has been successfully introduced. While initially wary, government workers and their unions have become adamant supporters of the concept. Attention must be paid to getting the work force involved in understanding production requirements and working together to make sure that basic needs are covered.

Other working time areas considered by QWL programs have been staggered working hours and compressed workweeks of four nine- to ten-hour days. Time may be a major issue considered within a QWL program. Clearly, these issues, however, fall into the realm of mandatory subjects for bargaining. The union needs to be involved in the design and setup of new working time arrangements.

One must temper enthusiasm about QWL with a sober look at the record.[22] Most of the experiments in the 1970s fell by the wayside after a few years. Internal cohesion or productivity has not always been generated by the program's implementation.[23] Union and management politics have flared over these programs. In large measure, we believe this is due to confusion that broad mandates mean vague implementation. Too many programs have been cut off at the knees by poor attention to implementation and too great a reliance on emotional halos. A QWL approach provides an opportunity to apply broad theoretical vision and wide-ranging technical application to resolution of common issues and possibilities.

CONCLUSION

Looking at new organizational structures in a cooperative manner generates opportunities for invention and a fresh review of how organizations should be structured. Quality circles can be a means of better involving shop floor employees in organizational problem solving. Introducing parallel structures, matrix organization, and/or union-management task forces can encourage greater flexibility and responsiveness in dealing with change in an organization. Sociotechnical systems, including autonomous work groups, requires a fundamental reexamination of the technological and organizational assumptions and foundations of an organization. The quality of work life (QWL) approach provides an umbrella for joint organizational revitalization, drawing broadly from theoretical and technical applications.

ADDITIONAL RESOURCES

Abrahamsson, Bengt. *Bureaucracy or Participation: The Logic of Organization.* Beverly Hills, Calif: Sage Publications, 1977.

Bass, Lawrence W. *Management by Task Forces.* Mt. Airy, Md.: Lomond Books, 1975.

Cleland, David I. *Matrix Management Systems Handbook.* New York: Van Nostrand Reinhold, 1984.

Cummings, Thomas C., and Suresh Srivastra. *Management of Work: A Socio-Technical Systems Approach.* San Diego: University Associates, 1977.

Davis, Stanley M., and Paul R. Lawrence. *Matrix.* Reading, Mass.: Addison-Wesley, 1977.

Herbst, Phillip. *Alternatives to Hierarchies.* Leiden: Martinus Nijhoff Social Sciences Division, 1976.

Ishikawa, Kaoru. *QC Circle Activities.* Tokyo: Union of Japanese Scientists and Engineers, 1958.

Kanawaty, George, ed. *Managing and Developing New Forms of Work Organization.* Geneva: International Labour Office, 1980.

Lawler, Edward E. III. *High Involvement Management.* San Francisco: Jossey-Bass Publishers, 1986.

Ronen, Simcha. *Alternative Work Schedules: Selecting, Implementing, Evaluating.* Homewood, Ill.: Dow-Jones-Irwin, 1985.

Stein, Barry A. *Quality of Work Life in Action: Managing for Effectiveness.* New York: AMACOM, 1983.

Thompson, Phillip C. *Quality Circles: How to Make Them Work in America.* New York: AMACOM, 1982.

10

Creating New Opportunities: Cooperation on Marketing, Service, and Product Development

COOPERATION FOR REVENUE GENERATION AND GROWTH

There are two sides to a financial statement—expenses and income.[1] For the most part, employee involvement (EI) or quality of work life (QWL) efforts have exclusively dealt with one side of the ledger—costs. Yet a healthy organization has to pay attention to the balance of the balance sheet.

The use of employee involvement and cooperation for cost containment is a legitimate and important initiative. Employees do have an incredible number of ideas about ways in which operations can be improved, and it is poor management not to tap into those ideas. Workplaces need to be efficiently run and produce in a quality manner in order to compete. And unions are correct to get involved, if only to intensify focus on nonemployment-related areas for cost improvements.

Yet such a focus is only half a loaf. Too many management strategies accept the status quo. More so, far too many organizations have focused solely on how to manage their decline. They fail to apply the vision necessary for growth. Healthy and vital organizations center on growth. For many companies, a great reservoir of talent and ideas sits dormant inside their own organizations that can be tapped for growth. Their employees can generate new markets, additional products, and a renewed entrepreneurial spirit. The reason is very simple. Employees often have the most contact with customers and thereby generate critical information about what customers need. Producers of the product develop intimate knowledge of current resources. These employees can be creative in the reconfiguration of these resources to produce new products at a lower startup cost. Employees have a clear and vested interest in seeing that their employer succeeds and therefore can be its best promoters. This motivation and knowledge can be used to help employers grow.

In all cases, a company starts with a product/service and a market. The organization then organizes itself to meet the demand for the product it offers. Product and market are in fact more important than cost structure. Many companies have gotten by even with bloated costs when they are fortunate to have a large unmet product demand. Companies cut to the bone on expenses cannot compensate for lack of demand. If a company is making an excellent product and no one knows about it, or if the distribution networks are not intact, then it will fail. This is true even if its pricing and cost structures are very low. Yet access to markets may not be enough. An apt example may be buggy whip makers. They could have had the best quality circle program in the world but that would not have made up for the lack of demand for buggy whips. In short, the first effort a company must make in seeking to grow is to expand the market for its current products. Next it must realistically assess the demand for and lifespan of its products and diversify prudently into other areas as product demand shrinks.

At first consideration, the connection to the public sector is not clear. However, agencies are created to meet perceived public needs. The stronger the perceived need, the better position the agency is in to command adequate resources. Legislatures are less convinced by the efficiency of the operation than by the nature of the public demand and the manner the agency services those demands. More than one inefficient agency has been saved by public outcry for need in the areas it is meant to serve. Again, "market" takes precedence. Public needs do shift, and intelligent agency management requires staying abreast of those changing demands and shifting resources and energy to the areas of highest concern. If the need for a public service ends, adequate plans need to be made to shift resources and people to emerging areas of need or to help the employees in the program's sunset.

For unions, involvement in the growth side of labor-management cooperation buys out of the inefficiency-unemployment dilemma. In traditional employee involvement programs, employees worry whether they are working themselves out of a job. If a static market or product base is maintained, efforts that improve efficiency must of necessity lead to loss of jobs through increased productivity. The problem is that maintaining inefficient or sloppy procedures in a competitive environment will eventually lead to being priced out of the market or losing market share—and losing jobs. The classic solutions are to avoid competition or to hope for natural market forces to work on expanding the pie. The first leads to market distortions and the second is based on prayer.

For employees and their unions, there can be another answer. They can consciously get involved with expanding markets for the products or services currently provided and look to revise the potential product/service base to deal with obsolescence and shifting demand. In addition to the obvious impact on job security, expanded markets and growth make collective bargaining easier. With more cash and a larger pie, more can be shared with the bargaining unit.

Employers projecting growth are more likely to reach favorable agreements than ones characterized by declining or stagnant balance sheets.

A complete approach to union-management cooperation enlists joint efforts not only in the effective management of the enterprise but also in the promotion of growth and development. This view goes beyond cost-containment concepts of participation but recognizes labor as a stakeholder in the enterprise's future. Labor can then be used to strategic advantage to position for growth of the enterprise. Labor can use its position as a partner in a joint venture to protect and expand the availability and quality of jobs.

When labor is viewed as a stakeholder, then the questions about labor are not simply cost reduction but instead center on asset maximization. Labor, instead of being a drag on profits, becomes a generator of profit potential. One looks at a company's human and technical resources not as obstacles to growth but as assets that when configured in appropriate ways can lead to operational improvement, innovation, and increased revenues. In a rudimentary sense, this has always been true. Large organizations are built on the premise that employing additional people adds to overall net worth. The theory is that by adding employees, products or services can be provided less expensively per unit, or more reliably, or markets can be better served. Unfortunately, the fit between theory and practice is not always snug. Most personnel planning asks how the least amount of people can be used to meet fixed targets. Stakeholder concepts state how people can be used to accomplish more widely and fully organizational goals. Targets are raised to accommodate market potential and internal asset capability, as in the highly successful Mondragon cooperative system in Spain. Overall, growth is obtained through market retention, improving the yield from current customers, increasing market share, product diversification, and capital investment.

JOINT CUSTOMER SERVICE IMPROVEMENT PROGRAMS

Every organization and every function has a customer. The customer is the reason why any unit produces a product or service. Customers pay for or justify the work that is done. In the public sector, the customer is the taxpayer or the user of the service. Inside an organization, there are many units whose function is to serve other parts of the organization, their "customers." A sign of trouble in any organization is when the customer loses the primary position. Smugness can lead to long-term problems, as customers eventually find other ways of meeting their needs. Not only does attention to customer service defend current relationships, it provides the venue for increased revenue and responsibilities through increasing the number of customers.

Customer service is not just a function of *what* is provided but also the *manner* it is delivered and the way the system adjusts to problems experienced by the customer. Employees are critical to the process. An area where management and union often agree is improved customer service. Again, this applies equally well to private sector workers who have contact with paying customers and in the public sector when they interface with their own patrons. However, most customer service programs consist of two parts: lofty statements about the importance of customer service and general rules about what employees should do to serve customers. They are communicated in a top-down fashion and have had very limited effectiveness.

In conjunction with Pantry Pride supermarkets and the United Food and Commercial Workers Local 1625, we developed a Participatory Customer Service Program. It tested a joint union-management approach to bottom-up customer service improvement. In retail food, customer service is the lifeblood of the industry. Working as a team, union, management, and the QWL staff implemented the program. A brainstorming session in each department was conducted to determine specific actions that could be done in each work area to improve customer service. These ideas were left uncensored. The ideas were posted on a checklist in the work areas, and employees made a commitment to themselves and the employer to carry out their items. The checklists are updated about every three months to reflect changing conditions.

Virtually all of the items were on target as within their control. Evaluated three months later, the checklists clearly helped improve the delivery of service to customers and gave employees a voice in their work. In addition, their use aided the whole chain by providing valuable data to management and the union on what employees think about customer service. The checklists were used as one way to orient new employees to how to work in each store. Most importantly, in a concrete, clear, and simple fashion, their use demonstrated joint union-management concern and action on customer service.

At Pantry Pride, problems of customer service were also addressed by a number of other joint problem-solving groups in more comprehensive and indepth ways, including surveying and interviewing customers about their reactions and suggestions.

In any organization, a variety of forums and mechanisms can be created for going beyond rhetoric and finger pointing to actually improving customer service. In a sales environment, if customers are more satisfied, they are more likely to buy more and more often. New customers will be attracted. This is money in the bank. In a public service role, stronger support is likely and a larger percentage of the client population will utilize the service if its "customers" are well treated.

JOINT UNION-MANAGEMENT MARKETING PROMOTIONS

Customer service looks to ways to improve performance with people who already do business with the enterprise. Marketing issues are critical in helping to generate new customers and new revenue. Management has a clear interest in expanding its market share, since it often results in economies of scale and additional profits. Labor sees marketing as important in order to maintain and expand jobs. Unions have a long-standing interest in marketing questions and have employed several traditional approaches. Advertisements imploring consumers to "look for the union label" are ways to market union-made products. In addition, the AFL-CIO's Union Label Department puts on an annual trade show to showcase products made with union labor, and it publishes a directory of these products. Unions and employers have "marketed" together in defense industries and other government-linked enterprises by jointly lobbying Congress and government bodies for contracts.

Several other approaches are possible. Joint union-management marketing teams to make calls on sales prospects can help in some industries. As part of the Labor-Management Action Group of the Milwaukee Road Railroad, several times a month teams of marketing representatives and labor officials call on potential shippers. The company marketer takes a lead in the discussions and they are backed up by the union representative. Having the backing of the union in a heavily unionized industry like the railroads provides important assurance to the shipper about reliability and quality. Contact of the labor union with the customers provides new insight into the difficulties of obtaining customers and their needs. It also has been very valuable to the marketing department to learn more about operations from those who actually perform the service. Invariably, the customer is positively surprised by the joint call and this makes a stronger impression. Opening up communications between sales and the unions has also led to funneling ideas about marketing possibilities from the work force into the sales office. In general, the Milwaukee Road experience has been very positive and has contributed significantly to new sales and new jobs for railroad workers.

The construction industry is also a heavily unionized industry where the ability to bid on jobs in a competitive marketplace is critical. The Building and Construction Trades Department and the National Construction Employers Council have developed a "Market Recovery Program" designed to promote cooperation in attracting new work. Throughout the country are an increasing number of local joint, multicraft, labor-management construction councils, such as PRIDE in St. Louis, Union Jack in Devner, and Operation MOST in Columbus. They have been credited with winning many millions of dollars of business for the unionized shops. Their efforts have been aimed at creating a better image of the unionized sector, hammering out prejob agreements to reduce or eliminate jurisdictional battles, and improving the quality and timeliness of unionized construction work.

In the construction industry, certain crafts also conduct their own marketing efforts. One model is provided by the International Masonry Institute (IMI), a joint program of the Bricklayers and Allied Crafts (BAC) and the Mason Contractors Association (MCA). Getting people to use stone, brick, and block is the goal of the marketing effort. Through the IMI a number of joint programs are promoted. IMI works closely with more than 70 local and regional joint promotion institutes in the United States and Canada. Materials are provided for their use, including a quarterly newsletter, a slide show, educational material, publicity releases, and advertising reprints.

A central facet of the marketing effort is providing information to civil engineers and architects as well as other construction specifiers and designers on the benefits of masonry construction and ideas on how to incorporate masonry materials into different kinds of building. Seminars are also conducted for building owners and public sector facilities managers. IMI developed computer software to assess the contribution of passive solar approaches to heating needs in the one-and two-story structures. The geographic focus of the institute allows it to target more than 300 large national firms. Generating positive publicity about the industry and keeping an eye on developments in building codes are other ways that markets are protected and expanded.

Joint marketing efforts can use union-management teams and sophisticated advertising and promotion campaigns or integrate the tasks of employees with customer contact to include a greater marketing awareness and function. In a few cases, workers affected by slowdowns have been retrained to become salespersons. When the demand increases, they return to production. In retail, "suggestion-selling" by employees can be increased and delivery people and repairers can actively promote new products.

NEW PRODUCT DEVELOPMENT AND INTRAPRENEURSHIP

One of the most promising areas for cooperation is new product development and intrapreneurship. Few products have an eternal life span. For our purposes here, product can either be a manufactured good or a service. Indeed, it can be new services in the public sector that are needed regardless of profitability criteria. For growth needs, current product lines may not be sufficient to generate the revenues necessary for bottom-line improvement. As such, looking at new products and new ideas for profitable areas of involvement is critical.

Union-management cooperation is helpful in two regards. Joint union-management cooperation can speed the introduction of new approaches especially when they hit the production phase. Second, the union membership represents a valuable ingredient in an ongoing product evaluation and renewal strategy. Most industrial innovations are not the result of dramatic breakthroughs but are incremental improvements in the product or some variation or combination of existing products. In production facilities, workers have an intimate knowledge of the process involved. They often have ideas about different permutations of the current product that could be developed. In addition, through a knowledge of the existing machinery, they often think of ideas about different products that could be developed using essentially the same technology. Product planners often are not aware of the range of product possibilities inherent in the current process and generally tend to consider more expensive options than what the internal work force might propose.

An example of product development surfaced in England where the Lucas Aerospace Combined Shop Stewards Committee, concerned about declining employment caused by declining demand for the product, worked with local technology experts to develop more than 150 ideas for alternative socially responsible products that could be made using essentially the same technology and workers in the plant.[2] The good part about the Lucas plan was its graphic demonstration of alternative possibilities in the facility and the imagination of workers. However, the Alternative Plan failed to gain the support of management and this shows that unilateral efforts by labor are unlikely to turn into reality. The issue became not what can be done but a power struggle.

New products can also emerge out of product research. Because of the prevalence of small contractors, needed research in the masonry area was minimal, especially in comparison to other building materials. In 1979, the Masonry Research Foundation was founded as a joint effort of four industry groups, two labor unions, and the IMI. The foundation has approached a number of areas. Its first task was assessing what research was being done in the industry. Subsequently, research has been conducted on the bonding qualities of mortar and masonry units. Other topics include water penetration of walls, compatibility of materials, comparative costs, development of new wall systems, and testing of prefabricated stone panels. IMI has also been involved with market research as well.

The particulars of the IMI approach are of less interest to those outside the industry than the process by which these efforts came about and the way they are managed. Included on the review committees for each research project are rank and file craftspersons, local business agents, and local contractors as well as others with a national scope. An effort is made to ensure that the research conducted is useful and understandable by those who would use it. Those with hands-on experience are brought into contact with the skilled researchers in the field. The union took a real leadership role in the development of the IMI foundation. John Joyce, president of the BAC, says:

> What happens in the area of promotion and research will go a long way toward determining job opportunities in masonry for our members. This is the arena of industry-level, or strategic decision making. We're affected which means we have a *reason* to be involved. We're concerned about decisions management has made in the past about these subjects, and so we *need* to be involved. We don't like the fact that when management made the masonry industry's promotion and research decisions on a unilateral basis, it decided to spend so little on these activities that we've lost markets and jobs. That's why we've gotten involved and plan to stay involved.[3]

Several additional mechanisms seem possible in the joint product development area. A joint union-management committee could attempt to investigate this area. Such a committee could review with a sample of the work force a proposed new idea to find out the reaction workers have to its feasibility and design. It could also examine market areas and creatively explore new product concepts. Another alternative would be to sponsor a competition for new product ideas among the work force and develop subcommittees to help work out the more promising suggestions. Joint union-management teams could meet with customers to find out what product innovations would be helpful. The same kind of survey could be done by training employees who have customer contact on how to generate this kind of information. In fact, a survey could be done with noncustomers to see what product innovations they would be inclined to buy. In organizations with product development groups, these efforts can be integrated. In those without that specific function, the union-management effort could help catalyze and implement activity.

UNION-MANAGEMENT COOPERATION
TO PLAN NEW FACILITIES

Keeping abreast of change to produce new products/services or to expand to meet rising sales opens the arena of cooperation on new facilities and ventures. In the past few years there has been an increase in joint activity in these areas, especially in the auto and metals areas. For unions, involvement is attractive because it provides new jobs for current and prospective members and initial input on the work environment. For management, the worker perspective can be a valuable asset in thinking through the new project. In new locations (that is, greenfield sites), it helps avoid costly union-avoidance battles and may test new procedures that could be used in existing unionized locations. In existing plants, union-management cooperation can be used to help plan and review changes in plant layout. In General Motors, for example, cooperation is being sought in model changeovers. In some plants, redesign teams have been established, and in some others the blueprints have been posted for all to see and comment on. In the public sector, the American Federation of Government Employees is working with management at the Social Security Administration to redesign most of the offices to fit new technology and work flow.

At the Carborundum Corporation's refractories in Falconer, New York;

> Plant management was acutely aware of the need to redesign the old facility as a means of improving working conditions and productivity simultaneously. The proposal was put before the plant labor-management committee, and a subcommittee comprised of both union and management was formed to direct the project. Department foremen called on employees to identify problems in

plant layout and make suggestions on how redesign could benefit their work, quality of working life and working conditions. One hundred sixty-seven responses were received, ranging from the relocation of a machine to the complete redesigning of a departmental layout.[4]

In Sarnia, Ontario, Shell Canada was considering the construction of a new chemicals plant and decided to invite the Energy and Chemical Workers of Canada (then the OCAW) into the design process.[5] The union's involvement has worked out well in practice for management, the union, and the membership. It has also resulted in an innovative collective agreement that maximizes flexibility in operations and calls for full union involvement in all aspects of the operation of the plant. In describing the process, two of the principals reported:

> The union accepted with two stipulations—1) that it be a full partner in the design process and 2) that it would maintain a high profile. This was quickly accepted. The participation of the union representatives provided the means for capturing and utilizing organizational learning at the shop floor level. Initial concerns were quickly forgotten as the high quality of union contribution unfolded and managers congratulated themselves for their statesmanship.[6]

In the auto industry, this kind of planning is taking place at General Motors with Saturn, at Ford with the Alpha project, and at Chrysler on the Liberty car. In each company, the UAW is working in partnership to develop whole new ventures and facilities. The Saturn Division of General Motors provides the best view on the process. It represents an exciting break with the past in manufacturing and in industrial relations. The Saturn Project's dimensions are staggering. The research costs will be about $1 billion and start up in the vicinity of $5 billion. GM is banking on this project to make the company competitive again in the small and medium-sized car market. Saturn will be the first new GM division in 66 years.

The United Auto Workers has been a significant part of that process. Fifty-two auto workers and union officials worked with 39 salaried GM managers in seven subcommittees to develop the plan. They worked for about a year on the design and initial plan submitted to the GM board and the UAW top leadership. The subcommittees examined technical and human systems innovations in North America and elsewhere, including Japan, Sweden, and West Germany. Their input went far beyond how the labor relations system should be constituted and touched every technical and operational area. The Saturn group put more than 50,000 hours of work into this phase, and many of these hours were taken up by intense discussions among labor and management on the pros and cons of the various alternatives. The final agreement for Saturn provides a wide range of innovations in automotive design, marketing, factory design, and labor relations. The UAW is to be an integral part of the entire process and involved in every aspect of the operations.

LABOR REPRESENTATION ON THE BOARD OF DIRECTORS

Though still far and away the exception, labor representation on boards of directors is increasing in the United States. In the last few years, union representatives have been seated on the boards of directors of Chrysler, Eastern, United Press International, Western Airlines, Pan Am, Republic, and other companies. They have been proposed seats on the Conrail board. Primarily this has been a result of trade-offs in distressed companies for wage and work rule concessions.

Employee representation on the board of directors is a common phenomenon under the codetermination systems of Europe. The situation in the United States is far from the circumstances in Europe, where the major issue is joint control of enterprises. In the United States, the issues have been communications and access to information. The unions have exempted themselves from discussions on the boards of directors that directly affect collective bargaining agreements in order to minimize the role conflicts inherent in their dual roles. However, role conflicts are not new to boards of directors. Banks and major investors are frequently included on boards. Like labor union leaders, they share a common interest in the success of the enterprise but have conflicting loyalties that influence decisions on resource allocation, divestment, new investments, and other critical decisions. The objectivity and singular concern of the membership of boards of directors is a myth.

Board level representation can in fact be an opportunity for cooperation. Despite the rhetoric, in most foreign countries the employee representatives on the boards generally do not act as opposition forces. In fact, many studies have confirmed that they aid in the quality of information and kinds of decisions made by the board. Such a system can provide a forum for union-employer cooperation at the very highest level.

Board representation, however, can be oversold, as can the benefits of employee ownership. Board representation does not necessarily imply that the quality of work life of the average employee will be better in ways that he or she can readily perceive. Many members of boards of directors recognize the limitations on their ability to influence broader forces and internal dynamics of companies. Board representation provides joint analysis at the highest decision-making body of the corporation, but how those decisions are carried out are just as important. In the day-to-day working lives of employees, many decisions other than those determined by the board are equally critical if not more so. Further, representation does not mean that difficult and painful decisions about resource allocation and employment may not still need to be made. As always, joint participation guarantees voice in the decisions but not the specific outcomes.

JOINT INVESTMENT DECISION MAKING

The allocation of capital affects both corporate health and jobs. Largely, investment decisions are made unilaterally. There are two examples of union-management cooperation on investments that demand attention.

The first is the effort of jointly trusteed pension and welfare funds. Found in a number of industries, though most frequently in building and construction, there are more than $600 billion in assets in union pension funds, representing the largest source of investment capital in the United States. By law, these must be jointly trusteed. Unions and unionized employers are asking whether the investments of some of these funds are being used in ways that undercut their own long-term viability. They are examining ways to use those funds prudently in unionized industries to provide support for the jobs that support the pension funds. It makes a lot of sense to consider this area so long as the funds are accountable and used wisely from an investment perspective. Joint trusteeship of pensions provides a forum for cooperation and an avenue for funneling dollars into socially desirable and job reinforcing investments.

A second joint investment program has just been started and its results are yet to be seen. A much smaller initiative, it may provide the framework for experimentation with joint labor-management approaches toward investment and job creation. In the 1984 GM/UAW contract, $100 million was allocated for a New Business Ventures Development Group. This is administered by a negotiated Growth and Opportunity Committee with equal membership from the company and the union. According to the *UAW-GM Report*, "The bold, new program marks the first time a major corporation and union will have an ongoing activity to develop and mutually direct ventures into new, non-traditional business areas—financed entirely by corporate funds, but providing full input by the union." The companies will, within the boundaries of labor law, recognize the UAW as the bargaining agent.

The latitude for the program is broad. Ideas for the use of the funds will in large part be generated from local JOB Security Committees, which are empowered under the contract to make recommendations to the national Growth and Development Committee and to develop, according to the report, "Employee participation toward bringing about new, competitive business." This fund, combined with the $30 million negotiated in the Ford agreement, provides a bank of funds for joint cooperation in investment in new enterprises.

CONCLUSION

Every employee involvement and labor-management cooperation effort should seriously consider the growth dimensions of their collaboration. It should be a part of the agenda in terms of building a complete approach to joint participation and part of joint strategic initiatives. Not to do so adopts a reactive approach to the future and squanders talents and possibilities of potentially great importance.

A task force or committee can be established at the highest levels of the organization to guide and spearhead efforts at growth development. Subordinate activities can be spun off that work on various aspects of service or marketing or different product or service ideas. Under the labor-management umbrella, training in the processes of union-management cooperation and the content areas of service, marketing, and/or product development can be carried out. Where this goes from here is limited only by the imagination of the partners.

A wide range of options could be pursued:

1. *Integration of tasks*: Jobs can be redesigned to include marketing and service as integral parts of their function. Rather than establish separate job categories such as marketers or customer service representatives, these functions can be incorporated into a whole job description. An example of this would be drivers in a package service who are also promoting the company's services and looking for extra loads.

2. *Alternation of tasks*: By switching off according to need, employees can be involved in marketing and production. In Japan, some factories have retrained and sent production workers out as door-to-door salespersons when demand was slow. When demand picks up they go back to the line. United Airlines had a program to promote its express service that used laid-off pilots as spokespersons. Think what that would mean in the American context if auto workers, instead of getting unemployment and supplementary unemployment benefits, which amounts to practically the entire paycheck, were trained and sent out to market American cars.

3. *Parallel activities*: The Milwaukee Road case is a good example of parallel activities where the basic functions of the job are not directly affected but joint labor-management teams supplement traditional marketing efforts. A parallel approach does not change basic responsibilities but adds an additional structure to complement those basic responsibilities. A parallel approach might also include a suggestion or reward system for ideas for product or market growth.

4. *Strategic approach*: A strategic approach would adopt the marketing, product development, and/or customer service issues as a common strategic goal. Then, through a joint task force or committee, a comprehensive strategy for joint efforts and improvement is developed. Approaches may include any of those described or additional ones such as advertising campaigns. The distinction of the strategic perspective is its clear and broad focus on the revenue side and an attempt to use internal resources as much as possible. The Saturn and Alpha projects at GM and Ford illustrate this approach.

5. *Joint contracting*: The International Masonry Institute is an excellent example of the joint contracting approach. The two parties agree on important marketing or research objectives. Experts, generally from the outside, are contracted to perform the work with review by the labor-management partners.

Each company and union presents a unique set of internal resources and aspirations and external market conditions and constraints. Factors such as the size of the enterprise, the capital base, distribution networks, customer contact level, location, skills levels of employees, degree of technological flexibility, and the like will need to be considered. Yet, as employee involvement and union-management cooperation evolve and the pressures of competition increase, there will be greater movement into the revenue and growth side of union-management cooperation.

III

The Design of Effective Union-Management Cooperative Efforts

11

First Steps: The Decision on Whether to Cooperate and Getting Started

The first steps are the hardest steps in developing a cooperative program. The initial segments of feasibility assessment, building involvement in the organization, setting goals and objectives, making deliberate choices on whether to proceed, and clear design are often rushed through or left out entirely. Later, these omissions and superficial treatment of important initial steps come home to roost. Lasting change rarely occurs overnight. Good cooperative programs need to follow a process that unfolds in a deliberate and systematic manner.[1] The issue is not the amount of time spent but making sure that all of the steps are thoughtfully and adequately addressed. The steps in the process of getting started are identified in Figure 11-1.

In the beginning, there is something or a set of circumstances which motivates one or both parties to look at cooperative approaches. Rarely do organizations take an anticipatory look at their situation and examine additional options for cooperation or ways to improve the management of the organization and the effectiveness of the union. More often than not, some precipitating crisis motivates either or both parties to suggest a cooperative approach.

A frank understanding of the motivating forces is helpful and will inform the selection of the goals and objectives. The range of possible motivations is virtually infinite. If the problem is an imminent cutback or shutdown of the location, then one set of strategies may be necessary. If the situation is changing market conditions or customer demands for quality, there may be other approaches. Sometimes the issues are bad morale and communication. If the motivation is to be in on the latest fad, then trouble is ahead. Most importantly, the parties should not let the pressures of crisis or anxiousness to see results cause shortcuts in the process.

DETERMINING MUTUAL GOALS AND OBJECTIVES

Cooperation should do something worthwhile or it should not be done at all. The basis for effective cooperation is to attain important goals and objectives.

FIGURE 11-1
Getting Started

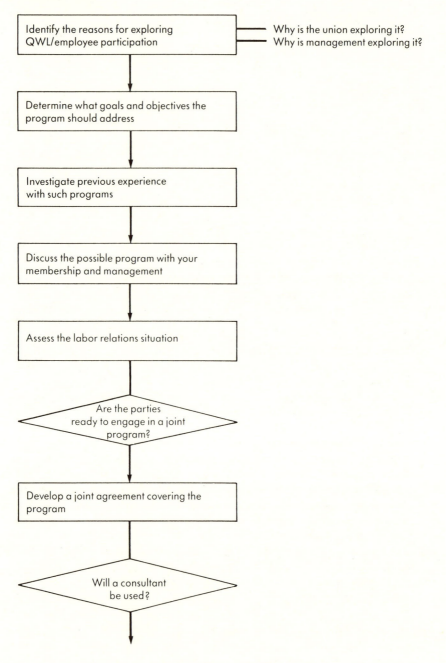

| Identify the reasons for exploring QWL/employee participation | ——— Why is the union exploring it?
——— Why is management exploring it? |

Determine what goals and objectives the program should address

Investigate previous experience with such programs

Discuss the possible program with your membership and management

Assess the labor relations situation

Are the parties ready to engage in a joint program?

Develop a joint agreement covering the program

Will a consultant be used?

If a cooperative program is entered into only to appease or solely to get along, then soon it will have to answer uncomfortable questions about what it has really accomplished. The rule of thumb is that the closer the goals and objectives are to the central goals and objectives of the union and management partners, the more likely the program is to maintain itself and to result in positive accomplishments. Tangential issues do not get the time and attention that central issues receive. Even if tangential issues are pursued "successfully," many do not care about the results. Some argue that cooperation should be built on first accomplishing something easy. This is generally wrong. All this proves is that cooperation can tackle the unimportant or facile issues and does not breed respect for the process or a desire to use it. On the other hand, goals for initial consideration should be within the span of control of the parties involved. It makes the issue more manageable and avoids tackling issues beyond the partners' jurisdiction and influence. Choose goals and objectives that are important and attainable. Programs should be tailored to meet real organizational needs, not squishing the real needs into the confines of a particular technique being presented.

Some of the important objectives that management may have in mind include an improved financial or market picture, better quality and reliability, and/or improved customer service. Management has a legitimate obligation to suggest that cooperative strategies be employed for cost reduction and productivity enhancement. Other objectives may be improved supervision, communications, skills development, and team work. Improved profitability is often an important management goal in the private sector. In the public sector, meeting legislated or departmental mandates better and handling political pressures more effectively can also be important goals.

The union also has many reasons to enter into a cooperative effort. These include a belief that workers should have a greater say in the workplace as a basic right and that their minds as well as their bodies should be employed. Additional objectives and goals are improved health and safety, reduced problems with supervision, increased job satisfaction, added access to information, and better union-management relations. Another objective may be helping to expand production or service in order to generate new jobs or taking a hard look at contracted-out services to see which can be accomplished better inside. Improving job security, working conditions, and the size of the pie available for bargaining often form the core objectives for the union.

To get started, there need be only one objective in common. With adjustments for complexity, the scope of cooperation is a function of the range of common goals and objectives. The parties do not have to agree on all of each other's objectives and goals. They can agree to disagree respectfully. Nor do they have to trust or like the other partner. What the initial stage needs to establish at the least is that the management finds that working on objective X is in its interest and the union finds that working on objective X is in its interest. They then agree to work on objective X together.

There is no more critical element to a successful joint union-management effort than the definition of common goals and objectives. If there are none, cooperation is impossible. Grandiose and florid statements may sound good, but they mean little in the long run. Without shared specific goals and objectives, then one group expects certain things to be done while another has different expectations. Real conflict between the union and management can develop over different expectations. The more vague or unstated the goals, the greater the potential for confusion in management and union ranks. In addition, unclear goals and objectives can cause problems in union and managerial internal politics. Rivals in either organization can seize on the general or vague statements to undercut accomplishments or credit.

The lack of specific objectives is often a cop-out from working through potential conflict to arrive at specific and mutually agreeable objectives. The temptation to leave it ambiguous almost always comes back like a boomerang and hits you in the head. Without specific goals and objectives, the parties cannot adequately design and plan, develop effective training, communicate clearly, and monitor and evaluate effectively. In short, they can't do well what it takes to make a program solid.

EXAMINING THE CURRENT ORGANIZATIONAL CLIMATE

Key to a successful program is a clear understanding of the current organizational climate and situation. This influences what kinds of cooperation are possible, if any. Often called a *feasibility assessment* or an *organizational diagnosis*, this can be conducted internally and/or with outside help. An assessment and diagnosis can be conducted separately and/or jointly by management and the union. In multiple union settings, each union may engage in its own analysis, but the various unions should coordinate as much as possible. The feasibility assessment lets the parties know whether or not they have a chance of success. An organizational diagnosis keys on critical problem areas for attention and the resources and constraints affecting any effort. These insights can be gathered through structured interviews, questionnaires, and/or review of existing organizational information sources such as profit and loss statements or summaries of grievance reports and safety records.

As normal practice, we have conducted structured interviews with equal numbers of people from both management and the unions to gather this information and feed it back to top-level decision makers to provide a data-based means for developing the program. We have found the following critical areas to be considered: possible goals and objectives; areas that need improvement and areas that go well; the labor-management relationship; previous knowledge and/or experience with cooperation or participation programs; organizational readiness, including the current level of cooperation and innovation; how a program could be structured, governed, and managed; existing training and training needs; communications patterns; time frames and staging of startup; what part(s) of the organization might start first; organizational experience with evaluation; available resources, including budget; and both the forces working in favor of and against the success of a program.

An open discussion of all the issues is necessary on each side of the table. Managers should seek the counsel of other managers at all levels on the potential nature of a joint effort. Make sure that all of the power brokers in management have some say in the initial decision and design. The union should discuss it with the membership and key leadership. It may want to hold special sessions to get input from the membership. The more open the process, the less long-term resistance to the program there will be on either side. Sometimes, seeking information from a diagonal slice through the organization chart is used to obtain varied and sufficient employee input.

Pay careful attention to timing. When new top executives come on board, they need to be involved and this may mean a limited waiting period until they become acclimated to their new positions. Just before a union election is generally a bad time for beginning this process. It requires delicate judgment if the issue is broached at the end of the contract period and the agreement is about to enter negotiation. There are always excuses about why now is a bad time. These reasons, some valid and some not, must be recognized as potential barriers and should be addressed seriously. However, the present is the moment to begin getting better. There is never a perfect time to begin, so you might as well start as soon as possible.

ANALYZING THE LABOR-MANAGEMENT RELATIONSHIP

There are two types of locations where employee involvement and cooperation programs seem to be most concentrated—places with very bad labor relations and places with very good labor relations. There have been remarkable success stories of workplaces with very bad labor relations over many years, such as the GM Tarrytown plant that used increased participation and cooperation to turn around that relationship.[2] The Relations by Objectives program of the FCMS draws on these circumstances to provide an opportunity to reexamine the labor-management relationship while improving the operations of the company. If this is the case, then the poor relationship must be recognized, and one of the objectives for the program has to be the improvement of that relationship. In these circumstances, it may take a little longer to get started so that a respectful relationship can be built up.

In other situations, the labor-management relationship is generally good, and these efforts are viewed both as a way to involve the union and the membership more fully and as a means to enhance organizational performance.

Frequently among those with good relations, an assumption is made that what worked well in the past is all that is needed to implement a new program and the necessary training and structures are watered down. This is a big mistake; new skills and structures will be necessary for the successful program *even in the best of circumstances.*

Sometimes there is an unrealistic expectation on the part of either party that before cooperation can be started there has to be sainthood in the traditional collective bargaining setting. This is unrealistic. Cooperative and adversarial labor relations can and will occur simultaneously. Hopefully, over time, a better relationship in the traditional adversarial setting will appear, but this is too much to expect from the start.

REVIEWING PREVIOUS COOPERATIVE EFFORTS

Past is prologue. Too often, lessons from the past are not assimilated into plans for the future. There is a large trash receptacle in the back of all organizations labeled "Past Programs." Vexingly, with each new program the same problems tend to recur time and again. Amnesia sets in, and the disasters of the past are not analyzed to avoid painful memories and recriminations. Often program proponents are at a loss to explain specifically why their program is "not like all of those other programs that failed in the past." It's no wonder that the lack of clear differentiation from past failed programs leads many to be skeptical of claims for new efforts.

Cooperative programs are no exception to the rule. For example, an organization considering a QWL program may previously have constituted a joint health and safety committee. Or an organization considering establishing an ongoing labor-management committee may previously have worked together on a community fund drive for the United Way. Previous and ongoing cooperative efforts must be examined to determine what outcomes or consequences occurred and whether they were desirable or undesirable. The parties need to learn if the program caused these effects or if there were other more critical factors. A simple technique is to have the parties make a list for each program and discuss what went well and what went poorly.

In addition to looking at the results of previous programs, review how it was done. Examine the startup, design process, governance, management, training, communications, monitoring, and evaluation to see what was done or not done right. These are the process issues in doing a program. Make a list identifying the critical areas for each program and again identify and discuss what went well and what could have been improved.

Mistakes and failures in the past should not be too disturbing or necessarily be barriers to the new program. The situations may have changed. The biggest mistake, however, would be not to learn from those mistakes. Use that learning to plan and implement a better program that meets the specified goals and objectives for the current effort.

LOOKING AT THE EXPERIENCES OF OTHERS

Though each organization is unique and may come up with a unique design, it is important to learn from others. There are generally two groups to seek out—in other parts of one's own organization and in other organizations.

Inside one's own company, government department, or union, there may be other segments that have engaged in similar activity. It is worth seeking them out and consulting with both management and the union to find out how they went about their activities, what went well with it, and what they would change if they could do it over again. In some large organizations, there are basic guidelines for labor-management cooperation and employee participation that must be followed, and these should be reviewed and discussed in terms of their impact on this effort.

Outside one's own organization, other companies, agencies, or unions in the area may have engaged in the kind of cooperation the parties are considering. Many are open to visits and sharing their experiences. Such groups can be found through directories of programs published by the U.S. Department of Labor and through Canada Labour. In addition, many states and provinces have associations dedicated to the development of labor-management programs and can help link organizations together. The union can contact the International and ask for information on other locals and other unions that have engaged in such a program, whether successfully or unsuccessfully. In addition, college programs of labor studies or industrial relations may have individuals knowledgeable of possible locations.

Visits are the best way to learn about what is going on. Management and labor can go together and may reserve some time to be alone with their counterparts. In the absence of a visit, a telephone interview and written case studies can be helpful. Put down ahead of time what questions the union and management would like to ask. Check out how they did or did not do the various phases of program development described in this Part. A word of caution is necessary about looking at other programs: The problems that other groups had may not be applicable to your environment. For that matter, their successes may be based on personalities and resources that may not apply to the visiting organization. Copycat programs rarely work. Learn from the experience of others but avoid mimicry.

GAUGING COMMITMENT

Determining the depth of commitment on both sides is very difficult. At some level, it comes down to whether there is enough respect between the two parties to proceed and an assessment of the importance of the issues. However, there are some tangible signs to look for. There should be top level sanction and involvement on both sides. If this is not the case, it points to limited commitment and a much more difficult road to implement changes. Potential participants in the initial stages of developing the project should be of sufficient status and caliber that success is possible. The union should be willing to discuss openly the issues and commit time and energy to the joint project.

Adequate resources should be available. A program run on the cheap will wind up with tinsel outcomes. Extravagance is not necessary, but the employer must be willing to pay for the time involved and the training needed for an effective program. Paid time for the program is critical, since if it is a way of meeting important business or operational objectives, then it should be included in work time. Managers who are too busy to find time for increased cooperation and participation are constantly fighting fires and digging deeper and deeper into ruts. Some of the ideas are going to cost money to implement. Management must be willing to give those ideas full consideration, especially when their usefulness is justified from a cost-benefit perspective.

SURVEYING THE RANGE OF OPTIONS

There is never just one way that things can be done. While the parties may reject out of hand certain types of approaches, others may be acceptable. Part Two describes the full range of cooperative possibilities. Refer to the options described there to outline alternatives. Use this as an opportunity to stretch imagination about what is possible. Possible combinations of the various approaches are practically endless. So long as the options meet the challenge of the goals and objectives then they are welcomed. Too many programs depend too heavily on one approach and are disappointed when the results fall short. On the other hand, an overly complicated approach could undermine the success of an effort. Determine at this point if it is possible to structure a program to meet the goals and objectives, but don't fixate on the techniques. The particular techniques will be refined much further during the design and planning phase.

ASSESSING THE RISKS AND BENEFITS

No situation is risk free, nor are two situations exactly alike. If all that is seen is cooperation's potential gain, then rose-colored glasses are being worn. There are always risks in any new enterprise, especially sensitive initiatives like cooperative programs. Yet, if all that is seen are possible problems, then too pessimistic and narrow a perspective is being adopted. It is essential, however, that the parties not stop at listing the benefits and the risks and then subtract the number of risks from the number of benefits to decide whether to proceed. There may be different weightings of the various entries based on their importance. For example, in assessing a team work proposal the risk of accidents while learning more skills may be more important than the risk that timecards will not be gathered correctly at the beginning. Further, there are often ways to maximize benefits and minimize risks. The parties have an obligation to see what can be done. Chapters 2 and 3 outline many of the risks and benefits for unions and managements, respectively. Some of the safeguards put into the agreement may be strategies to reduce the potential risks.

When all of the information is in, a "go or no-go" decision needs to be made. If the decision is "no go," then having engaged in the previous steps the parties know exactly why. If the decision is "go," then they have made a considered judgment. The process of reaching that decision will inform everything the parties wish to do in the future. No one can make the decision for the labor and management parties at a location. They need to accept responsibility for the decision to proceed and to make it work. Shortcutting the necessary steps leads to lower levels of commitment and less informed choices. From here on out, we make the assumption that the parties have decided to proceed, recognizing that some may choose to bow out at this time.

ARRIVING AT A WRITTEN AGREEMENT

If the program is worth doing, it is worth putting in writing the basic understanding and safeguards to make sure that there is clear understanding.

The first part of an agreement should be an expression of the willingness of the two parties to work jointly and equally on all aspects of the program. A second section should specify the goals and objectives of the joint effort. This defines what the union and management want to accomplish. Next should be clear statements on the basic safeguards built into the program. Often included are prohibitions against intrusion on collective bargaining, violating the grievance procedure, loss of employment, downgrading of positions, or increased worker stress due to the program. In some cases, this agreement specifies whether the program is an experiment with a limited time period or a permanent commitment. Some agreements also contain an exit clause that specifies how the parties will get out of the program should they so decide.

CONSIDERING A CONSULTANT

Consultants are not always necessary for the development of a cooperative project. The need for a consultant has to do with the complexity of the program and the situation. If the relationship between labor and management is bad, a mutually trusted third party might be helpful. If the skills needed to accomplish a program are not resident in the employer or the union, a consultant can help fill the gap.

Jointly interview potential consultants to determine their perspective, experience and approach. Beware of consultants who will do everything for you and have quick easy solutions. This leads to consultant dependence and simplistic analysis. In the union-management cooperation field, the consultants should be knowledgeable about collective bargaining and understand how to handle healthy conflict. Too often human resources or organizational development consultants have little understanding of unions or the collective bargaining process and have a Pollyanna perspective on conflict. This kind of consultant may be personally endearing but has a philosophy that unions are only necessary because of bad management. For them, the union is not integral to the success or operation of the project.

Seek consultants who are evenhanded and able to deal well with both sides. Sometimes union-busting firms work in unionized workplaces and try to portray themselves as friendly to unions. They should be rejected because discovery of their activities can blow a program apart and cast aspersions on the real motivations for the effort. More importantly, they really don't believe in union-management cooperation. Consultants who can see only the union perspective should also be avoided. Check out consultant references with both management and labor at places where they have worked. The consultant should be agreeable to both parties and perceive both as equal clients even if management is picking up the cost. Remember when hiring them that the program must remain controlled by the labor-management partners, not the consultant.

Good consultants will have a clear plan of how they will work with you and work themselves out of a job at your location. They should be building the skills internally to maintain the effort in a quality way. As clients, the union and management should have a clear idea of what they want the consultant to do, thereby being more cost-effective and directed. The greater the clarity of the contracting between the consultant and the labor-management partners the better the working relationship.

CONCLUSION

Good union-management cooperative efforts stem from a realistic understanding of the motivations for working together and the mutually acceptable goals and objectives. Setting important and realistic goals and objectives provides the centerpiece for the construction of a viable program. The decision to proceed with a joint effort should also take into consideration the current organizational climate, the labor-management relationship, previous cooperative efforts, the experience of others, the level of internal commitment, and the range of possible options. All of these factors should be reviewed to determine the possible risks and benefits to the employer and the union of engaging in a cooperative effort. The parties should seriously consider ways to minimize the risks and maximize the benefits and make a go or no-go decision. Finally, this should be crystallized in a written agreement setting out the directions, understandings, and safeguards of the joint effort. In some cases, consultants will be used to help aid the process. Adopting this way of entering a program informs the entire process. For those stopping here, they know what the barriers to cooperation are. For those continuing on, they are firmly grounded and ready to undertake a serious and important joint effort.

ADDITIONAL RESOURCES

Burton, Cynthia, and Edward Cohen-Rosenthal. "Implementing QWL in Unionized Settings: The Basic Steps." In *Quality of Work Life: Perspectives for Business and the Public Sector*, ed. Daniel Skrovan (47–56). Reading, Mass.: Addison-Wesley, 1983.

Communications Workers of America/Bell System Joint National Committee on Working Conditions and Service Quality Improvement. "Roadmap for Successfully Managing Quality of Work Life." February 1983.

Mansell, Jacquie, and Tom Rankin. *Changing Organizations: The Quality of Working Life Process*. Ontario Quality of Working Life Centre, September 1983.

Ontario Quality of Working Life Centre. "Starting Up a Redesign Project," *QWL Focus* 1 (March 1981). 1–7.

12

Setting Clear Direction: Designing and Planning an Effective Union-Management Cooperation Program

With a decision in hand to proceed with a union-management cooperative effort, it is now time to turn it into reality. Designing and planning the program are opportunities for the union and management to apply their energy to make their commitment to joint participation happen. What was decided earlier were the areas of common interest and the basic safeguards and boundaries. If the union and management find themselves agreeing first on the techniques, then they are way ahead of the game. The joint objectives come first and the appropriate approaches come next. Agreeing to a design presented by outside parties or internal proponents before the preliminaries are worked out can be a major mistake. Especially beware of the outside consultant who pushes only one approach as the right approach. Later, if the program doesn't deliver what was promised, it may have been that valid objectives and goals were suited in the wrong clothes, it was poorly tailored, or the way it was made was incorrect.

CONDUCTING A JOINT UNION-MANAGEMENT DESIGN PROCESS

The program design describes the particular approach to union-management cooperation and fostering participation that the union and management partners will use. The design also describes the specific techniques that will be used in the program, such as quality circles, labor-management committees, autonomous work teams, task forces, bargaining study teams, or the like. One can think of the program design as the blueprint of the program. It lays out the broad framework for what will be done in the future. The design process ensures the closest fit between the organizations involved and the desired goals.

The highest level of the union and management concerned with the issues jointly targeted should be involved in the design of the program. These people are the union and management partners to the program, the same people who formulated the agreement to go forward described earlier. Other management and union representatives from the location can also join in this phase under the direct supervision of the top leadership.

The union and management designers should be directly and equally involved in every step of formulating the program design (see Figure 12.1). The design process should build on the union-management cooperation generated during the initial decision to proceed. The designers should work together as a group in smaller subcommittees and/or in union-management pairs to accomplish the tasks required at each step in the design process. An internal or external consultant may assist the union-management designers in the design process. However, the consultant(s) should be working for and with the union-management designers. The program design absolutely should not be put together solely by a consultant. The union-management designers should draw on the consultant as a technical resource to assist them in the design process. It is the internal parties' program and it must fit their own situation.

Exactly how long it will take to design the program will vary from location to location, depending on the range of common objectives and the scale of the cooperative agreement, as well as on the particular characteristics of the employer and the union. In any case, adequate time must be set aside to do this well. For a simple program, design need not take long, but for more complex challenges full attention to design is a necessity. Careful design of a cooperative program is an essential and critical step in the successful program. Too often, this step is rushed through or skipped over in favor of accepting a prefabricated design. This is usually done for understandable reasons. The parties do not trust their own knowledge of how to do it and want to get things moving quickly. While they may need to learn some new information and skills, the premise of a union-management problem-solving activity is that experience and knowledge inside the organization can be drawn on for decision making. This knowledge of one's own workplace, which even the best outsider cannot know as well, is critical to a tailored program. One can learn much from others, but application inside is an internal decision. Rushing into a program willy-nilly or without proper adjustment to the local environment can cause long-term delays, muted performance, or outright failures.

The design process works best by following the steps outlined below:

1. Use the goals and objectives for the program outlined in the decision to proceed. The design is meant to put these into practice. We may sound like a broken record throughout all of Part Three, but the goals and objectives generated at the start provide the reference points for every part of the development of the joint program. The design process is the first area where they are put to use.

2. Identify all of the cooperative and participative techniques that could be used to meet all or part of the goals and objectives. These techniques and approaches can be found in Part Two of this book and in some of the resources that are identified. Table 12-1 shows the range of objectives/problem areas and possible approaches. The chart is intended to steer the user in the right direction. Not all of the approaches will work in every organization or they may need to be linked to other or new approaches. Exercise

FIGURE 12-1
Designing a Program

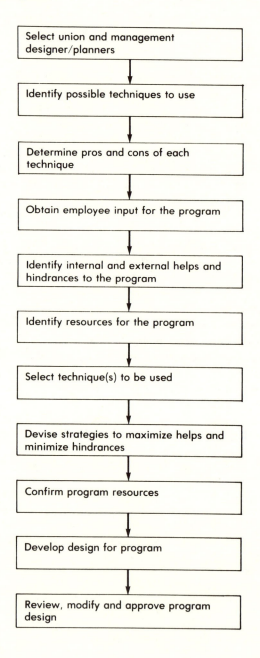

Select union and management designer/planners

Identify possible techniques to use

Determine pros and cons of each technique

Obtain employee input for the program

Identify internal and external helps and hindrances to the program

Identify resources for the program

Select technique(s) to be used

Devise strategies to maximize helps and minimize hindrances

Confirm program resources

Develop design for program

Review, modify and approve program design

TABLE 12-1

Union-Management Cooperative Approaches to Use According to Specific Problems or Objectives

Problem Area	Possible Approaches Include
Organization Problems	
Market	Labor-management promotion institutes
	Labor-management marketing teams
	Joint advertising programs
	Construction market recovery programs
	Job redesign
	Customer service programs
	Joint seminars for customers
	New product development
Financial	Profit sharing
	ESOPs
	Productivity gain sharing
Investment	Joint investment funds
	Pension fund investments
	ESOPs
Adapting to change	Strategic collective bargaining
	Labor-management committees
	Sociotechnical redesign
Community image	Joint promotion campaigns
	Customer service programs
	Joint United Way campaigns
	Joint volunteer efforts
	Adopt a school
Labor-management relations	Relations by Objectives (RBOs)
	Problem-solving grievance handling
	Strategic collective bargaining
	Integrative collective bargaining
	Union-management conflict resolution
	General labor-management committees
	Quality of work life programs
Operational Problems	
Facilities	New plant design task forces
	Plant redesign joint committees
	Sociotechnical redesign
Technology	New technology joint committees
	Union-management task forces
	Sociotechnical redesign
	Quality circles
	Autonomous work groups
	Joint meetings with vendors
Productivity	Individual and group incentives
	Productivity gain-sharing programs
	New technology committees
	Labor-management committees
	Flextime
	Quality circles

(continued)

153

TABLE 12-1 (continued)

Problem Area	Possible Approaches Include
Quality	Labor-management committees
	Union-management task forces
	Quality circles
	Sociotechnical redesign
	New technology committees
Resources use	Cooperative conservation committees
	QWL programs
	Union-management task forces
	Quality circles
	Autonomous work groups
	Job redesign
	New technology committees
Structure	Parallel structures
	Matrix
	Sociotechnical redesign
	Autonomous work groups

Employee Problems

Problem Area	Possible Approaches Include
Security	Strategic collective bargaining
	Contracting in task forces
	Joint marketing efforts
	New product development
	QWL programs
	Board level representation
	Joint investment activities
Working conditions	Strategic collective bargaining
	Integrative collective bargaining
	Problem-solving grievance handling
	General labor-management committees
	Health and safety committees
	Quality circles
	QWL programs
	Job redesign
	Flextime
	Sociotechnical redesign
Career development	Joint orientation sessions
	Apprenticeship committees
	Training committees
	Autonomous work groups
	Pay for knowledge
	Preretirement training
	Joint layoff preparation
	Plant closing assistance
Communications	Board level representation
	Labor-management committees
	Union-management task forces
	QWL programs
	Quality circles
	Autonomous work groups
Substance abuse and personal problems	Employee assistance programs
	Problem-solving grievance handling

imagination in looking at the possibilities and be open to examining inventions that combine features of several kinds of cooperative programs or adds necessary modifications. The best way is to assemble a packet of information about each of the techniques under consideration. Subgroups of the design team could divide up the task of gathering information. There may be a need to do additional research on some of these techniques. The information can be obtained from books and articles available through an in-house library at the employer or union (if available) or at libraries at a local college or in the community. Written material and other insight and information may be obtained though state, provincial, and regional productivity and quality of working life centers, labor studies centers, industrial relations programs, business schools, union or corporate headquarters, consulting firms specializing in this area and/or federal sources such as the U.S. Department of Labor or Commerce and Canada Labour. Several of these sources may need to be used to get a complete picture. Each member of the design team should have a complete collection of information on each technique. For complex programs, third party assistance will probably be necessary to do a thorough job.

The team wants to have a full understanding of how the technique works, what it can accomplish and what it usually doesn't accomplish. Critical areas to look at include the level of the organization where the approach operates, necessary sanction level, what kinds and numbers of employees are or can be involved, resources needed, issues addressed, time commitments, training requirements, success and failure record, kinds of results generally obtained, impact on collective bargaining, staffing requirements, length of the problem-solving process, potential use with different kinds of employees in the organization, costs, impact on employment, and effect on personnel allocation and compensation.

3. Determine in detail the pros and cons of each of the techniques as measured against the goals and objectives. The designers should discuss what it is about the technique that will aid or block the achievement of the overall objectives. For example, if one of the goals is to promote interdepartmental cooperation, quality circles would not be an appropriate technique since they are by definition inside of a common work area. But they would help with product quality improvement or internal teamwork. Or if an objective was greater communication with hourly employees, labor-management committees may be one way to spread information via the union to the membership. Before-work startup meetings or a joint newsletter may be other approaches to the same end. In one company where we were working, the major common concern was customer service. This issue was addressed by middle-level problem-solving groups of managers and union business agents, by store committees with employees from every department, and, under the leadership of the union and management, directly with each employee in the store working together with other members of their department. They felt that only one way to look at the problem would have been insufficient.

4. Obtain input from others throughout the organization. The designers, based on their discussion, will develop hypotheses about the best ways to meet the objectives. These should be listed in priority order or bundled in ways that seem the most effective. The opinions of managers and employees at all levels should also be solicited about whether these would be effective ways to achieve their stated objectives in their particular location. This information may be available from the earlier stages of getting started or may be new data for the consideration of the designers. That people may resist an approach does not mean it cannot work but that its implementation will require attention to the reasons for resistance.

There are several ways to obtain the input of employees at all levels. One way is to use the input gathered during the feasibility stage of getting started. Often employees consulted at this time gave ideas on whether to do a program and what such a program should look like. Another way is to gather information through a series of information-giving/information-getting meetings with employees. One program we worked with used this strategy for design by holding meetings with every fifth person on the seniority roster in order to get a fair and accurate distribution of opinion. At these kinds of meetings, the management and union designers would explain to the employees what has been decided about the program thus far, such as the goals and objectives, boundaries, and safeguards. Also, examples of other similar efforts can be described to give them a basic idea of what is being discussed. The employee group can be solicited as to their opinions on key items of importance to the designers. Small focus groups could also be used for this purpose. A third method is to obtain input via the traditional management and union channels. Management can use its usual forums, such as staff meetings and memos, to solicit ideas. The union can bring it up at the union meeting or print some information in the union newspaper.

5. Next generate a list of the motivating and restraining forces that will affect the implementation of a joint program. Based on the data from employees and other opinions and information available to the designers, the internal and external helps and hindrances the various approaches to the program might encounter should be identified. An internal help, for example, may be funds already earmarked for improving operations and a hindrance may be lack of a specific budget. In identifying the hindrances, think of all of the things that could go wrong or get in the way of that particular approach working inside the designated work setting or organization. Finding all of these negatives is often easier than being aware of the things that can help make the approach fit. Often taken for granted, it requires real concentration to identify the helps fully. In both the helps and hindrances categories consider the impact of resources, internal and external pressures, market conditions, suppliers, legal requirements, forthcoming events, timing, finances, size of work units, organizational structure, seasonal adjustments, reporting relationships, shift work, geographic location of employees, customer needs, attitudes of employees, and other essential factors. Looking at both sides should provide a realistic assessment of the forces working in favor and against the workability of a proposed alternative. This assessment is called a force field analysis.

6. Identify the potential resources upon which the program might draw. The designers should examine such areas as training professionals within the employer or union, space for meetings, skilled internal employees who have worked on similar programs, and/or available budget funds. There should be a comparison of the resources available and the resources needed to apply any particular strategy. Maximum use should be made of internal resources. Cost-effective approaches should be pursued. If two techniques will achieve the same objectives, choose the one with the lower cost and/or a more streamlined design.

7. Consider all of the above information to make a judgment on which strategy or set of techniques should be pursued. The designers should also consider the list of features from previous programs inside the organization that affected the process and outcomes positively or negatively. The experiences of other organizations can also provide key clues to design features. In locations part of a larger organizational effort, factor in the guidelines established by corporate, union, or departmental authorities. In many cases,

the final result will be a hybrid version of various kinds of approaches to cooperation and participation.

8. Brainstorm and decide on various ways to maximize the internal and external helps and minimize the hindrances to best ensure the success of the program. The list of helps and hindrances was developed earlier. It is too time consuming and unnecessary to conduct this analysis for every single technique, which is why it appears after the initial cut has been made. However, if there is a relatively close call on an either/or choice between options, then this analysis could be done earlier to see which would be most feasible. An example of addressing a hindrance may be responding to a resistance to the terms "quality of work life" or "cooperation." The design group may decide that a new description should be applied. Or it may be aware of the changeover in a key position and develop ways to get the new person involved. Some hindrances cannot be completely removed or ·circumvented. The designers should determine what can be done to minimize the hindrance most effectively. Some issues will reflect items over which there is little control and hence great uncertainty. For example, work forces whose availability are weather-related, may require backup people and times. In another case, there may be uncertainty on funding of various parts of an organization due to legislative inquiries or potental buyouts. Clarification and flexibility may be necessary.

9. Confirm the resources needed to conduct the approach identified. Check them out to see the extent to which the program can count on them. In addition, a listing of needed additional resources should be prepared and costed out as much as possible. In most union-management cooperative programs, the most precious commodity is time. Supplies and consultants usually are a minor cost compared to the time spent by internal employees in the activities of the problem-solving groups.

10. Prepare and deliver a design report to the entire group of top union-management decision makers about the recommended approach. The report should cover the techniques to be used, the structures to be established and their responsibilities, the management and staffing of the project, location of the initial activities, training, communications, monitoring, evaluation, and resource requirements.

Going through this process provides these decision makers with a clear idea of what the alternatives are and why the one(s) chosen best address(es) the primary goals and concerns of the program. If lays out a realistic assessment of what will help it along and what may get in the way, as well as strategies to manage these factors. The accounting of the resources available and the resources needed completes the picture for informed decision making. Checking in at this point and getting approval allows the effort to proceed to planning confident that common understanding about the fundamental design has been reached.

PLANNING THE PROGRAM JOINTLY

After the initial design, the success of the entire project hinges on proper planning. The best ideas mean little if they are not implemented or if they are done wrong. Some program developers are loathe to plan. They prefer to let things happen as the process unfolds. People avoid planning in order not to look wrong or off schedule. The reasoning goes that if no one knows what should have happened it is difficult to criticize when "something" doesn't occur. Frankly, people are rarely fooled by this ruse. Paradoxically, people who do not plan make more mistakes and vary more from the perceived schedule. Further, sometimes people don't plan in a rush to get things done. Yet poor planning usually results in more time needed to complete a significant task rather than less. People also don't plan to avoid conflicts over what to do. Yet, in fact, the process of planning deepens the common relationship and lessens conflict over diverging unstated agendas and approaches.

Most people have limited experience with structured planning. Their most structured is a "to-do list." While a list can be a reminder of things to accomplish, it is not a plan because it isn't broad enough. It misses essential factors and does not provide a sequence for action. Planning is absolutely critical to the success of a union-management cooperative program. Overwhelmingly, the reason for programs that do not succeed is lack of adequate planning. Conversely, a well-planned program is confident of its direction, secure in the knowledge of what will be done, and clear with others about expectations. Plans are used as a way to conceptualize an entire process, as a way to identify needed steps not initially apparent, as an orientation tool to let others know what is being done, as goals to spur the process, and as a means to identify more clearly future implications if changes are necessary.

The program plans details exactly how the effort will be done. In general, plans do three things. They specify exactly what it is that needs to be done, they define the process for reaching those goals, and they identify strategies and techniques to accomplish the effort. For example, a plan for a union-management cooperative effort should specify how it will be started, how it will be maintained over time, and how it will be evaluated. The program plan takes the basic program design as if it were the skeleton for the program and adds the flesh to that skeleton in the form of descriptive detail. The plans brings to life what was only concept.

The program plan answers the following questions: who is to do what, when, where, for what purpose(s), and with what resources. A program plan should cover at least one year. It may be best to devise an initial 18-month plan covering a six-month startup and a one-year operating period for large-scale programs. The later rounds are also very important to plan clearly, especially in regard to reviewing and renewing the major program design features.

DEVELOPING THE PROGRAM PLAN

The management and the union designers should also be the planners of the joint effort. Together, they should develop the program plan using the steps

FIGURE 12-2
Planning a Program

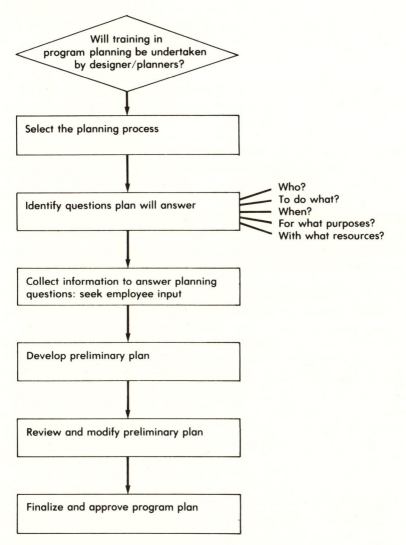

shown in Figure 12-2. They may want to use the services of an internal or external consultant to help in this process, but, again, the consultant assisting the planners works for and with them during the planning process. The consultant should be a technical resource and/or provide staff support to the planners. The more complex, the more necessary is competent third party assistance.

Just as with program design, the planners should seek input from all levels of the organization while constructing the plan. Much information useful for planning will already have been obtained through earlier activities. However, it is important to have a clear process for getting additional needed input from employees for planning at this time. Key items to check again are timing and resource issues.

Two elements increase the probability of successful planning. *Specificity* brings out all of the details about what needs to be done. Statements like "I know what I mean but can't put it down in writing" or "Don't worry about it now" signal trouble ahead. Generalizations in planning are not helpful. Second, all plans change due to circumstances that arise. The parties should *learn from miscalculations or unanticipated events* to ensure more realistic planning for the future. The fact that plans will change over time should not deter the parties from planning; the plans provide the framework for any reconsideration of the program. Plans are meant to be dynamic documents that help respond to changing conditions. In estimating the time that it will take to complete tasks, keep in mind that the probable time frame is somewhere between the optimistic and the cautious estimates.

The overall process for planning a joint union-management program is as follows:

1. Set out the major categories that need to be planned. These may include the selection of groups, meeting locations and times, completion of governing documents and plans, startup, training, recognition, communications and publicity, monitoring, and evaluation. Each area should have its own plan and be integrated into a master plan. Staff for the program should plan out their communications, backup contingencies, supplies, coordination with governing bodies, and other logistics. Each problem-solving group should develop a plan for the development, carrying out, and tracking of the problem-solving projects within its responsibility. The governing body monitoring the groups should be able to tell at any point where each group is in the process. There should be separate sets of plans for each level of the program—top, middle, and shop or office level. Planning should be built into the problem solving itself, including plans for data collection and the implementation of solutions.

2. For each of these plans, collect information for answering the planning questions. All six of the following categories need to be answered. Plans that fail to address any one of these questions are unquestionably weaker.

- *Why*: Specify the statement or purpose of the effort, the need the effort is supposed to meet, and the goals and objectives that it helps meet. If there is no clear answer to these questions, then the task has to be clarified before being included. Fuzzy or no answers to the why questions should lead to reconsideration about the inclusion of the activity.
- *What*: What exactly is to be done (that is, the tasks and activities to be accomplished).
- *Who*: Who is involved in the effort and what role each person plays.

• *When*: Over what period of time this activity occurs and when the planned activity begins and ends.

• *Where*: Where in the organization are activities located and what physical space will be used.

• *How*: What processes, procedures, methods, and techniques will be used to accomplish the task and what additional resources will be necessary.

3. Develop a preliminary plan. Carefully look it over to see if one can move smoothly from step to step. Particularly review it to locate illogical or unnecessary activities and periods in which too many activities are scheduled at the same time to be adequately handled. The plan should shadow what would actually occur and describe each step that will be taken. Someone unfamiliar with the program should be able to piece it together from the plan itself with little difficulty. However, don't overcomplicate the issues. Use simple language or an outline. Look for comprehensiveness, not complexity. Sometimes the answers are very obvious. Even the obvious should be included in the plan if it answers a critical question. At all points, the plan needs to be evaluated to ask whether it makes the most sense in terms of efficient use of time and resources and promotes effective performance of the tasks and meets the overall goals and objectives of the joint initiative. The pacing in a plan should be brisk. Too rapid or too languorous a pace will harm the development of a program. As much as possible, the means used to accomplish the tasks should mirror the values inherent in the overall effort. This means that a participation program should be participative in its implementation throughout and that joint union-management initiatives should mirror jointness and equality in all of its process.

Use a common format to outline the plan. A form we have used successfully is the action plan log. The action plan log is a chart with columns down the page for critical planning elements. The first column is the "item" category, which lists what and why. It provides the general category. The next column is "action," which describes how the item will be done by noting all of the tasks and subtasks necessary for completion. For each action, an entry is made under a "who" column, indicating who will be responsible and who will be involved. "Resources needed" is a column that specifies the materials, equipment, or funds needed to accomplish the task. A final set of entries on the chart is "when." Specific dates can be entered into three subcategories of "startup", "target," and "actual."

4. Share the plan with the top union and management decision makers involved in the effort. Doing so generates additional information and input into the plan. It also creates sanction for the implementation of the plan. These decision makers should finalize and approve the plan. This serves as an agreement about what will be done, by whom, when, and with what resources. If difficulties arise in the future, then this document serves as the basis for reserving resources and maintaining commitments. The top-level sanction means they can help ensure close adherence to the plan. These documents should be shared with others interested and involved in the effort.

5. Use and review the plans. Plans do no good if they are just filed away. They must be reviewed on a regular basis. Every committee, problem-solving group, and staff person associated with a program should review their plans at least once at month. When changes are necessary, they should be discussed and agreed to by both the union and management. Communicate the changes to those affected by the ammendments and to the governing committees to whom the group reports. Mark down when parts of the plan are

accomplished. Doing so will generally provide a sense of accomplishment along the way to completion of major tasks or activities. If the date targeted is frequently different than the date accomplished, then in the future planning needs to be more realistic or other problems may need to be addressed.

TRAINING THE JOINT DESIGNER/PLANNERS

A number of planning processes could be used to develop the program plan, including Action Plan Logs, such as PERT (Program Evaluation and Review Technique) and Critical Path Analysis. The union or management may have little experience with structured planning of this type. Frankly, the precise techniques used are less important that the fact of a conscious and systematic effort to plan jointly. Both union and management planners often will need to have training in program planning processes and skills. Such training can take the form of a workshop conducted on site for the planners by an internal or external consultant/trainer. Regardless of who conducts the training, all of the union and management planners should participate in it. The training should be a mixture of theory of planning and application to the tasks at hand. The training should be sensitive to the various information sources and experience bases of the union and management. The parties should come away confident that they can plan the program together. Learning and acting more on planning not only benefits the joint program but enhances the capabilities of the employer and the union in their separate responsibilities.

CONCLUSION

The design and plan for a union-management program give it form and direction. The design provides a realistic tailoring to the actual organizations involved. It, at the same time, asks the parties to consider broadly the possibilities and exercise imagination in its creation and molding to their particular circumstances. By using a joint approach to designing the program, the first steps are being taken in actualizing the union-management cooperative commitment made earlier. A new process, skills level and spirit, is being engendered.

The planning anchors the program in concrete actions. It sets specific directions and clear expectations. The planning describes how an idea will become reality. The plans are the specific goals for implementing the overall goals of the program. Working together on establishing directions uncovers important decisions and resolves them. Later on the plans provide important tools for training participants, communicating about the program, monitoring progress, and evaluating results.

13

Taking Charge:
Governing and Managing a
Union-Management Cooperation Program

WHY JOINTLY MANAGE AND GOVERN
A COOPERATIVE EFFORT?

Programs work better when both parties are working together in an equal manner. Think of a rowboat. If only one oar is in the water, it is more difficult to advance quickly and steer effectively. If there are two oars and they go opposite ways, the boat comes to a standstill or revolves in circles. But if both oars are in the water and pulling together, then the boat moves more quickly and directly. The analogy holds true here as well. A program with both the union and management pulling equally is a more effective program since it draws on the strengths and resources of both parties. It has a clearer sense of direction and usually can accomplish tasks quicker.

Unfortunately, too many programs have been undertaken unilaterally by management or with only token union involvement. These tend to be much weaker efforts. Where management and labor work well together in joint programs, they provide complementary perspectives. When either side is having difficulty due to organizational pressure, they help each other out. Not only is co-management much better practically, it also recognizes the institutional responsibilities of the management and union for exercising leadership and oversight. The best way to manage a joint project aimed at mutual gain is jointly and equally. This process is shown in Figure 13-1.

THE ROLE OF GOVERNING BODIES
OR STEERING COMMITTEES

The kind of governing structure to establish depends on the kind of cooperation the design calls for, the size of the organization, and the dispersion of the

FIGURE 13-1
Governing and Managing a Program

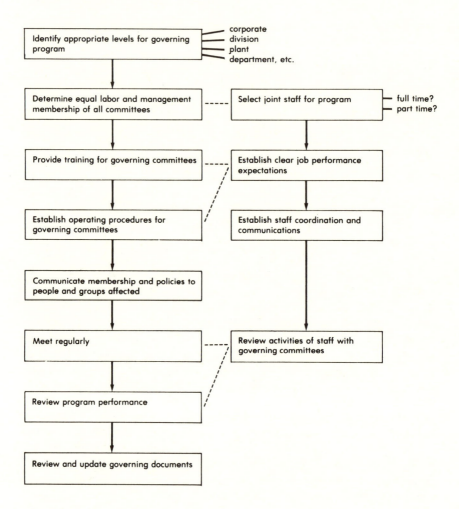

work force. If an organization is large, then there may be several levels of governing committees. These make a better fit between the program and various tiers of the organization or functional units. If an organization is very spread out, there also may be various governing bodies to correspond to the geographic dispersion. However, if only very few employees are at each location, then some rethinking on an appropriate structure may be in order. Of course, the kind of program is the central variable. If the program is a labor-management committee or a way of conducting the bargaining session, then this deserves a different response than establishing quality circles at the shop floor or office level.

All programs need to be sure that they have effective governance to guide and nurture the effort. When the program extends beyond the activities of one or a few small groups, then some sort of coordination and governance is necessary. The comanagement of the process requires formal structures to keep it going. Informal agreements or laissez-faire approaches simply do not work beyond the short term. Too many programs become the domain of consultants or particular personalities on either side and no structure is established to run the program. Such programs have a very thin or tenuous base of organizational support and guidance. If something should happen to the prime shakers, then the program will collapse. Good governing structures shore up the framework of the program.

A joint steering or governing committee overseeing a cooperative employee participation program may have to relate to many different audiences. Such committees need to work with the various problem-solving groups to support them, set guidelines, troubleshoot problems, monitor their activities, visit periodically, recognize accomplishments, and evaluate them. If there are facilitators and staff within their jurisdiction, steering committees should serve as a support system that provides constructive feedback, reviews their plans, monitors their activities, and evaluates performance. The committee should interact with local management to ensure open communication, encourage technical assistance, squelch rumors, ensure that adequate time is being allowed, and ensure that respect for management authority is being maintained. In relation to local labor, the steering committee has to maintain open communication, answer rumors, and ensure compliance with the contract. It also has an internal obligation to try to work together as a team, hold effective meetings, plan for the activities in its area of juridiction, and monitor and evaluate all activities under its purview, including its own functioning. A steering committee helps plan the next steps or expansion of an effort. In some cases, the steering committee selects those who will have other roles in the program such as facilitators or leaders.

Governing bodies rarely make good facilitators for small group activities and should not interfere directly. In most cases, these steering committees make decisions about the program but do not make the final decision on the recommendations for improvement or changes in the employer. If the decision would normally be a management decision, then the normal decision maker should render a decision. This is important both out of respect for management's decision-making authority and to contain union liability questions. In almost all cases, steering committee membership is not a full-time responsibility, and the group needs to manage itself in a way that balances these activities with other responsibilities.

TOP-LEVEL INVOLVEMENT

All levels of an organization have to be involved in a comprehensive project. One group for which this is especially true is the top level of management and the union. An executive or top-level committee provides the view from the higher rungs of the organization. The top level of the program establishes overall guidelines for the effort, provides guidance and leadership, demonstrates support, establishes and ratifies an overall plan, and monitors and evaluates progress. It is best if the top level is also engaged in joint problem sòlving on issues and concerns at its level of the organization.

Efforts to "end run" the top levels of management and the union rarely succeed in the long term. Top-level involvement means not only the top of the organization chart but also the people with clout. It does no good to have a committee that has to keep looking elsewhere for decisions. The deliberations in the committee will not be meaningful.

To say that the top level has to be involved does not mean that it has to be 100 percent committed or involved all of the time. But people at the top must fully understand what is going on, sanction the process, and be willing to give it a fair chance. On some occasions, senior-level people may have to step in and use their formal power to make sure that those below them are also giving the program their full support. There are ways to manage the time commitment so that upper level officials can attend meetings and functions as much as possible.

Often, top-level participants are reluctant to engage in training or to attack specific problem areas and use structured problem-solving methodology to reach conclusions. While impressed with the impact of this approach in the lower parts of the organization, they exempt themselves. Though understandable, it unfortunately prevents spreading new skills and problem resolution at higher levels. The problem solving at the higher level can be adjusted to the time constraints and responsibilities of the participants. A consistent program would model cooperation and thoughtul problem solving at all levels.

MIDDLE-LEVEL INVOLVEMENT

While sanction from the top is critical, real involvement of those in the middle is equally important. Perhaps the biggest stumbling block to cooperative and participative programs has been middle-level resistance. There are several important reasons to have middle-level management involved. First, they usually have a tremendous amount of knowledge and expertise in the problems under consideration and therefore add to the problem-solving capabilities. Second, they are likely to be involved in approving and putting into place changes and therefore will be key to successful implementation. Third, no one likes to have his or her position eroded, and sometimes there is an impresssion that these kinds of programs aim at showing up the mistakes of the people in the middle and circumventing their authority.

Middle-level managers and unionists can be involved in several ways. In large organizations there can be one, two, or even more layers of committees that oversee the program's application in various parts of the organization. These groups are composed of middle-level labor and management members who are closer to the situation and can provide closer monitoring and adaptation to local conditions. The aim of these committees is not to bureaucratize the process but to assist the successful introduction, maintenance, and growth of activities. It is a shame to use this resource only for program monitoring of lower level activities. It is best if these middle-level groups become problem-solving groups in their own right and address significant issues at their level. This adds real substance and respect to the task of middle-level involvement.

For a large organization, the middle level may include various levels of the union hierarchy. For example in auto plants, there are zone committee persons who work with a higher level in the plant; in railroads, there are local union chairpersons who handle a location. Too often, the participation only involves the top elected union official. In both small and large locations, consideration must be given to how to involve the stewards. They can be members of the shop floor level problem-solving committees or cochair them to provide union visibility and involvement.

On the management side, while projects are best when they are "owned" by line management, some way of involving support staff and technical experts needs to be addressed. Their expertise can be used by linking them actively into task forces and other flexible problem-solving teams.

SELECTING PARTICIPANTS

Some argue strongly that all cooperative programs need to be based on voluntary participation. We dissent from that opinion. While we agree that if the members are willing participants, it makes things easier, easier is not always what is necessary. Organizations have hierarchies and power structures. These need to be respected and used. Groups composed of top levels from management and the union need to acknowledge that they represent positions in their organizations. If they were to die or leave, someone would be hired to fulfill their roles (if not, then maybe the position shouldn't be there in the first place!).

Union-management cooperation is the cooperation between two institutions and their agents. While participative programs deal with people, the people are there because they are parts of an organization, not as individuals, and their interactions are within the context of their organizational affiliations. Programs based on personalities suffer from mood swings, but programs meshed with the organizational structure stand firm. Furthermore, the agreement to proceed becomes the policy of the organizations involved, just like any other policy decision. Once a decision is reached, organization members are expected to adhere to the policy of their organization. If cooperation and participation are ways of doing business, then managers should be required to implement faithfully this policy. If the union has agreed to cooperate in certain areas, then this agreement must be lived up to by the union. In cases where there can be a choice of participants, it is best to take the most willing. However, when there can be no choice, as in total system change activities, then reluctant participants must be expected to contribute and their performance should be monitored.

The governing committees should be drawn equally from labor and management. In some cases that may not be possible, such as on the railroads where there may be 20 different local unions at a location. While some locations have separate committees for different unions, it is preferable if there is cooperation on a joint committee at the top. There may also be separate groups for subsections of the organization represented by the various unions. By definition, shop floor groups will not be equally balanced. Whatever the composition, the groups should aim for consensus on decision. In the absence of total consensus, they should agree on a fair way to make decisions that doesn't play one side off against the other and builds the broadest agreement.

The employer should select its representatives for any part of the program calling for management. Delegation of tasks is a normal management responsibility. As its elected representative, the union should select any representatives of the employees. Selection by the powers that be on each side makes for a stronger program. Being on the outs with the influential leadership can cause disaster or gridlock. Linking to them reinforces the notion that union-management cooperation is important and central to the missions of both sides. This should not lead to cronyism, and leadership should look for diverse input and a way to involve new people. Sometimes the best help can come from unexpected quarters. In a few programs, elections have worked out. At the Minneapolis *Star-Tribune*, the union representatives were elected. In general, this is unnecessary since the union is already a result of elections and it splits the union into two groups of elected officials, the cooperators and the confronters.

In programs with quality circles, employee involvement groups, or other shop or office level groups, there are leaders designated for the groups. Traditionally, these have been the first-line supervisors. There are good reasons to install the supervisor. The program generally teaches new skills that will enhance the abilities and standing of the supervisors. Since good supervision is key to the success of an enterprise, this opportunity for skills development should not be overlooked. In most of these groups, the leader's role is to ensure that the process is followed and not to interfere on the content. Segregating the role in this way helps remove the supervisor from dominating the group. Some programs, like the Labor-Management Participation Teams in the steel industry, insist on having the bottom-level groups cochaired by a supervisor and a union designate, usually the steward. So long as teamwork is demonstrated, this can also be a good situation. Some programs have elected rank and file leaders for their groups. We think this is a bad idea. It undercuts the role of the first-line supervisor as a problem solver and in the union sets up political rivalries with the steward by creating a competing elected office.

Large and complex programs do not just happen. They need people to help make it work and to take care of the day-to-day tasks. The principle of each side choosing its own holds true for the selection of coordinators and facilitators who staff the project. There may be some sort of joint interviewing process, but the final choice should be up to each party. One criterion that should be used is the ability of the people selected from both sides to work as a team. Staff should be able to work well with people, collect and analyze data, understand collective bargaining, and be able to adjust to many different situations. They should also be able to handle planning, monitoring, and other program management skills.

For shop floor or office level teams, when there are more employees than openings for participation in the program, the selection should be as fair as possible to avoid favoritism. One successful technique is to have all who want to volunteer put their names in a hat. The participants in the problem-solving group and backup alternates are determined by the luck of the draw. In every company we have worked with, to the surprise of the local handicappers, some of the most effective participants turn out to be people who would not have been appointed because of their reputations. Often the more negative person will become one of the best members because he or she now has a positive outlet for his or her frustrations and energy.

In the development of sociotechnical design and new forms of work teams, consideration needs to be given to seniority to ensure fair access to the groups. When another system cannot be agreed upon by the joint partners, seniority should be the prevailing way of making selections.

DEVELOPING GOVERNING DOCUMENTS

Clarity in a program about where it wants to go, the way it should work, and the areas to stay out of provides essential guidance to the participants. Too often, these things are left unsaid. This mistakes vagueness for flexibility and inserts confusion where the parties thought they had trust. Each level of the governing structure should have a clear governing document to outline its position. In general, these fall into three levels in a top to bottom joint participation program: project principles statements, policies and procedures statements, and codes of conduct. While these do set boundaries for activities that are not allow-ed, the primary objective of these governing documents is to encourage and sup-port the program. They should be enabling documents, not naysaying in-struments, and should be clearly communicated to all members of the program having copies. It is best if the governing committee that propagated the docu-ment presents it in person and explains it to the groups below. Also, these documents can be used to orient other employees not yet involved about the pro-gram.

The top level of an organization must clearly establish its support and understanding of an employee involvement program if the program is to be a success. A *project principles* statement provides guidance and leadership to the top committee and other levels of the organization(s) involved in the process. It also demonstrates in black and white that the union and management are work-ing together cooperatively. These top-level governing documents are rarely lengthy but articulate the basic principles of the program.

The first section sets out the basic goals and objectives by listing what it is that labor and management want to occur as a result of the joint effort. It also may explore the basic motivations of the two parties for the program. Next comes an outline of the basic structure of the program describing the various levels and activities and delineating the responsibilities and authority of each level. Another section defines the basic boundaries such as noninvolvement with collec-tive bargaining or supplanting management and union responsibilities. This also may exempt the union from liability for management decisions made by the pro-gram. Another boundary frequently used is restricting problem-solving groups to addressing issues within their own areas of responsibility. The safeguards for the program (discussed below) are then laid out. Finally, the general expectations of labor and management are put forward, including a pledge of good faith effort to make the program successful, that adequate time will be devoted to the effort, and that information will be provided fully and promptly. The top level also needs to develop clear operating procedures for undertaking its tasks of gover-nance, management, and problem solving, where applicable.

At the next level, *policies and procedures* are developed that adapt the general principles to specific locations. It helps mold the program to local objec-tives, structures, practices, barriers, and language. The policies and procedures statement cannot be in conflict with the project principles statement. The follow-ing sections are generally included: purpose of the document; specific objectives of the group in the area of responsibility of the governing body; the organization of the governing body, including purpose, composition, and meetings; defini-tions and limitations of participants, including the selection process to be used; roles of nondirect participants in management and labor; information and publicity; recognition; procedures for handling recommendations; and monitor-ing and evaluation.

At the shop floor or office level, problem-solving groups often develop their own codes of conduct, which cannot contradict the other higher level documents.

This may sound restrictive, but in practice it is not. These codes set the ground rules for behavior within the group and establish the framework for the group managing itself and enforcing its own rules.

It is very important that each group develop its own guidelines without copying from or using another group's document as the basis for discussion. We have seen this done both ways and measured the effectiveness. Our review showed clearly that borrowed documents are much less effective. Internally generated norms and rules have much greater impact and adherence. When writing these documents, small subgroups of the governing body could be used to draft sections. The drafts should aim for comprehensiveness, not length or complexity. An outline format is easiest to work with. In each case, the entire group has to agree to the overall document before it takes force.

BUILDING SAFEGUARDS INTO PROGRAMS

Basic safeguards are a necessary ingredient for union-management cooperative programs. These help establish the boundaries of the program and remove some of the worries people have about participation. With this clarity, more participation can take place. The basic areas often covered are protection of collective bargaining and management rights, no character assassination or retaliation, job security, wage protection, no downgrading of classifications, and no increase in worker stress.

In most programs, setting down in writing that the program will not intrude on collective bargaining is an important principle. This protects the right of both parties to bring any issues to the bargaining table. The bargaining route can be taken by either party and hence any issue removed from the cooperative program setting. Second, the grievance procedure and the right to redress concerns through that process remain untouched.

Ensuring no character assassination of management or labor at any level focuses the cooperative process not on personalities but on issues. One group we worked with stated it as "fixing problems, not blame." Too often, groups dissect problems by psychoanalyzing personalties without looking at behaviors and what can be changed. Amateur psychiatry is a poor way to solve problems. Further, a commitment to nonretaliation helps reduce the fear of those below that they will be punished for what they say in a cooperative setting. Too often the messenger of problems is shot instead of taking aim on the problem itself. If employees are punished for what they say in the cooperative context, then trust is wiped out and the overall program is effectively sabotaged.

Job security is one of the most difficult issues. No worker should be asked to participate in a program that threatens his or her job. There needs to be some overall protection against job losses due to a program's recommendations. This does not mean that workers will necessarily be doing the same tasks. Probably jobs will change as a result of a successful program, and change for the better.

Further, protection from job loss from the impact of a cooperative program does not mean that unemployment cannot occur because of general economic conditions or unrelated management decisions. Unfortunately, cooperative programs are rarely in themselves sufficient protection.

It is in the interests of both parties to consider job security language. For labor, the membership will not be receptive to a program that threatens employment. Union leaders would not be reelected if they promoted a job-cutting program. For management, it has been shown that excellent returns on investment can be attained without layoffs. The fear of job loss leads workers to be less open with their ideas for change. Frankly, a job security pledge pays off to management in the quantity and quality of ideas. Yet such a clause should not lead to featherbedding. Considerable thought has to be given to how to utilize the time freed up from improvements for other activities that will be of benefit to the employer in the short and long term. Here is an opportunity to look more into market development, new product and service development, preventive maintenance, and community service. In one General Motors location in Flint, Michigan, workers adversely affected by changes were placed in nontraditional jobs in the community until openings for useful work were found inside the plant. This was a model for the Job Security Bank in the 1984 automotive industry contracts providing alternative community-oriented jobs if internal positions are not available. Many programs also wind up recommending new positions that will be cost-effective. At the very least, the gain and loss of jobs should balance out, and no one person should lose his or her job as a result.

People want their working conditions to improve as the result of a joint program. We frame the issue in terms of "worker stress." In some locations, this refers to speedups. Cooperative programs should not object to productivity improvement per se. In some cases, poor productivity makes a job less safe and more aggravating and demanding. Programs should not diminish the quality of the work environment and reduce job satisfaction. The problems with productivity for the union include the impact on jobs, pay rates, safety, and job satisfaction. These issues can be addressed without taking broad aim at productivity as a concept. An unproductive workplace will shortly work to the disadvantage of those employed there. It is through productivity increases that capital is available for improvements in wages and the business or the agency without inflation or large borrowing costs.

Losing a job and fear of the unknown that might bring worse conditions are the biggest worries of workers. Other concerns include the loss of wages due to a program, especially if there is a reassignment of personnel. This involves ensuring no downgrading of classifications. In general, the goal of a union-management cooperative program is to find win-win solutions. Adequate safeguards help make that possible.

JOINT MANAGEMENT OF COOPERATIVE PROGRAMS

Just as a program needs to be jointly governed, it also needs to be jointly managed. The more extensive and complicated the process, the more the need for people to manage the process to ensure that tasks are being performed. In a truly joint program, this is also conducted in a joint manner.

For labor-management committees, the union and management cochairs of the committee can be its "staff," or management and union people can be assigned to run its activities. In larger programs, there is often a need for *coordinators*, who are responsible for administering the program. In many joint programs, one person is selected by management and one by labor. They jointly run the program and report to the top-level governing body. Whether they are full or part time depends on how much work there is to do. In some cases, they will be trained to train others to work in the program.

Another type of staff person in many cooperative programs is a *facilitator*, who works with problem-solving groups to make sure that they are adhering to the process, to monitor their activities, and to aid in overcoming obstacles. In some programs, coordinators are called by this name. Whatever the nomenclature, these people should be drawn as equally as possible from labor and management to demonstrate a balance and to provide complementary orientations.

Regardless of whether they are management or union, they should be accountable to the governing body. In their staff roles, they bring different perspectives, but they should strive to be mutually supportive. Too often, the staff takes over the leadership of the program or too much decision-making authority is delegated to them. The governing bodies should remain firmly in charge of a program and the staff serves in a support role. The staff should neither be glorified clericals on one extreme nor dominating policy setters on the other.

SETTING PERFORMANCE STANDARDS AND MONITORING PROGRAM STAFF

Being clear about what it is that staff people are to do in a program is often overlooked, but it is essential to a smooth-running effort. Good business practice involves setting performance standards and measuring performance against those standards. If one of the goals of a joint program is better management of the workplace, then it should model good business practices in the management of the program.

We have successfully used a participatory approach toward setting performance standards and monitoring staff for joint union-management programs.

At the outset, the staff members develop a draft job description and a behavioral checklist describing what it is they do. These include such items as the ways to support the problem-solving groups and to communicate with key parties. These lists should avoid vague statements or general platitudes. Each behavior listed should be specific and observable in some way or other. The draft description is shared with the governing body to whom the staff reports, modified as needed and approved.

At the end of a year (or some other interval), the governing body can set up union-management review teams for the purposes of reviewing performance. The team can use a variety of techniques such as interviewing the staff person privately, including items on staff performance on evaluation questionnaires and/or observing them in action. The focus of the inquiry should be on how well staff people fulfilled their job description, not whether or not the review team likes them. Further, emphasize finding ways to improve performance in the future. The review should be shared with and signed off by the staff person and placed in his or her personnel file if that is the normal practice.

At the end of the review process, the staff group and the governing body should review the job description and behavioral checklist to see if they need modification and update them as necessary. The review team should assess the process it used for review and learn how to do it better the next time around. Since staff may come on at different times, there may be several review periods in the course of a year.

CONCLUSION

Governance and management of a project help assert the principles of joint and equal union-management cooperation. Using the joint process, projects run much better than using unilateral management-only approaches. The particular needs for governance depend on the cooperative technique(s) being used. Governing committees should be designed to meet the particular size, location, and functions of the employer and unions. The governing body serves as an enabling group to help ensure success for the effort. The top level has to be involved in the process. Depending on the particular approach, strong roles for the middle and lower levels of the organization should be introduced with an emphasis on problem solving. The methods of selection of membership on the groups should be fair but recognize institutional prerogatives. Clear governing documents such as project principles statements, policies and procedures documents, and codes of conduct articulate the processes, boundaries, and safeguards of the program.

Program staff should also be drawn equally from both sides. They should work cooperatively and act as the staff of the joint governing committees. There should be clear and shared expectations of their performance, which is monitored by the labor-management partners at least each year. Applying these approaches to governance and management helps ensure high levels of program performance and maintains control of the process in the hands of the union and management partners.

14

Building Skills:
Developing and Delivering Training
for a Union-Management Cooperation Program

Good results come from knowing what you are doing. Most union-management programs require new skills and understandings. Some believe that it is as easy as sitting down together and talking. While this is a start, the most effective forms of joint activity demand new understanding of content areas and cooperative processes. Without training, many programs hang on goodwill and good luck. Training does the following four things for any joint union-management effort:

1. *It explains what the program is and how it will work.* The training lays out the framework for the cooperation for all to understand. Without this basic background, moving forward to meet common goals is extremely difficult. A foundation for this aspect of the training is explaining the overall goals and objectives and structure of the joint endeavor.

2. *It teaches the basic principles, processes, and procedures by which the activities of the program will be run.* In other words, this facet of the program tells how the program will be put in place. The basic safeguards and approaches to be used are laid out for the trainees. The training itself should model the values and underlying principles involved in a joint effort.

3. *It provides skills training in the specific areas necessary to meet the goals and objectives of the program.* Different kinds of union-management programs require different kinds of skill training. For example, if the program uses labor-management committees for joint problem solving, the committees will need training in union-management cooperation processes, in joint problem-solving procedures, in meeting management, and in other similar topics. If the focus is on creative ways to undertake collective bargaining, skills in generating and costing out alternatives are helpful. If the focus is on product quality, training is called for on the various ways to analyze, improve, and monitor quality.

4. *It builds support for and commitment to the program.* In some cases, training could be provided by self-paced instruction through reading or by viewing tapes. Though such approaches may be appropriate media in some instances, remote instruction loses out on the important objective of building group involvement in and commitment to the joint process. By learning together more about what is going on and participating in group-based learning activities, an intangible but necessary element of support is added to the program. People feel empowered and enriched by good training. This positive association spreads to the program.

While clearly training is important, in practice it is often given short shrift. Designers of some programs believe that all the parties need to do is meet together and everything will go well. Unfortunately, the landscape is littered with well-intentioned programs that broke down in areas where proper training could have made a major difference. However, the biggest loss from the lack of training is the diminished potential of untrained programs. If group members had a better sense of how to go about their work and ways to conduct joint problem solving, the results would be stronger and the process more directed.

Most forms of union-management cooperation by their very nature require the development of new skills. These new skills are developed most effectively through quality training. People might be able to pick up some of these skills on their own without training. However, they won't do it systematically and not everyone will pick up the necessary skills. People participating in the program deserve to have the proper training to make their participation effective and rewarding.

Developing and delivering effective program training require time and money. Too often, programs skimp on the time available to develop or deliver training or they budget inadequate funds. These are serious mistakes. It is best to determine what training is needed and then how much it will cost rather than having a set amount for training and then figuring out how much training can be covered. The training development process is shown in Figure 14-1. If there is truly a budget crunch, then the goals and scope of the program should be cut back before the training is watered down. The costs and benefits of training need to be weighed. Obviously, training can be overdone, but there are real costs to underdoing it in terms of poor quality and waste of time in the application of necessary skills.

Frequently, there is a rush to get things done and therefore many take short-cuts in the training. Patience with the process is necessary because less will get done in the medium and long term if sufficient training isn't provided. The other manifestation of the "get it done fast" approach is to cram all the training into a short period of time and overload the trainees. Getting it all in at one time is a waste since the trainees can't absorb it all. Prudent pacing of the training is a necessity.

FIGURE 14-1
Developing Program Training

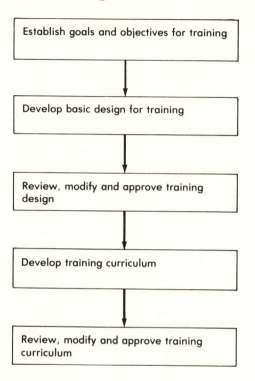

ESTABLISHING JOINT TRAINING GOALS AND OBJECTIVES

The union-management governing body at the top establishes the goals and objectives for the training. It also specifies what training is to be offered and how it will be given. The establishment of training goals and objectives is crucial to the development of the actual training. While third-party experts can help out by providing options, the decisions should be made by the union-management partners.

The general goals and objectives of the training for a union-management initiative should parallel the goals and objectives of the overall program. Those aspects of the overall objectives and goals of the program that require additional understanding, skills, or commitment should be incorporated into the training. Think in terms of what the participants should be able to do and what kinds of attitudes they should exhibit. These provide critical clues to the training needed. It is through reference to the program goals and objectives that the training program takes shape.

After the overall learning objectives are identified, each item should be reviewed to determine if there are various components that need to be learned to fulfill that objective. For example, if a general learning objective would be to learn how to function as an effective steering committee, there might be a whole range of subobjectives, including learning how to conduct meetings effectively; to identify the full range of roles and responsibilities of the group; to plan, monitor, and evaluate activities in the group's area; to work well together as a small group; to discern the relationship between collective bargaining and the cooperative program; and other similar specific objectives.

Write out the general learning objectives and specific sublearning objectives. They are critical for those designing, delivering, and evaluating the training program. They should be shared with the trainees to give them a clear idea of the objectives of the training, of what they are being asked to do.

DEVELOPING THE BASIC DESIGN
FOR COOPERATIVE TRAINING

The basic design of the program flows directly from the goals and objectives. The design provides the framework of who is going to teach what to whom and under what conditions. Not every participant in every program needs to know the same things. Some goals apply more to some groups than others. The union and management designer/planners should be clear about whom each goal and objective is directed to. Some apply to all and some to only parts of the group. Delineating this specifies the target audiences of the training. Table 14-1 lays out some of the audiences and the general kinds of training they might receive.

The designer/planners should next set the goals and objectives and the training audiences and the various options for the ways the training might be conducted. The options include group training, one-on-one coaching, self-paced instruction, films, attendance at external seminars or classes, videotapes and audiocassettes, and observations. These represent the training methodologies. The choices will be influenced by resources, content needed, and the nature of the potential trainees. Training for the initial group may be different than training for employees who join the process later. In geographically or occupationally diverse work forces, innovative solutions may be necessary.

The next order of business is to outline the topics that should be covered. This lists the content to be included. Many people who set up training jump first to a list of topics to be taught. The better way to develop training is to see that the topics flow from the objectives and audiences rather than vice versa. Eventually, the time frames for the topics and the identification of who will deliver the training should be specified.

Last, the designers should lay out a sequence for the delivery of the training. For example, in quality circles training, the steering committee would be trained

TABLE 14-1
Who Receives What Kinds of Training?

Audience	*Training*
Labor-management governing bodies	Labor-management cooperation processes and skills—problem-solving processes and skills; program governance and management processes and skills
Key union, supervisory, and management personnel	General orientation to and training for the program—what the program is and how it works; background on labor-management cooperation and employee participation; how key people can assist the program
Cross section of employees at all levels	General orientation to and training for the program—what the program is and how it will work; background on labor-management cooperation and employee participation; how employees can be helpful to and/or participate in the program
Labor and management coordinators and facilitators	Program coordinator/facilitator training—what the program is and how it works; background on labor-management cooperation and employee participation; roles and responsibilities of coordinators and facilitators; how small groups work; problem-solving techniques
Labor and management group leaders	Leader training—what the program is and how it works; background on labor-management cooperation and employee participation; roles and responsibilities of leaders; how small groups work; problem-solving techniques
Program participants (rank and file)	Participant training—what the program is and how it works; background on labor-management cooperation and employee participation; problem-solving techniques

first, facilitators second, leaders of the circles next, and finally the circle members. Dates are attached to the training schedule. Program training may have several cycles or phases as the program progresses and each cycle should be clearly planned.

All of this information is brought to the governing body for approval. The governing body has an opportunity to review the training program, ask for clarifications, challenge sections, make suggestions, and modify the plan as is necessary. Its involvement provides both insight and sanction for the training process. With the governing body's concurrence, it will be easier to develop the specific training curriculum and to implement it effectively.

DEVELOPING AN EFFECTIVE TRAINING CURRICULUM

A tailored training curriculum takes considerable thought. The basic rule of thumb is that participants in a joint program need to know more about what to do and how to do it. The particular training needed is a function of the gap between what the group needs to know or be able to do and what all of them already know or can do prior to the training. In some cases, materials are already available to help build the specific information that will be provided. For example, the explanation of the program can rely on the project principles statement and the policies and procedures document to outline what the program looks like and what it intends to do. However, there will be other generic topics, such as problem solving, motivation, listening, group dynamics, facilitation, planning, organizational change, and conflict resolution, for which it is unnecessary to go back to scratch to develop a curriculum. Preexisting exercises, lecturettes, films, instruments, and other learning aids may be available. These need to be carefully reviewed to make sure that they fit into each particular program. Just plucking a canned program off the shelf is a serious mistake. There may be elements that are on target and these could be used. Other parts may need to be scrapped or reshaped. Here, again, expert assistance can be helpful to the designers in determining if the curriculum fully addresses the learning objectives.

The union-management environment poses special challenges to curriculum developers. Most of the materials and exercises developed for teaching the skills of problem solving or organizational development do not fully or realistically incorporate the union. Those drawing up the curriculum must pay careful attention to make sure that the training provided supports and strengthens union involvement in the training and the union's legitimate role in the workplace.

A corollary issue in curriculum development is how to address the topic of collective bargaining. Usually, the issue is handled like sex education was 50 years ago. If it is mentioned, the trainees are told to stay away from it and the topic is dropped. It becomes taboo. Actually discussing collective bargaining and its relationship to the particular joint effort is the best approach.. Trainees in any program should have a common base of understanding about the particular nature of collective bargaining and contract administration in that location. They should learn how labor relations works from the employer's and union's perspectives. This provides common ground for working with it if the cooperative program is focused on the collective bargaining situation or staying clear of it if that is the objective. Knowing where contract negotiation, grievance handling, and discipline operate and how makes sure that they avoid interferences. In this case, trainees should clearly set out the clear areas and the gray areas where the issues are not clear-cut. A process for resolving the gray areas quickly and fully should be presented.

Another major area of curriculum concern is the problem-solving process. In essence, all union-management cooperation is a problem-solving effort. Though there are many variations, any approach should incorporate building facility with problem identification, problem selection, problem analysis, solution development and analysis, and preparation of a recommended solution and implementation plan. It also should include later evaluation of the efficacy of the solution identified and implemented.[1] The analysis section of the problem-solving process requires strong attention. Findings on the success of employee involvement groups and quality circles convincingly show that those who collect and use data well are much more successful than those who put little emphasis on data. Even more important than identifying the problem is the clarification of the issue at hand through data-based descriptions of its dimensions. Second, since there is never just any one solution to a problem, examination of alternative solutions needs to be facilitated. Alternative solutions need to be double-screened to make sure that they are both workable and desirable from a cost-benefit perspective. Quick and dirty problem solving, while attractive in terms of responsiveness and time, are almost always less effective than well-researched and well-analyzed solutions.

In an attempt to tailor a program to the local situation, broader perspective should not be neglected. Knowing about the history of union-management cooperation and what is being done in other locations provides important insights for any location. The long and broad view helps anchor one's particular efforts within those of others. Understanding what others have done can generate innovation and permutations in one's own location.

The curriculum should be as rooted in reality as possible. Adults seek learning to make an impact on their actual working and living conditions. Over-reliance on games, simulations, and hypotheticals should be avoided. If there is a possibility to link learning to real situations at work or in the program, then this approach should be taken. If this is impossible, then fictionalized versions can be used. Training in union-management cooperation programs should avoid the psychotherapeutic. The focus of joint programs is behavior or what it is that the union and management will do, not their innermost psyches and feelings. In some programs, workers are asked to "bare their souls" as part of the training for trust building. This information can be misused and shows a basic lack of respect for the privacy and feelings of most working people. Leave psychological analysis to competent professionals.

The curriculum should be expressed in clearly laid out training agendas whose relationship to the objectives and design are straightforward. Topics, time frames, and methodologies should appear on the agendas. The trainers should be able to present the backup documentation of the materials and content that they will use in the training. The curriculum, the agendas, and backup material should be reviewed and approved by the union and management partners before they are used. Suggestions for improvement should be considered and implemented if necessary.

SELECTING AND PREPARING JOINT TRAINERS

Once the training is identified, it must be delivered well. The steps are outlined in Figure 14-2. Trainers for a union-management program should be drawn from the union and from supervision and management as much as possible. In this way, union-management cooperation can be modeled in the trainers' group. These program trainers will need to be specially trained to provide the training for the program. For most, it will be a part-time responsibility that they would perform on an as-needed basis according to the program plan. Ideally, they would work in union-management training teams when actually providing the training.

The trainers should be selected by each party after consultation with each other. The final selection should be confirmed by the joint governing body. The union should put forward its nominees and management its candidates. They should consult each other to check for compatibility and the opinions of the other group. The first trainer group is the most difficult because the organization may have little or no experience with these kinds of programs or the training to be presented. Prior training experience is helpful but "know-it-alls" should be avoided. Trainers should be able to speak clearly and distinctly, respond well to a group, take pride in the learning of others (not strutting their own expertise), and be credible within the workplace.

An important criterion in selecting those who will be teaching is the willingness to learn. Good trainers learn from their training environment, examine new ways of presenting the material, and are open to new experiences and new ideas. Training is hard work and requires attention, preparation, and a willingness to listen to feedback. Hence, great care should be exercised in the selection of the joint trainers. After the initial startup, exemplary participants can be given a chance to become trainers.

Large organizations may have internal trainers who are familiar with many of the necessary topics. Where possible, their expertise should be used. They can

FIGURE 14-2
Delivering the Program Training

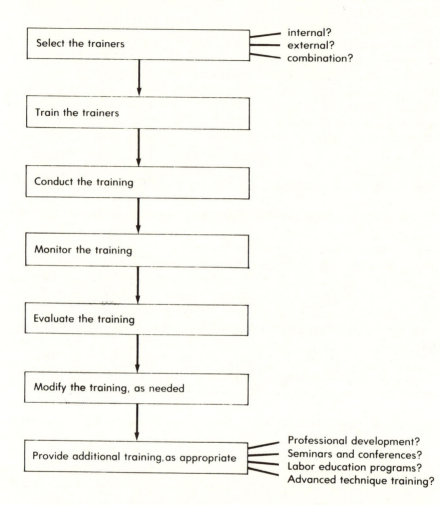

be excellent internal consultants to the training development. It is important to determine their credibility with the union because their primary responsibility may have been in management development. Despite their position with the employer, they should still abide by the process described here which places the training under the review of the union and management partners.

At the initial stages of training or for one-time training events, outside trainers can be retained. They can put on specific training that requires particular expertise not resident in the organizations directly involved. They also can help train the internal trainers so that they can take over responsibility for the training. The best kind of outside trainers to get are ones who understand the needs of a joint program and are responsive to both management and the union. For many professional trainers, working with a union will be a new experience. Outside trainers should be carefully monitored to make sure that they are working out well in the client's environment. Especially make sure that they are teaching in ways that meet the internally developed goals and objectives and that they do not have agendas that are in conflict with the internal demands. Except for highly technical subjects requiring a particular expert, any outside trainers should present the governing body with a clear plan for transferring the knowledge and quality capability to the internal union and management trainers. While their initial help can be welcome, their role should diminish over time. Quality checks to make sure that the internal trainers are maintaining a high level of delivery and effectiveness are necessary.

CONDUCTING EFFECTIVE COOPERATIVE TRAINING

Exactly how the training for the union-management program will be conducted is determined by the top governing committee as part of the design and planning process. There are, however, some basic principles to keep in mind. The training should be given as much as possible to joint union-management audiences and should use both union and management trainers to model union-management cooperation. Doing this maximizes the appeal of the training to the trainees and ensures that the trainers understand where the trainees are coming from. The fact of joint participation in the training can be just as important as the content of the training about cooperation. While there may be some limited elements where the parties are addressed separately, this should not be overdone. Having teams teach the material also makes it easier to manage the training session and makes it more interesting for the participants.

Training should be given not only to the people directly participating in the program but also used to orient other employees, supervisors, managers, and/or union officials. These may be key people at a particular level and/or may represent a broad cross section of the people at a location. The mix will maximize understanding of, support for, and commitment to the program.

Very importantly, the training should pay attention to the principles of adult learning. This means understanding that the trainees are not empty receptacles waiting to be filled. They bring experiences, ideas, knowledge, and opinions all of which can be valuable learning tools. Rather than a passive lecture style, the trainees should be engaged in training that uses more participative and experiential methods. Adult learners want to know how to apply their learning; therefore steer away from heavy emphasis on the theoretical and take aim at the practical application of concepts and skills. Adult learners also require direct feedback on their performance. Clear and constructive feedback to the trainees on whether they are grasping the knowledge, skills, and values being taught is essential. If there is difficulty, then additional attention or new strategies are needed.

Training is best done in small, "digestible" chunks or segments. There is a limited tolerance for learning new things. When that tolerance is passed, even the best presented material will not be absorbed. Breaking the training into various segments will not only make learning easier for the trainees but will also make the program easier to manage and conduct. With some time between segments, adjustments can be made to make the training more effective. Use of training segments also minimizes the disruption of the normal work responsibilities of the management and union participants.

Within each segment of training there must be adequate time to conduct the training. Rushing through items without sufficient time for coverage, comprehension, and integration is a total waste. In general, adult workers learn best when they are told what they are going to learn, have a chance to experience the skills and apply them in a safe setting, and then reflect on the experience to develop general principles and understanding. Simply saying something once and expecting it to be remembered is a pipedream. A full cycle of learning makes a more lasting impression. However, more is not necessarily better. Operating in a work environment where time is money, training should be maximally efficient and effective. This can be done by setting and adhering to realistic time frames.

The trainees often come from many different educational, age, and cultural backgrounds. These differences mean that there may be a wide range of skills and abilities in any given group. Trainers should be prepared to work empathetically and respectfully with those whose reading and writing skills may be limited or who are worried since they have not been in a class in many years. Extensive reading and writing and $20 words should be avoided. Handing out the basic notes on each topic removes stress, allows the trainees to concentrate, and provides a reference for later review. Improvement in basic skills may be a topic chosen by the joint committee to attack. Language barriers may not be indicative of intelligence but rather the inability of the instructor to speak the trainee's native language.

To conduct the training, the trainers need to be aware of the importance of an unflustered presentation. The mechanics as well as the content should go smoothly. The keys to achieving this result are prior planning, early preparation, and flexibility. The training rooms need to be up to the challenge of setting a good learning environment. Having conducted training in frozen rail yards and next to noisy machinery, we've seen the problems that a poor environment can create. A training room should be convenient for the trainees, free from distraction and noise, and fairly comfortable. Finding such locations is not always easy, since it is best to locate it somewhere on or near the workplace. Trainers should be proficient in using various training tools and equipment, such as flip charts, overheads, videotapes, and slide/tape presentations. Sufficient training materials and handouts should be provided in advance and be ready for distribution with a minimum of fuss. Remember to have extra supplies handy for shortages or breakdowns of equipment.

MONITORING AND EVALUATING THE TRAINING

The union-management governing bodies at the various levels should monitor the training as it is given. Specifically, they need to compare the actual training to the initial goals and objectives. It is best to incorporate the monitoring of the training into the regular monitoring activities of the governing bodies. Such monitoring can be done through direct observations of the training and/or by seeking information from trainees regarding their reactions to the training. At the conclusion of each segment of the training, the trainees should be asked on anonymously written evaluation forms how well they thought the training met its objectives, how useful they see each part of the agenda, and how well the trainers did, as well as additional comments. With the group, the trainers should lead a discussion at the end of the training period about what went well and what could be improved about the training. The particular results and trends should be analyzed to make sure that the training is as on target as possible. If there are problems then adjustments should be discussed and implemented if appropriate and possible. This kind of evaluation is called "reaction evaluation."

The subsequent effectiveness of the training should be evaluated particularly during the initial phase of the program. Evaluation of the training should be oriented toward identifying specific strengths and weaknesses and successes and failures. The parties may want to modify the training in subsequent segments to make the necessary improvements. The top governing body should have the final responsibility for the evaluation of the training. This body may want to call on other governing committees to assist in the evaluation.

Assessments of the adequacy or effectiveness of the training may change when the trainees attempt to apply the skills in practice. To conduct a "use evaluation," which assesses the impact and relevance of the training after it has been put into practice, use the methodology described in Chapter 16 specifically applied to the training issues. The parties will need to determine relevant questions, identify indicators, select methods of data collection, analyze the data, and draw conclusions about the effectiveness of the training. The use evaluation should assess how well the training worked and determine other areas of training or aspects that need further attention.

A training or evaluation professional can help in the framing and discussion of the questions, but it is essential that the union-management partners analyze the evaluation information themselves and draw their own conclusions.

TRAINING AS AN ONGOING FUNCTION

Training is not a one-shot deal whose need comes and goes at the beginning of a program. Training should be an ongoing commitment to excellence and learning. In addition, new people will become involved in the program and turnover will occur. Some programs deliberately rotate membership on problem-solving groups. The parties may decide to expand the program to cover new topic areas or new locations and thereby have new focus and/or participants. As basic techniques for problem solving or addressing the content areas designated in the effort are learned, then more advanced techniques can be taught.

Ongoing employee problem-solving groups should receive a brief refresher course mixed in with some advanced skills training to help regenerate long-term groups. The program facilitators and coordinators should receive ongoing continuing education on their responsibilities. Participants in the program may want to attend classes and seminars at colleges in their area or conferences sponsored in this field to broaden their perspectives. Labor studies programs and industrial relations departments may have offerings that will help maintain updated knowledge.

CONCLUSION

Overall, training makes a critical contribution to the success of a joint program. It provides the wherewithal to implement the goals and objectives of the program. It provides a setting for personal and organizational growth. It provides a forum for the explanation and resolution of key points in the cooperative program. It offers valuable skills that can help overall operational performance of the management and the union. It models the basic values of cooperative efforts that much can be learned together that will empower the organization to better address its problems and opportunities in an ongoing way.

15

Creating Awareness:
Communications and Publicity
in a Union-Management Cooperation Program

THE IMPORTANCE OF EFFECTIVE COMMUNICATION

At one level, the whole idea of union-management cooperation and employee participation is communication and awareness. It represents opening up the avenues of communication and creativity within and between labor and management. Consequently, the less effective the communication, the less effective the program. Awareness about what is going on in the organization and its possibilities for improvement is a parallel basic principle. Awareness brings inclusion of a broader range of ideas and data for helping resolve problems.

Communication is a two-way process. Each side must share information and ideas with each other and listen to what the other side has said. There must be clear communication from the program to others outside of it and within the program to and among its various participants. The key elements are presented in Figure 15-1. When others outside the program are kept in the dark, conflict can erupt or misunderstandings occur. Keeping important others informed ahead of time usually creates more leeway for action than more restricted styles of communication. For those within the program, lack of communication creates confusion, wastes time and energy, and reduces the cross-fertilization of experience and ideas.

Rumors occur in all workplaces. Sometimes the rumors are true; sometimes they are not. To a cooperative program, rumors can be fatal. The goal in a cooperative program is to maintain communication on as open a basis as possible to help contain potentially damaging rumors and demonstrate trust and welcoming. The foundation of a union-management cooperation effort is inclusiveness, not exclusiveness.

FIGURE 15-1
Communicating About and Publicizing a Program

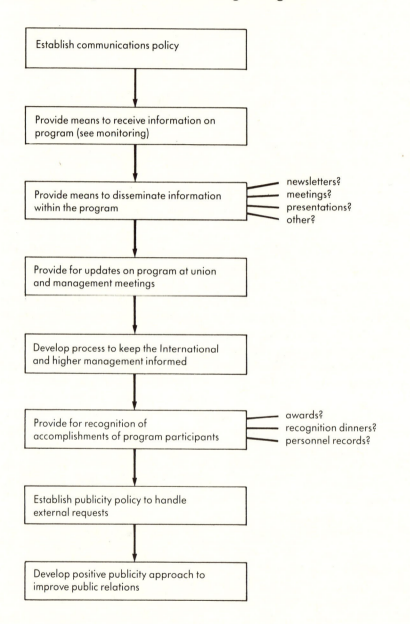

KEEPING PARTICIPANTS INFORMED ABOUT PROGRESS

Several mechanisms can be used to keep the participants in a program well informed. One is scheduling regular meetings with key groups within the program. If a QWL or quality circle program is developed, facilitators of the program should meet on a regular basis to share their experiences. This is particularly important when peer facilitators are used. These meetings provide an outlet for discussing feelings and frustrations that may not be appropriate to share with the groups they aid. Similarly, leaders or coleaders of shop floor groups should get together. When shop floor groups are used, a popular event is to get together all of the participants once a year for the presentation of awards and review of the highlights of the program. Adequate recognition is an essential part of any program. If the program is a series of labor-management committees, it is helpful for the cochairs to meet and discuss common concerns. The frequency of the meetings will depend on the groups involved.

Some programs jointly publish newsletters to keep people informed and to acknowledge and recognize achievements. Issued on a quarterly basis or on some other interval, they give an update of the program activities and accomplishments. These newsletters can be handled by coordinators of the effort or a special committee.

Minutes of meetings are critical instruments for communication about a program. Every meeting of a cooperative program should have written minutes taken. By having good minutes, groups ensure that accurate perceptions are being reported and that action items are being met. Key persons in management and the union will have the information they need to be of assistance and/or keep abreast of developments in the program. Some programs develop lists of people inside and outside the program who should be kept informed through the circulation of the minutes. Minutes should record who attended and missed the meeting to encourage participation. As a rule, minutes should not be verbatim accounts of what was said and by whom, but they should be specific about what was done. They should record major decisions of the group and report on findings that were shared with the group. Minutes should not be editorial instruments of the recorder nor used to embarrass members for what was said.

KEEPING EMPLOYEES NOT DIRECTLY INVOLVED INFORMED

It is important to keep those not directly involved informed of program developments. They should also be encouraged to express their ideas and concerns to the groups.

The mechanisms used to maintain internal communication can also be used to communicate with others in the organization. Either special meetings or parts of regularly scheduled events can provide updates and explanations of what is going on for both management and labor. The union should have an update on the joint efforts at regular union meetings. Newsletters can be distributed to the general work force or a broader range of people in the workplace, or a column included in regular internal publications. When groups are composed of part of a work unit, minutes should be posted in the work area for all to see. Minutes can be a very good way to keep people who weren't there informed. Posters can be used to raise awareness and explain key points.

Inviting visitors to the activities can be an excellent way of spreading understanding. In one company we worked with, at the end of each meeting the group decided who would be invited for the next week. They started with the more skeptical workers so that they could get a firsthand view of what was really going on. In addition, they have had visitors from inside and outside the company sit in on the sessions. The only restrictions are that visitors let the coleaders know in advance and that they should respect the rules of the group. Frankly, paper approaches to communication are much less effective than firsthand exposure.

KEEPING THE MANAGEMENT CHAIN OF COMMAND INFORMED

Particularly in large organizations, it is important to keep higher-level management informed of the process and the results being recorded. High-level management's sanction and involvement contribute to ongoing success. Too often, senior managers are involved with the early discussions but are left out in later stages. Incorporated in early startup, they move on to other projects and their potential contribution is lost to the program. Higher management should be presented a balanced perspective on accomplishments and future challenges for improvement. Overly rosy pictures of what is taking place are out of place. Continuing involvement also allows the use of the authority of higher management when problems develop for which their status or expertise is necessary. Honest and periodic updates help ensure their assistance when needed. Visits to program activities also spread understanding and support.

There are two principles for respecting management hierarchy. First, projects should not be end runs from lower in the organization around the formal organizational structure, especially in the middle, as a means to avoid certain decision makers or to undercut their authority. Second, projects should not be end runs from the top to get around middle managers directly to workers. By keeping everyone in the management chain of command informed about what is going on, broader involvement and sanction are developed.

In large corporations or agencies that have a variety of cooperative activities or many locations where these are being conducted, it is very important for the learning of the whole organization to share accurate information on local activities. Developments should be reported regularly to the higher level liaisons. This spreads good ideas and raises common problems that may call for new solutions or additional resources.

KEEPING THE LOCAL UNION LEADERSHIP INFORMED

Not every union officer is involved in every cooperative program or at all phases. But it is very important to make sure all of them are kept informed on what is going on. In a few instances where only a limited number of union leaders at the top were privy to information on the activities of a cooperative program, later they were ousted in union election battles. The union should review the progress of activities with its executive committee, bargaining committee, or board. In addition, the steward structure as the union's communications network should be included in information sharing. These two groups also provide a key link to learn of concerns and dissatisfactions with the effort. It is better to learn about them early and deal with these problems before they escalate.

KEEPING THE INTERNATIONAL UNION INFORMED

Just as the corporate or departmental chain of command needs to be kept informed, so too does the International union for several important reasons. Other parts of the union may have tried similar things or encountered the same problems. Sharing information may help come up with new ideas on how to handle issues in one's own setting. The other parts of the union will also be concerned about precedents that would affect other locals in the union. These issues cannot be shrugged off but need to be worked through.

At the local level, communication is particularly important with International representatives who service the locals and the officers of the union in the region. There is a tendency not to share information on cooperative programs with these officials. Since a large part of the image of union leaders emphasizes conflict, the description of the cooperation that takes place is ignored. Further, since higher level representatives cover a large area and unions are understaffed, they generally spend most of their time fighting fires and dealing with real conflict. There is also a fear at the local level that the union hierarchy will step in and squelch the effort. To be sure, many of the representatives got to their position because they were successful in managing conflict and may not be familiar with the particular cooperative approach. It often takes careful explanation and a working-with attitude to make best use of the International respresentative. A well-planned program with clear union goals will not worry the International union. The same is true with International officers. They can be a tremendous asset if informed and involved. Yet, when kept in the dark, they are embarrassed when they hear about the cooperation program in their area from the International office or through other sources than the local union.

The International office of the union also needs to hear about what is going on at the local level. Other locals may be facing similar situations and they need to know how (and if) the local overcame its difficulties and the good ideas and approaches used. Further, some activities may form a pattern that may not be evident from the local level. Usually the research department or education department of the union keeps tabs on these issues. In some unions, the president has appointed someone else to monitor what is going on. Local unions should be forewarned that the International may not have answers to particular questions since others may not have shared the necessary information.

HANDLING INFORMATION SHARING AND PROPRIETARY INFORMATION

One of the great opportunities of union-management cooperation and increased employee participation is information sharing. Organizations that do not share important information about the performance of the organization or upcoming changes breed rumors and foster distrust among the work force. A common complaint among employees is that they don't know what is going on. The periodic general labor-management meeting is one form of union-management cooperation whose primary purpose is information sharing. Yet each meeting of any form of union-management cooperation provides an opportunity for this sharing to take place. Management should keep the union and the work force abreast of developments and key indicators of organizational performance. In organizations with high levels of cooperation, there is a great willingness to share information. Some organizations have made it a matter of practice to answer all requests for information from inside and to be forthcoming in giving important information. Each side can decide on the limits to information sharing, but the greater the cooperation the greater the sharing of information.

One organization we worked with built information sharing into the agenda of every meeting. Management reported on what had taken place since group members last met and what was planned for the future. The union shared information on what it was doing and what it had heard from the work force. In addition, sharing of personal information, such as retirements, weddings, births, and other events, was also brought out. The mixture of institutional and personal information was well received. The members of the groups found these sessions useful and looked forward to them at each session.

The sharing of information can bring up proprietary or very sensitive issues. It is very important for both sides to exercise restraint and discretion in the spread of information. The union should pledge that proprietary information will not be shared with outside parties. Violating this principle on either side undercuts the trust and respect the parties need to work with each other.

Getting accurate and timely information to the problem-solving groups is absolutely essential to success. Poor information going in can ruin entire projects. If major changes in budget, personnel, equipment, or policies are already planned, the problem-solving groups should be advised. Information delays can substantially slow up progress. There has to be a clear understanding that information will be supplied promptly, fully, and accurately to the joint groups.

BUILDING RECOGNITION INTO JOINT PROGRAMS

The contribution of employees who participate in joint efforts needs to be recognized and nourished. Some regard this as unnecessary when these kind of activities are viewed as part of the way business is conducted. However, the normal conduct of work should include appreciation, personal contact, and acknowledgement. Placing a letter in the personnel file of participants in the joint effort notes accomplishment. Some companies have hung plaques with the names of the participants engraved on them. Pins, jackets, caps, and other small gifts and promotional material have been distributed. Certificates on the completion of training recognizes new skills. Recognition breakfasts, lunches, or dinners can provide a way to honor the participants. Governing committee members should visit the activities within their jurisdiction and offer words of praise. Pictures of the groups can be placed in program newsletters and/or in other internal employer and union publications.

There is a word of caution on the use of recognition devices. They should not be so time consuming that it hurts the performance of the program. Fancy recognition programs cannot hide deficiencies in a program's design or performance. Also, competitions should be avoided in order to value all of the activities of the participants. Avoid ostentatious or showy gifts, which may cause jealousy. The biggest recognition program should be the increased awareness of the positive impact of the program on the workplace.

HANDLING EXTERNAL REQUESTS FOR INFORMATION AND THE PRESS

Good news travels fast. There may be requests from employers and unions in your local area or even far away to come and learn about your program. The program should have a clear policy about such requests. A certain amount is courteous, and often one can learn something from the visitors as well. But make sure the visits are acceptable to both parties. Some unions have objected to visits from nonunion locations. Allowing a company on the AFL-CIO boycott list to visit can cause problems with the union. Second, there should be a limitation on how many are done because the primary responsibility is the maintenance of your own program. It is flattering to be asked by many to come visit, but internal responsibilities should come first and external requests handled as time allows. If there are many requests then an information packet can be put together to send out. The same principles apply to appearing at conferences and meetings on union-management cooperation. In moderation, these can be very helpful but should not obscure primary responsibilities.

It is not uncommon for the local newspaper to want to do a story on a cooperative program. This can be welcome so long as both parties are agreeable to the publicity and both discuss their perspectives with the reporter. It is very damaging to the program to find a description of your program in the morning paper with one side left out. The same is true of academics and students who want to do papers on your program. They should be minimally intrusive and touch all the bases.

In all cases, publicity is best withheld in the early stages of the program. There are other more pressing issues that need to addressed and the shakedown period is hardly the time for the glare of the public eye. For the observer, later on will be better because there will be more to report.

USING UNION-MANAGEMENT COOPERATION TO ENHANCE EMPLOYER AND UNION IMAGE AND MARKETING

A successful union-management cooperative program is a source of pride. Television commercials such as the Ford advertisement on "Quality Is Job One" and the General Motors promotion that "GM Is People" are examples of the use of cooperative programs for positive publicity efforts. Wheeling Pittsburg took out print ads to tout its new union-management relationship with the steelworkers. Publicity can show teamwork and dedication in the organization and that everyone is working together to produce quality products or services. For organizations whose public image may not be the best, touting the cooperative program can help improve the public image. The fact that many of these promotions also mention the union by name points to their possible use to improve the union's public image.

One task of a developed joint union-management effort may be to consider creating strategies for positive publicity on the effort for marketing purposes, to enhance the image of the units involved within their own organization, or for community awareness and approval. These can take the form of advertisements or presentations. People prefer to deal with responsive and reliable organizations. Showing that your organization has a commitment to these principles can help a lot.

CONCLUSION

Communications undergirds the effort at union-management cooperation. Awareness between and among the partners creates the best conditions for success. Information and concerns need to be regularly and systematically shared by all of the participants in the program. Those who are not directly a part need to be kept informed of progress and problems. All levels of the management and union hierarchy should be included in the information loop. The need for recognition of effort and accomplishments should be part of the fabric of a program. Information sharing between the union and management is a critical component of cooperative programs. Communications in a program sometimes involves matters of a sensitive or proprietary nature that need to be handled with discretion. Getting timely and accurate information needed to solve problems helps improve the results of joint problem solving.

How to handle publicity should be addressed in the planning of a program. Attention from the press, academic world, or other employers and unions can be welcome so long as both parties agree to it and it does not divert necessary attention from the program itself. Positive use can be made of the joint program to help improve the marketability of the product or service and/or the community image of the employer and union.

16

Keeping Tabs:
Monitoring and Evaluating
Union-Management Cooperative Programs

Setting up a program is one thing. Keeping it going and making sure that it is doing what it is supposed to do is quite another task altogether. To keep tabs on how the program works in the real world, effective mechanisms for monitoring and evaluating what has been set up and how it works need to be designed and deployed. The union and management entered into a program because they wanted to get something done. All of the hard work up to this point would be for naught if it bogged down in the program's actual implementation. Monitoring applies directed attention to the process to keep it running smoothly. Unless this ongoing attention is directed at a program there is a danger that it can slide into conflict cycles and bad habits without anyone knowing it. Some programs suffer the doldrums after the initial excitement of its introduction. Adequate monitoring and evaluation help to revitalize the process without the catalyst of program-wrenching crises. The partners want the program to be a success. The final outcomes of a program must be visible and measurable. They should make a real difference in the operation of the organizations involved and the lives of the people within them. Adequate evaluation checks to see that this occurs.

ESTABLISHING JOINT MONITORING POLICIES
AND PROCEDURES

Monitoring simply means keeping tabs in a purposeful, systematic, and periodic manner on what is happening inside a program. A variety of mechanisms can be used to ensure that things are going according to plan or to determine when the program is off track (see Figure 16-1). As a starting point, the governing body needs to establish a clear policy for monitoring and write these out as part of its governing document.

FIGURE   16-1
Monitoring a Program

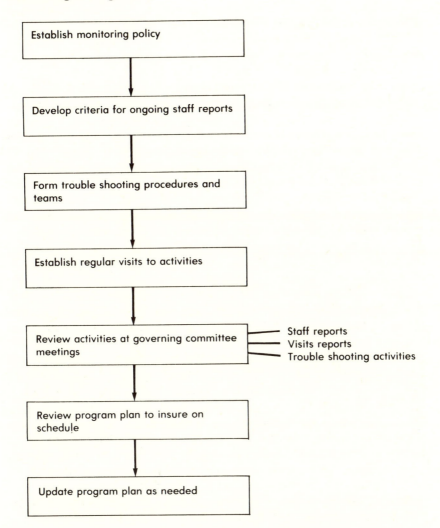

Monitoring checklists is an excellent way to determine what it is that the parties want to look at on a regular basis. Frequently, governing bodies are enjoined to monitor what is going on. Left out usually is monitor what and monitor how. By brainstorming and agreeing on a monitoring checklist, the group is clear on what it wants to review—and what it doesn't want. The more specific these lists are the better. Clues to what should be included on the checklist are found in the governing documents of the group. Items can include such topics as understanding where the goups are in the problem-solving process, attendance, and whether there are any potential interferences with traditional collective bargaining.

Reports by the staff of the program, whether they be coordinators or facilitators, provide critical information on where things stand, how the groups are functioning, and what is planned. The staff should primarily address the items listed on the monitoring checklist. If there are other items of burning importance then they should be relayed. However, the staff should avoid long and boring reports on issues of little interest to the governing body. They also should not be tattletales on what is said by whom in the groups. The staff should be candid about the problems they are facing. Hiding difficulties only boomerangs when the issues surface. In some programs with a large staff, a schedule is developed for staff reports from various locations.

A second and very important way to monitor the activities of a program with multiple levels is to *make visits*. If a governing body has jurisdiction over other problem-solving groups, a union-management team should be scheduled to visit them at regular intervals. There is no need to be there all of the time, but periodic visits demonstrate interest and provide firsthand impressions. It is best when the group knows about the visitors ahead of time and the visitors stay for the duration of the meeting. By doing this, the group will feel genuinely supported rather than spied on by the team from the governing body. All of the members of the governing body should have a chance to sit in on problem-solving groups within their jurisdiction. Visits have two-way benefits. They increase the commitment of the visitors and shore up the morale of those visited and open up communications between them.

A third method is to make sure the minutes of the various program components are shared with those who need to know what is going on. *Review of important documents* such as charts, plans, minutes, and surveys helps to determine whether the program is going as planned. The content of what is going on inside the groups is just as important as the adherence to the process. The sharing of content information about the topics under consideration with appropriate parties can generate additional information that could help the problem-solving process. The governing body should not preempt or undercut the problem-solving group's efforts. They should not be prejudging preliminary data or draft documents. Instead, they should be reviewing them to see if they can assist in any way and to see if the group is on target.

An area of particular importance in monitoring is the use of the problem-solving techniques. Program coordinators and others better versed in the techniques should see not just the minutes but the application of the techniques. Early intervention to correct mistakes, oversights, and tangents can save later on an incredible amount of time and aggravation. The various components of a program should be operating in a quality manner. Many advocate quality control intervention before the end of the line so that quality defects are caught and corrected early. The same should be true with these programs. High-quality standards need to be maintained. Ongoing and early assessment of the quality errors in the problem-solving process and the adherence to the governing documents improves the quality of the final results and avoids failures and blowouts.

USING JOINT TROUBLESHOOTING
PROCEDURES AND ACTIVITIES

In every program's life a little rain must fall. Inevitably, some difficulties arise when the union and management are trying to do something different. There is literally no way to anticipate every situation or problem. The aim, however, is to manage these difficulties as early as possible, at the lowest possible level with the least disruption to the program and the organizations involved.

Several counterproductive strategies are often used. When trouble looms, some programs do ostrich imitations and stick their heads in the sand. However, one major part of the anatomy remains exposed by this approach! Few problems go away by ignoring them or wishing them away. In some other locations, magnums are drawn to shoot at minor issues. Top-level people are sucked in to solve petty issues that could have been resolved at a lower level. They generally resent this intrusion on their time, especially if it occurs with any frequency. Practitioners of this approach have a favorite troubleshooter and call on him or her all of the time. These "favorites" tire quickly of this role. When the big guns are brought in immediately, particularly to confront middle management, there is a residue of resentment left over carrying long-term negative consequences. In some cases, program staff are nervous nellies and call meetings of the governing bodies for every little thing. Such meetings are unnecessary and a waste of time for the group.

A system of joint labor-management troubleshooting teams designated on a rotating basis from the governing body can help find the necessary solutions and avoid the traps discussed above. To set up the team, the governing body designates a team of one management and one union representative from the committee to be on call for a period of time, such as three months. When the team is needed, it is called on by any member of the program to examine a potential problem and help solve it. Both team members consult together on the possible solutions. If it is a labor problem, the union person is given first crack at solving it. If it is a management problem, then the manager tries first.

An example of a labor problem would be when a group refuses to go forward with problem solving due to the slow processing or unfavorable outcome of a grievance. The union has to inform them of the separate processes for cooperative problem solving and grievance resolution, the different agreements that have been made, and the fact that not all grievances can be won despite the union's best efforts. This situation is often referred to as "hostage taking," that is, holding the cooperative activities hostage to try to get something in the traditional collective bargaining arena. While hostage taking does not happen often, it can and does happen. The labor approach can work best when trying to get accurate information from employees about the real situation.

On the management side, the most common problem is resistance from middle management who put up roadblocks to the accomplishment of the task, forbid or discourage attendance of group members, or have frequent "emergencies" that just happen to fall at the same time as scheduled meetings. The management member of the troubleshooting team informs the resisting manager of the overall commitment of management and counsels him or her to desist. Hopefully a word to the wise will be sufficient, but sometimes intervention from a superior is necessary. From time to time, problems occur with delays from technical support groups that provide information to the problem-solving groups. Their slowness is generally due to not being used to responding to requests from nonmanagerial employees. A friendly reminder from the troubleshooting team is usually sufficient.

If after consultation the team feels it cannot resolve the problem, the problem goes to the full committee. Preferably this is in a regular session, but it may be a special meeting if absolutely necessary. If the full committee can't resolve it, the issue gets bumped up the ladder to the next higher level in the program for resolution. In some cases, the issues may not be clear-cut and the appropriate level of governing body may need to establish or clarify the policy on the matter in question.

Troubleshooting brings up the issue of authority. As much as possible in a program, voluntarism and the wisdom of good sense should be used. But, unfortunately, in some situations this is not enough. Individual players cannot be allowed to sabotage overall institutional cooperative policy. On management's side, if a subordinate manager is undercutting the agreed-upon policy of cooperation, then traditional managerial hierarchical authority will need to be enforced. On the labor side, while individuals may have legitimate reservations, when agreements are made, the membership should abide by those agreements. Selective application of agreement by labor opens the door for the other side to do the same. The enforcement mechanism is generally stronger on the management side—your job. If union-management cooperation is a way of doing business, it ought to be enforced like any other basic policy of the organization.

In some programs there has been too much of an emphasis on the voluntary nature of the process. Managers cannot volunteer not to produce the product or service of the employer or to make up their own way of doing things fundamentally counter to the policy of the employer. They go along or leave. The same principle should apply here. Too many programs have gotten the image of being pushover efforts shielded from the reality of the work world. Some organizations have built in reviewing how the manager works with the joint process as part of the management performance appraisal. Cooperation is then highlighted as a standard operating procedure and given concrete reward.

USING THE PROGRAM PLANS TO MEASURE PROGRESS

The plans developed earlier are the critical instruments for program monitoring. Without them, the criteria for monitoring can shift from moment to moment, there is little sense of comprehensive reviews, and future implications of changes are left dangling. The plans for the entire program, the work of the staff, and the activities of the problem-solving groups provide the bases for the review.

At each meeting of the governing body, these plans should be reviewed to see if planned activities are being implemented, if they are occurring on time, and what the next steps should be. If there is a difference between the plan and what is taking place, then that must be discussed. Sometimes a difference is a result of an unavoidable problem. In that case, this needs to be acknowledged and adjustments made in the next steps. The mere fact of being off the plan is not a problem. Not becoming aware of why and what to do about it is a major mistake.

In most cases, monitoring the plan helps flag problem areas early and clearly. If there is a consistent lag between plans and actual progress, either the planning was unrealistic or there are barriers impeding progress. If the planning skills are lacking, the group should learn from the mistakes, perhaps get some training, and look at the planning challenges more realistically. However, often the deviations from the plan are symptomatic of problems inside the group. There may be problems in task accomplishment, in group maintenance function, or because outside conditions are making things difficult. Sometimes the problem is a lack of adequate training for group leaders and members. Fingers are usually pointed at the outside influences first, but in reviewing groups behind schedule, a careful look at their internal functioning is in order. The plans should be clearly communicated to all members of the group so that all can aim for clearly understood goals. A troubleshooting team should be used to diagnose a group with significant problems meeting its plans.

In actuality, plans provide a source of pride and accomplishment in a group. Rather than waiting to the end of the process and a presentation to experience a sense of accomplishment, setting and meeting plans that accurately describe the necessary tasks provide important intermediate milestones. Monitoring plans should include praise for those who set and meet their plans as well as warning signals for problem areas where progress does not keep pace.

ESTABLISHING A JOINT EVALUATION PROCESS

For many people, evaluation is a scary word. To some it rings too academic; to others, it conjures painful memories of bad report cards. Management may remember the use of evaluations as a prelude to major changes, harassment, delays, or punishment. It really doesn't have to be all that bad. Evaluation is absolutely essential to long-term success of cooperative union-management programs. Without knowing what the program's results are or what went right or wrong in implementing it, people can keep marching in the wrong direction. Organizations that do not evaluate what they are doing are like people walking down blind alleys. They might get to where they want to go—but then again, they might not! If the program stumbles along the way, the parties have no reliable idea of why and what to do about it next time. The governing bodies have to make a clear commitment to evaluation at all levels of the program—and carry it out. Make assessments of the particular solutions being implemented, each element of the process of the group, and the overall results. Evaluations too often fall by the wayside as programs get underway and get lost in the shuffle of institutional priorities. When those affected learn that no one is evaluating the program or their participation, the quality of performance suffers.

Evaluations should measure both the process for introducing and maintaining a project and specific results—including those results anticipated in the goals and objectives set at the beginning. The goals of an evaluation are really very simple. Evaluations ask if the program is doing what it set out to do and if it is doing it in an acceptable manner. They go on to ask how we can do what has been done well still better and how the aspects that were not right can be corrected.

As such, good evaluation provides not only important answers to where the program has been, but even more importantly, clues to where the effort should go in the future. In addition, by adopting a joint union-management approach toward evaluation, understanding and teamwork are strengthened. We have seen eye-opening awareness of the program develop from previously reluctant internal union and management evaluators. The usual end result is a stronger commitment from both parties to make their program work even better and a pride in identifying the accomplishments they have brought into being.

CONDUCTING A JOINT PROGRAM EVALUATION

Most formal evaluations are done by outside evaluators in order to preserve the "objectivity" of the research. While this is understandable for academic papers and formalized comparisons, the objective of evaluations inside a union-management cooperative project is different. The people inside want to know in terms they can understand what has gone on. We have tested the approach described in Figure 16-2 and it has been shown to provide the kinds of process and answers that help strengthen a joint program. It is not an academic approach and probably would not stand up in most college classrooms—but it works!

The fundamental principle is to have the union-management partners do as much of the evaluation as possible. While external assistance can be helpful in

FIGURE 16-2
Evaluating a Program

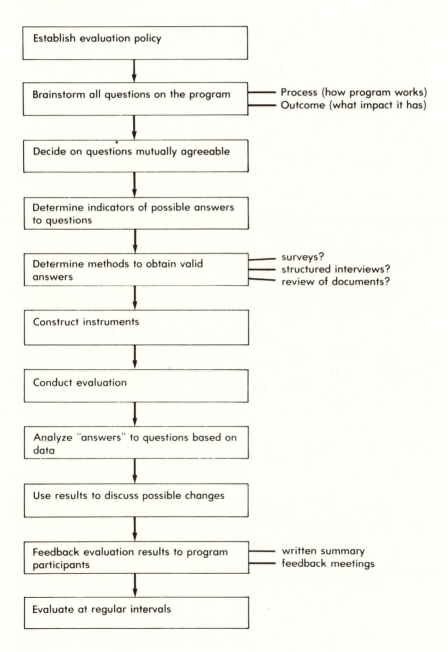

the design and administration of the evaluation, the union and management principals maintain control over the process. The magic of this approach is the relationship of the internal parties to the learning, not the degree of statistical reliability.

Who should evaluate whom and what should be reviewed must be clearly understood at the outset. Every group in a program should evaluate itself and its subordinate groups. These various evaluations should be integrated into an overall plan for evaluation. The groups should work together maximally to ensure that they are in sync in terms of timing, areas of investigation, and methodology. For example, in a program with three tiers, the top level should evaluate its own functioning and the overall performance of the program as well as top-level staff. The middle level should look at its own activities and subordinate groups and reporting staff. The lowest level on the organization chart should also review its performance. The evaluation can flow upward with the next higher level using the results of the assessment at the lower level as a starting point and then examining additional questions that seem important and incorporating them into its own self-assessment. This helps avoid duplication. However, in some cases, the group may want to conduct its own review of similar questions to those addressed at the lower levels, especially when they are subjective answers rather than based on hard data.

The first step within the group is to brainstorm all of the questions the union and management partners have about the process of their effort. While these should be internally developed questions, it may be helpful to look at some generalized evaluations of joint projects or the efforts of others to give the group additional ideas. Outside aids should supplement and not replace the group's own questions.

Process refers to the way the program has been established, or the how of the program. Included as general categories under process might be the overall design process, management of the project, relationship to nondirect participants, development of program staff, development of the governing bodies, communications approaches, implementation and development of shop floor or office level groups, and/or the use of consultants. Preferably, the group determines the major categories of program implementation and brainstorms questions within these categories.

In terms of the outcomes, this is where the results are addressed, or the *what* of the program. The primary necessity is to measure the impact on the goals and objectives set by the governing committee. These should include a balance of areas that affect operation and the work force. In addition, there should be an accounting of the sum results of various groups associated with the program, such as top- and middle-level committees, task forces, shop floor problem-solving groups, and other joint mechanisms.

A surprisingly large number of questions may emerge during this brainstorming. The next step is to review this list and determine priority questions to have answered that are agreeable to both sides. By setting a minimum number of votes, each question needs to be included, the list can be reviewed for clarification, and votes taken to determine priorities. At the end, a final list of questions for the evaluation should result. These questions represent the most important questions for the evaluating group.

With the questions in hand, the next step is to figure out how to determine answers to these questions that would be accurate and complete. This means identifying the "indicators" of the possible answers. The group should not jump ahead to answers at this time. For example, indicators of impact on organizational performance could be results on unit profit and loss statements, production records, or quality scoresheets. An indicator of customer satisfaction may be found in the level of customer complaints. Indicators of the labor-management relationship may be the number of grievances and when they were settled. An indicator of interest of employees in participating may be attendance at the meetings. The ways in which the answers to each question would be exhibited should be listed under each question. The aim should be to look for hard data indicators before relying on composites of opinions.

Knowing what the parties want to know and how they would recognize the answers, the next step is to determine the methods for collecting the information. Take each question and its indicators and see whether review of documents, surveys, structured interviews, and/or observations would be the best way to answer the question. An obvious and important way to get information is to review records and documents available within the organization. These include production records, summary grievance reports, productivity assessments, minutes of meetings, attendance logs, and other similar internally available documentation. Use these sources first.

Surveys and structured interview may be necessary to get additional information. Surveys are a good way to get information confidentially from a large number of people. The questions included should be clear about the options provided. Too many open-ended questions make analysis difficult. In developing surveys, it is wise to consult texts or experts on the construction of surveys to minimize the bias of the questions and to ensure that the information generated by the survey will in fact answer the general evaluation questions asked by the group.

Structured interviews are ways to elicit more open-ended discussion with key parties as to their reactions and assessments. A structured interview carefully plans out the questions to be asked in advance. Similar kinds of interviewees should be asked the same set of questions. A structured interview is not a general conversation or a rap session but a clear way to pose and probe questions of concern to the overall evaluation. The interviewer needs to be careful not to lead the person being interviewed or interject his or her own opinions. It is not a good idea to have immediate supervisors or subordinates do the interviewing.

Having the overall questions, the appropriate indicators, and the methods for gathering the data, the ensuing step is to construct the appropriate instruments for gathering the data. Checksheets may need to be developed for reviewing organizational documents or gathering new information. Surveys and structured interviews need to be prepared in advance and tested to make sure they will accomplish their intended tasks. If it doesn't quite work, it is best to work out the bugs before everyone uses the instrument.

Then the actual evaluation is conducted. When a sample is being used, pay careful attention that the sample is representative of the whole group or set of documents. In the actual conduct of the evaluation, smaller subgroups of labor and management teams might be assigned to particular groups, kinds of data, or evaluation questions. The group must guarantee confidentiality of surveys and structured interviews if it wants the most accurate data. By using identification codes, no one beyond the interviewer will know the name on any response sheet.

With the data collected, the answers need to be summarized and analyzed. Again, there may be subgroups of union and management evaluators who summarize the interviews or particular surveys, and/or work on particular evaluation questions. Finally, all of this needs to be brought together and each one of the overall evaluation questions answered based on the data collected. Some questions will have simple answers. Others will require more analysis, combination, and/or comparison of data from different sources. Some will be judgment calls. The final evaluation report should be a listing of the questions and the answers. If methodology is a concern, an explanation of the approach and the instruments can be appended.

Evaluations do not end with the results tabulated and reported. The most important part of the evaluation is to use the results to learn how to do the program better. The evaluators and the entire governing body need to review carefully what has been uncovered and collected to determine what improvements are needed where. Improvements should have a clear plan for implementation. Then the next evaluation will determine how well these improvements were applied. In addition, the evaluation process itself should be evaluated to see what went well and what could be improved for the next time it is done.

The results of the evaluation should be reported back in some form to the participants in the evaluation. This can be through a summary report listing the major findings. The entire report can be made available to those who would like to review it. Feedback meetings can be scheduled with the problem-solving groups within the jurisdiction of the study to let them know what was found and what is planned based on the findings. Making this a two-way process allows those who were subjects of the evaluation to ask additional questions about the evaluation results.

This process may seem like a long and involved procedure. It is a considered process that need not take major amounts of time if it is managed well. But then again, when asked to comment on the success of the program they will have concrete answers. The results go beyond the specific answers that are derived in the end. It teaches leaders in the union and management how to do systematic evaluations, which will have positive impacts on their other work. The teamwork of the union and management in the process helps build a stronger commitment to the joint process. They understand much more about the program than they would if the evaluation were contracted to another group or outside evaluator. The subjects of the study know that it is important because they see important people in the organization involved in the process.

Evaluation should not be a one-time event but an ongoing commitment of the joint partners to assess how well they have done in every aspect of the joint effort. Subsequent evaluations should be easier to manage than the initial review. Many of the questions will have surfaced and can be updated, bugs in the methodology have been worked out, and the members of the governing body will be more experienced. Usually once a year, a thorough evaluation should be done, but this may vary depending on the kind of program initiated.

CONCLUSION

Planning, monitoring, and evaluating are key elements in successful joint union-management initiatives. They are linked because each requires careful thought, agreement between the partners, and real reflection on what should or did happen. Initially the partners plan together; along the way they monitor to see if this has occurred; and periodically they systematically evaluate the progress to see what has happened. To complete the circle, the evaluation leads to new goals and plans for continuing what has been done well and making necessary improvements. By making sure the parties have covered all of the bases for program development, it then leads not only to a more secure representation of the interests of the union and management but an exceptionally strong program. This can influence effective performance in other areas of management and union responsibility. It will be a program that delivers on its promise.

It may seem like a formidable task to do all of the things discussed in this Part. In many ways it is. But doing things right is not always easy. Unless all the areas of program development discussed in this part are covered, there will be long-term costs in the form of aggravating problems for both the union and management; the potential for the program will be diminished, and the possibility of failure increased. Avoiding these risks makes the extra energy it takes to engage in a complete approach to cooperation more than worthwhile. A new and stronger creative energy will be unleashed inside the organizations involved. The reason why the union and management entered a joint effort is because they have important objectives in common. This approach gives them the best chance for realization.

IV

The Financial
Side of Cooperation

17

Sharing the Pie: Financial Gains, Collective Bargaining, and Profit Sharing

Efforts combining finances and cooperation appeal to two basic human needs: self-interest and the desire for common purpose. Companies are motivated to engage in this form of cooperation when it helps meet the basic need for successful financial performance. Employees are motivated to engage in it when there is a clear monetary benefit to them. Together employees and the company can cooperate to their mutual financial benefit.

The union and management partners are linked by a basic cooperative relationship in the financial area. Management must manage employees so that operations are maximally effective to enhance and secure organization finances. The union must represent employees in such a way that they obtain the best compensation for their contribution to the organization. Traditionally, the union and management divide up the financial pie at the bargaining table by setting basic compensation. Recently, the union and management partners are examining more closely cooperation in such financial aspects of the organization as profit sharing and employee stock ownership plans. Also, the union and management partners are assessing cooperation in the area of overall employee compensation through such approaches as productivity gain sharing, pay for knowledge, and pay for performance.

This part examines employee participation in the financial aspects of organizations and in the less traditional forms of employee compensation. The four chapters describe ways in which management and unions have worked together to increase financial return to employees and employers in both the public and private sectors.

HOW ARE FINANCIAL GAINS TRADITIONALLY SHARED?

Traditionally, employees have shared the financial gains of their organizations through increased pay and benefits. In unionized workplaces these are among the key items addressed at the bargaining table. Additionally, there have been various bonuses devised to reward employees for extra effort and raises to acknowledge employee tenure, skills, or performance. With few exceptions, the sharing of financial gains has operated on the "trickle down theory," that is, the organization gains through increased profits or a higher budget and employees eventually get their share of it as it works its way down from the top of the organization. The union wants to obtain more for its members and management wants more for its own compensation, dividends, investments, and growth. In recent times this search for more has been conducted in contexts of declining profits or organizational budgets. Such organizations haven't had greater financial resources to be shared by those seeking more compensation. Historically, the search for more has concentrated on getting a greater share of the existing pie rather than on increasing the size of the pie. Employee involvement in the financial aspects of organizations and the less traditional forms of employee compensation contribute to building up both the employer's and the employees' financial resources. For this reason, greater attention is concentrated on these arenas of union-management cooperation.

HOW IS PARTICIPATION LINKED TO FINANCIAL INCENTIVES?

The New York Stock Exchange's 1982 survey on the connection between employee participation and financial incentives determined that a majority of companies using financial incentives gave improving overall company performance and/or productivity as the main reasons for using them. The rationale is that employees participate in the company more intensely especially through their job performance when that participation is tied to some kind of financial reward. Group-based forms of financial incentives are on the increase while individually based forms of incentives are on the decline. This is consistent with the notion that employee participation is more easily and effectively fostered in the context of group-based activities. Further, many employee participation and quality of work life programs were initially isolated from the areas of employee compensation or financial incentives. Now these programs are either linked to compensation or other financial incentives or at least peacefully coexisting with nontraditional compensation and/or financial incentive programs.

WHAT IS THE FRAMEWORK FOR THE VARIOUS FINANCIAL GAIN SHARING APPROACHES?

The term financial gain sharing is being used in its broadest sense to describe an entire array of approaches. These approaches can be organized into five categories according to the aspect of the organization with which the employee becomes involved. First, profit sharing involves employees more directly with the organization's overall profitability. Second, there are approaches that involve employees with organizational output. Through individual financial incentives, employees concentrate on their individual productivity. Through productivity gain-sharing programs, employees as a group concentrate on organizational productivity. In these ways, as output increases more money is shared with employees. Third, pay for performance or merit pay involves individual employees with overall organizational performance by providing incentives to individuals to raise their overall performance. Fourth, pay for knowledge involves individual employees and groups of employees in human resources management and planning. By investing in the knowledge and skills bases of the employees, the company seeks to increase its worth. Fifth, employee stock ownership plans and employee buyouts involve employees in capital formation in private sector organizations. Employees invest in their companies, and the value of their investment fluctuates with the value of the business. The chapters in this part describe all of these approaches.

COLLECTIVE BARGAINING AS A FINANCIAL GAIN SHARING MECHANISM

Collective bargaining is the most common mechanism whereby management and the union decide how to share the results of improved financial conditions. It is a very effective way for the union and management to reach agreement about how to divide up the financial pie. Monetary items or items affecting employee compensation by far comprise the bulk of the items addressed through collective bargaining.

Collective bargaining has a much longer and broader track record as a mechanism for joint decision making about financial issues than all of the other less traditional mechanisms described in this part. Both workers and management have benefited by using collective bargaining to decide how to share financial resources. It is important to note that when these other less traditional mechanisms are adopted in unionized workplaces, they are rooted in collective bargaining. In many cases they began as items introduced at the bargaining table. In other cases they grew out of nonfinancial union-management cooperative efforts such as employee involvement or labor-management committees and were later incorporated into the agreement.

Last, collective bargaining has several distinct advantages over these other mechanisms for employee involvement in the financial area. First, collective bargaining has equity and fairness as guiding principles. Financial benefits to rank and file employees are shared in a fair fashion among all of the workers. This approach recognizes that each employee has made a unique contribution to the organization and that employees as a group have made a contribution greater than that constructed by adding up the individual contributions. For this reason, unions advocate dividing the financial benefits among workers on an objective, fair, and equitable basis. Also, because of the guiding principles of equity and fairness, supervisory and middle management compensation packages are usually adjusted by management to keep pace with additional financial benefits obtained by agreement-covered employees working under them. If anything, union insistence on equity and fairness through collective bargaining has had the effect of supporting teamwork within organizations and has mitigated against the "every man for himself" attitude, which some of the less traditional mechanisms for employee involvement in organizational finances can foster.

Second, collective bargaining is a process by which management and the union examine the complete organizational picture. This joint building of a comprehensive organizational perspective is in part the explanation for the effectiveness of collective bargaining. But collective bargaining also allows all of the various factors affecting the organization's financial picture to be taken into account. Financial resources and gains are divided up with an eye to the total organization picture. None of the other financial gain-sharing mechanisms identified here is based on such a broad inclusive perspective. Most of them zero in on one or more measures relevant to the approach being used. This narrower, less comprehensive perspective has real limitations as the basis for dividing up the financial pie. For management, gain sharing through collective bargaining provides predictability and an opportunity to weigh different factors and cost out the different options specifically. However, tying gain sharing to one factor such as productivity can be risky and undesirable if, for example, revenues decline while productivity is enhanced. Or the skills and knowledge of employees could increase through pay for knowledge, thereby resulting in higher labor costs while revenues remain the same or decline. Collective bargaining is the best joint process by which management and the union can divide up the organization's financial resources equitably and fairly based on an analysis of the total picture of the organization.

WHAT IS PROFIT SHARING?

Profit sharing is a scheme whereby the company shares its profits with employees participating in the profit-sharing plan. There are more than 350,000 firms in the United States with profit-sharing plans.[1] Procter & Gamble pioneered the use of profit sharing by establishing its plan in 1887. Major companies such as Kodak, Sears, Johnson Wax, and Harris Trust established profit-sharing plans in the 1920s. In 1939 Congress passed a law allowing tax deferments for qualified profit-sharing plans. More than 90 percent of the profit-sharing plans of today began as a result of this 1939 tax provision.[2]

Under profit sharing the company contributes to the plan out of company profits once a year. The amount contributed may be a fixed percentage of before-tax profits, a discretionary amount decided upon by the board of directors, or a combination of a fixed and a discretionary amount. These profits become bonuses that are credited to all employees participating in profit sharing. Usually the employee's share of the profits is based on compensation or years of service. A majority of profit-sharing plans defer actual payment of the employee's share until retirement or termination. The trustee of the plan then invests the profits earned in the individual employee accounts. In this way employees gain investment earnings. When the employee retires or leaves, he or she receives both the profits allocated to the account and the earnings from the investment of those profits. Some profit-sharing plans distribute all or a part of the employee's share as cash once a year. Also some plans allow employees to add to their profit-sharing accounts.

From a tax viewpoint everyone benefits through profit sharing. The company deducts its contributions to the plan. The trust handling the plan is tax exempt. Employees do not pay taxes on the funds in their accounts until they actually receive them. Most employees obtain their profit-sharing bonuses upon retirement when the tax liability is usually less because of a lower tax bracket. Such mutual tax benefits make profit sharing a popular form of employee participation in the finances of the company.

Most profit-sharing plans provide for no real, direct participation in management of the company. As a result the employee share of profits is affected by management decisions in which employees have little or no say. Some profit-sharing plans encourage employee participation through traditional channels such as suggestion systems. Others have regular communications to employees about the financial status of the company but this is primarily one-way communication. Many profit-sharing plans coexist alongside employee participation programs with no real direct connection between them.

HOW EFFECTIVE IS PROFIT SHARING AS A MOTIVATOR FOR ORGANIZATIONAL PERFORMANCE?

Profit-sharing plans can give employees a feeling of having a greater stake in the company and its success. In this way it can indirectly have a positive impact on employee productivity and morale. However, employees are usually aware that company profits are influenced by many factors, both internal and external to the company, most of which are divorced from their control or influence. Such factors can be changing commodity prices, political upheavals, currency fluctuations, liability losses, and the like.

It is not wise to convince employees that by improving their performance they will necessarily enhance profits and thereby gain a financial reward through profit sharing, for if profits decline due to factors outside their control, employees will be dissatisfied and disillusioned. Further, employees may fall into the trap of counting on a profit-sharing bonus as part of their regular income when there is a cash distribution of those bonuses. Financial rewards from profit sharing may be too unstable or insubstantial to be positively motivating to either employees or the organization.

When a majority of the profit-sharing plans defer payment until retirement or termination, this makes the financial reward from profit sharing very remote from day-to-day work and performance. For any incentive to be motivating it must be distributed as close as possible to the time period in which it was earned. Profit-sharing bonuses may not be motivating in the deferred payment plans. Even with cash distribution, this is done annually after the end of the year for which those profits were earned. Again the incentive is given out long after the period in which it was earned. These circumstances can make profit-sharing incentives too remote to be strong motivators.

There may be valid reasons that union and management partners wish to share financial gains through profit sharing. This is very likely in the small to medium-sized firms where an individual's performance would seem to count for more in the company's overall performance. However, the union and management partners should understand that profit sharing in and of itself may not be an effective motivator for employee or organizational performance. Also, profit sharing is not really a direct, active form of joint participation; therefore, all of the positive benefits that do accrue to successful employee participation programs cannot be expected of profit sharing. Profit sharing does provide mutual financial gains but with certain limitations.

In conclusion, it is important to examine the impressive track record of collective bargaining as a financial gain-sharing mechanism. Further, for union and management partners collective bargaining is the foundation for any of the other gain-sharing and financial participation programs that they might undertake.

ADDITIONAL RESOURCES

Doyle, Robert J. *Gainsharing and Productivity: A Guide to Planning, Implementation, and Development.* New York: AMACOM, 1983.

Frieden, Karl. *Workplace Deomocracy and Productivity.* Washington, D.C.: National Center for Economic Alternatives, 1980.

Lawler III, Edward E. *Pay and Organization Development.* Reading, Mass.: Addison-Wesley, 1981.

18

More for More:
Individual Incentive Plans,
Pay for Performance,
and Pay for Knowledge

Three kinds of wage incentive systems are presented here: individual incentive systems, pay for performance or merit pay, and pay for knowledge. All of these have been examined, negotiated, and implemented by unionized organizations to improve organizational performance and to share financial benefits with employees who contribute to this improvement. In all three systems the employee's wages or compensation are structured to provide stronger financial incentives for his or her performance and development on the job. Individual incentive systems focus on individual output as the defining context. Pay for performance systems focus on overall individual effectiveness. Pay for knowledge systems focus on individual skills and knowledge. In all three cases individual employees do more and therefore obtain more. What is significant is that the financial gains obtained by the individual employee are primarily up to what the individual employee does. These individually based systems are very different from the group-based productivity gain-sharing programs described in the following chapter.

Wage incentive systems are controversial though relatively common. When the burden for accomplishment rests so completely with individual employees, it raises questions of basic equity and fairness. The time, energy, and costs of administering wage incentive systems can be substantial. There are also questions about their motivating power over time. Further, wage incentive systems are often seen as a way to lower overall labor costs, and there are real questions about whether this actually happens.

WHAT ARE INDIVIDUAL INCENTIVE PROGRAMS?

Piecework is probably the most well known of the individual incentive programs. An employee is paid according to his or her actual output. A price or piece rate to be paid for each unit completed or processed is established for each job. Piecework is effective only when employee output is easily measured on an individual basis and where production is standardized so that the piece rates or prices will be relatively stable over time.

Standard hour plans or the 100 percent incentive plans are other individual incentive programs.[1] First, a methods study is done to ensure that a job is being performed in the most efficient fashion. Then the job is time studied to set the standard for it.[2] For each 1 percent performance over the standard, the employee is awarded a 1 percent over base wage. Base wage is guaranteed, and the employee receives 100 percent of the gain made.[3] Standard hour plans are applicable in more complex production operations where piecework is not applicable.

In both piecework systems and standard hour plans, time studies are used to establish standards against which individual output is measured. These measurements determine the wage incentives to be paid. Time and motion studies affect incentives further. Improved methods developed as part of the study are used by employees to obtain their financial bonuses. Time and motion studies, then, are a critical part of these two wage incentive systems. The union and management partners considering either of these individual incentive programs must agree on both the time and motion study methodology and the industrial engineer(s) being used. Further joint training on industrial engineering methods can help the partners to analyze the situation competently and reach agreement on methodology and specialists to be used. Some international unions such as the International Ladies Garment Workers Union or United Rubber Workers have industrial engineers on staff.

To link successfully wage incentives and labor standards established by time and motion studies, all of the following should be done: develop the best practical method for doing the work/performing the job; train the workers to use the best method; accurately measure the manual work and the machine time; have employees participate in changes affecting their jobs; and follow up after the standards are issued to ensure their proper application.[4] While piecework and standard hour plans may seem simple and therefore appealing as wage incentive systems, there is more to successfully applying them than may first meet the eye.

A third, less common individual incentive system is leisure time incentives. Time off or leisure time is given in lieu of additional wages or financial bonuses. In parts of the transportation industry when a run is completed more quickly than the standard established for it, time off is allowed, that is, an "early quit." In other industries when a certain level of production is reached, then time off is earned. Other names for this are stint work, task work, or sunshine bonuses.[5]

In one of the early joint quality of work life experiments, leisure time incentives were a major part of the program. At the Harmon Industries-United Autoworkers project at the Bolivar, Tennessee plant, one of the ways productivity gains were shared was through the Earned Idle Time (EIT) experiment.

Initially, EIT was a one-year experiment whereby individuals or groups could go home or produce extra production after production goals were met. Employees could leave early with a full day's pay; earn extra pay for extra work based on group performance; or earn bonus hours for whatever they wanted to do in the plant.[6] Through EIT, experimental groups of employees increased their productivity and changed work methods. Eventually the EIT was expanded plantwide. A free, inplant education program was begun to provide courses requested by the workers that could be attended during "earned idle time."

Probably the greatest controversy about individual incentives is how much is needed to be motivating. Experts suggest that 15 to 35 percent above the hourly base rate paid to day workers on similar jobs is the necessary level for an individual incentive to be motivating.[7]

WHAT ARE THE ISSUES CONCERNING INDIVIDUAL INCENTIVE PROGRAMS?

There are a number of issues raised by individual incentive programs. Many production processes are machine-paced or computer-paced, which can limit how and to what extent an employee can affect production. Individual incentive programs ask employees to affect their production or output directly. The limitations of machine- or computer-paced operations affect that output. Jobs have different potential for applying work methods improvements or production shortcuts. Differentials such as these seriously challenge the equity and fairness of wage incentive systems. In effect, different employees would have different opportunities for improving their output and obtaining the gains therefrom.

Industrial engineering sets the standards on which the incentives are based. It is not a precise science with absolute answers. In fact, giving industrial engineering a key role in American production over the last 40 years has not necessarily resulted in the highest quality products or the most effective production processes. Often management and the union have very different levels of belief in the competence residing in and the credibility of industrial engineering. Employees often have negative opinions of industrial engineering as a source of assistance in doing their jobs well.

Workers can manipulate these incentive systems. They can restrict output to convince management to revise the standards downward. They can also keep production at a certain level above standards and no higher so that the standards will not be revised upward. Initially, incentive rates can be motivating. However, standards can become outdated. Some employees resist changes. Finally, individual incentives can become counterproductive at some point.

Management administers the incentive plan. This requires accurate record keeping and bookkeeping, good supervision, and excellent communications. In some situations these requirements can't be met because the organizational wherewithal is just not there. Management misjudgments, incompetence, and failures can so adversely affect operations that the workers' chances for meeting the standards and obtaining the bonuses are reduced or eliminated. This raises a real potential conflict area for union and management partners in such a program. Finally, the union will probably demand a role in setting the incentive standards. In most industries, management alone has traditionally set standards. Reaching agreement on the process for setting and the standards themselves could be a serious challenge to management and the union. Either partner may also desire independent verification of the standards.

Despite these issues, individual incentive programs can result in greater daily output. Improved work methods resulting from time and motion studies enable workers to produce more with the same effort. Employees try to eliminate wasted time so that they can exceed the standard and obtain a bonus. Most qualified workers can easily meet reasonable work standards. Because of this they are encouraged to increase their speed and turn out more work. The average output of a group of qualified workers operating under an incentive program normally exceeds the standard by 14 to 45 percent.[8]

An outstanding example of how a union and management can successfully cooperate to institute an individual incentive program is the Productivity Incentive Plan undertaken by the International Brotherhood of Teamsters and Certified Grocers of California in 1980 and described earlier in Chapter 5. The union and management jointly established the work standards after hiring an outside company to do the necessary time measurement and analyses. Performance standards are devised for individuals and the crew. The average worker performs at 139 percent of the standard. At the same time some employees can perform at only about 90 percent of the standard and still retain their jobs because this lower performance is balanced by the higher performance of others on their crew. Time off or cash is given for exceeding the work standards. The combination individual and crew definition of performance was developed jointly to ensure that all employees be given fair treatment under the incentive system. Both the union and management are satisfied with this joint incentive program.

PAY SYSTEMS AND ORGANIZATIONAL CHANGE

Pay systems are significant in any organization. Pay is extremely important as an organizational cost. In manufacturing, payroll costs are estimated to be as high as 40 percent in many cases. In service organizations, payroll costs can be as high as 70 percent of total organization costs.[9] Pay systems are also significant because they are tied to other major aspects of the organization, such as organizational structure, superior/subordinate relations, job design, organizational climate, management philosophy or style, information and control systems, management training and development, and performance appraisal. Pay affects pricing structure and competitiveness. Input from these other aspects of the organization is needed to administer the pay system, and the administration of the pay system is affected by them.[10] The pay system impacts on the entire organization and literally involves everyone within it.

The union and management should consider the relationship of the pay system to an organizational change effort. It can be the primary system in which such an effort is concentrated initially. There are some compelling arguments in favor of that:

1. Pay is important to all employees and affects all.
2. By beginning with the pay system, the organization can demonstrate its commitment to real change.
3. Most organizations have problems within their pay systems, such as perceptions of inequity, rewards not contingent upon performance, and overall inadequate administration.
4. Dealing successfully with the pay system can lead to measurable differences in individual performance and organizational effectiveness.
5. Beginning with the pay system can provide a model of how to deal with other significant problems and can lead to the identification of those problems through the pay system's connection to the other major organizational systems.[11]

In any case, compensation issues are bound to arise in a long-term organizational change effort. The pay system can hinder that effort by not rewarding the behaviors necessary to make the required changes. Pay for performance and pay for knowledge are increasingly being adopted within the overall organizational change effort.

WHAT IS PAY FOR PERFORMANCE?

Pay for performance is a compensation system in which some portion of an employee's pay is dependent on his or her individual performance. It is also called merit pay. A study of pay for performance in U.S. industry completed in 1984 by the Conference Board revealed that of 500 firms surveyed 95 percent use pay for performance with their exempt (nonhourly) employees. Eighty-two percent of these companies consider their pay for performance programs to be successful.[12] In 1981, the Personnel Policies Forum conducted a survey to determine the status of merit pay in the United States. Of the 183 organizations responding, more than 80 percent were using merit pay to some extent.[13]

Pay for performance plans can vary along three dimensions: whose performance is to be rewarded, how performance is measured, and what form the reward or pay is to take. Essentially, pay for performance can cover individual employees, groups of employees, or entire organizations. Performance can be measured by productivity, cost effectiveness, or a superior's evaluation. The reward of pay can take the form of a salary increase or a cash bonus.

The general rationale for pay for performance is that by linking compensation to the employee's performance, job performance and satisfaction are enhanced. Social psychological theories support the concept of pay for performance. The expectancy theory maintains that an employee is motivated to perform based on three perceptions: "expectancy," the perception that a certain level of effort will lead to a certain level of performance; "instrumentality," the perception that certain performance will produce certain outcomes; and "valance," the attractiveness of the outcomes. The stronger these perceptions the more motivated the employee is.[14] Through pay for performance the employee directs performance toward the desirable outcome of pay or increased pay. In some ways pay for performance is an extension of the concept of a fair day's wage for a fair day's work. Pay for performance also has been more widely used among exempt employees, that is, supervision and management. However, increasingly pay for performance is being applied to hourly employees.

HOW DOES PAY FOR PERFORMANCE WORK?

The key element in a pay for performance system is how performance is measured. In most cases measurement is through a performance appraisal process. An employee's performance is appraised by his or her superior and in some cases by peers. An overall performance rating is obtained from ratings received on the various elements of the appraisal. This overall rating determines the actual amount of merit pay to be received. Most organizations rely primarily on subjective ratings. They are easy to gather; don't require an elaborate and expensive management information system; and can be an inclusive measure of all of the significant job behaviors an employee needs to perform the job effectively.[15] However, a subjective performance appraisal process requires a high degree of trust for credibility and effectiveness. The union and management partners must recognize that an effective performance appraisal process is key to a pay for performance system and that trust is in fact the foundation for what is usually a subjective appraisal process. In reality, the union and management can cooperate or clash over the elements of the performance appraisal.

Experts in performance appraisal have identified organizational conditions that must be present for the performance appraisal process to be effective. These are

1. Concentration on behavior and objectives
2. Use of a predetermined set of goals and/or job functions
3. An opportunity for subordinate input into the evaluation process
4. Regularly scheduled appraisal cycle that fits in with the nature of the jobs being appraised

5. Different meetings to discuss performance, pay, and career development
6. A due process with appeal procedures that allow a subordinate to discuss an unfair appraisal
7. Evaluations of managers on how well they carry out appraisals[16]

Inadequate or ineffective performance appraisal can be a real barrier to having a pay for performance system.

The second element of pay for performance is the size of the merit pay. An employee should be able to obtain a substantial increase in pay based on enhanced performance. At least a 3 percent increase is needed for an individual to really respond. Further, during periods of high inflation, the increases in pay that are necessary for an employee to respond have to be greater than 3 percent in real terms in order to have an impact.[17]

The third element of pay for performance is the frequency of the payout. The payout period should be short enough to be maximally motivating but also long enough to allow for useful, accurate performance appraisals or other performance measurements to be made. Usually merit pay systems evaluate employee performance and award increases or bonuses on an annual basis.

The last element in operating a pay for performance system involves whether employees participate in the design of the performance-based pay system. Employees should participate in designing the system in two particular situations: new plants where employee participation is built into the overall operation and in change efforts that involve the pay system in the move to a more participative style of management.[18] The GM/UAW Saturn Project is a good example of union-management cooperation in this regard. Union-management committees have been used to specify the pay for performance system being installed in this new GM division. By involving employees in design they will be more committed to it and more knowledgeable about it; will have more control over how it is implemented and operated; and will trust the system in which they have a stake. A joint union-management study team could be used to analyze each of these four elements in relation to a possible pay for performance system.

WHAT MAKES PAY FOR PERFORMANCE EFFECTIVE?

Research on the effectiveness of pay for performance has drawn several conclusions. Managers like to have their pay based on performance. The relationship between merit pay and performance is likely to be positive outside the federal sector. Pay for performance has been shown to be very problematic in the federal sector. Merit pay will have the greatest positive relationship with performance and motivation when the pay for performance link is clearly perceived and understood by employees. Motivational impact of merit pay is lower when inflation is high. Satisfaction with pay for performance may depend on the amount of the merit increase and on the demographic characteristics of the recipients.[19] Also, merit pay increases must be larger for employees with higher earnings than for employees with lower earnings for the same level of performance. For this reason pay for performance programs calculate the increases as a percentage of base pay.

Pay systems expert Edward Lawler rated the effectiveness of pay for performance programs as follows:

1. Programs that evaluate and reward individuals are most effective followed by group and then organizational programs.
2. Programs that reward with a bonus rather than a salary increase are more effective. Bonuses offer greater flexibility in responding to changes in performance. Salary increases tend to become permanent and less mutable.
3. Group and organizationally based program are more effective in promoting cooperation than individually based programs.
4. Employees are least accepting of individually based programs.[20]

The implications of these conclusions should be considered by union and management partners.

Other organizational conditions affect program effectiveness as well. The organization must be able to measure performance accurately and consistently. All relevant job behaviors and employee contributions must be taken into account. Furthermore, objective evaluative criteria should be established for all jobs. The budget for pay for performance should be large enough to finance adequately merit pay increases significant enough to be motivating and to administer the system properly. Employees must be able to impact on the evaluative criteria so that they can reach the desired performance level and must believe that their performance is being accurately measured and that the merit pay decisions reflect their real performance. Finally, employees must be at least willing to participate in the pay for performance system and want the kinds of increases available to them. These five conditions should be a kind of checklist for the management and union partners to use in establishing an effective pay for performance system.

WHAT ARE THE BENEFITS OF PAY FOR PERFORMANCE?

The most obvious benefit is that employees can be motivated to have improved performance on the job. People who perform well on the job will be attracted to and more easily retained by an organization that rewards them for their high performance. Pay for performance requires clarification of performance roles and measures. Further, it requires clear, structured supervisor/subordinate feedback on specified performance measures. These strengthen relationships and the organization. Last, employees may be more satisfied with their jobs because they see a clearer link between what they do on the job—their performance—and at least part of what they get out of the job—their pay.

WHAT ARE THE ISSUES AND PROBLEMS OF PAY FOR PERFORMANCE?

The first key issue concerns where performance will be measured: the individual, work group, department, plant, division, and/or organizational level. Many plans generate a bonus pool at some level above the individual and then allocate actual reward for performance on an individual basis. This issue affects performance measurement and the plan's costs.

The second issue is who participates in what plan and how many plans there will be. Traditionally, there were different plans for different levels of an organization. Often only certain categories of employees have pay for performance. Some organizations have developed pay for performance systems to cover vertical slice performance units.

The third issue is that of using performance bonuses or pay increases. Many plans use a combination of these. Performance pay increases can come to be viewed as a permanent portion of compensation, and therefore, may be less useful as a performance reward over time.

The fourth issue is how motivating pay for performance is. A merit pay system may put too great an emphasis on money as a motivator to the exclusion of other motivators. This may diminish the importance of the job itself, which also has been demonstrated to be a very powerful motivator.

Fifth, what are the limits to pay for performance? In other words, just how much can on the job performance be improved over what period of time, and what happens once a person is performing optimally? How does such a person stay motivated within the pay for performance system?

There are two potentially serious problems in a pay for performance system: costs and impact on teamwork. An effective pay for performance system, especially performance appraisal, can be very costly. There are no conclusive data available about the potential return on investment from merit pay. Pay for performance systems may work against group cooperation and teamwork. In fact they may foster intragroup competition and conflict, which could have a negative impact on overall organizational effectiveness. In this way a pay for performance system could defeat its own purpose.

Pay systems are significant parts of the work organization. The union and management partners need to assess carefully whether their organization has conditions that favor a pay for performance program and how to resolve the critical issues and problems such a system can present.

WHAT IS PAY FOR KNOWLEDGE?

Pay for knowledge is a wage incentive system in which employees are paid for the range of jobs that they can perform. It rewards increased human resource potential in an organization and not operational outcomes. Recently, unions and management have been looking at pay for knowledge systems as one approach to reorganizing the workplace to make it a better place to work. Actually, pay for knowledge is not a new concept. The garment industry has been using it for years.[21]

There are three kinds of pay for knowledge systems: multiskill-based pay systems, increased knowledge-based systems, and combination systems. In multiskill-based pay systems, employee pay is linked to the number of different skills they learn and perform—horizontal skills building. An employee increases his or her earning power by literally learning all of the jobs in the work area. In increased knowledge-based pay systems, employee pay is linked to increased knowledge and skill within the same general job category—vertical skills building. An employee increases earning power by learning all there is to know up and down within the job category. Usually multiskill-based pay systems are designed to apply to production employees, and increased knowledge-based pay systems are designed for mechanics and other skilled trades.[22] The third kind of pay for knowledge system combines opportunities for both vertical and horizontal skills building.

HOW DOES PAY FOR KNOWLEDGE WORK?

In the multiskill-based pay systems an employee must show mastery of one job before moving on to learn another. Employees are required to demonstrate periodically their mastery of the jobs that they have previously learned. How such a program works is shown by the pay for knowledge program operating at the GM Delco-Remy battery plant in Fitzgerald, Georgia. Hourly employees increase their wages by increasing their knowledge of the jobs within their team until they reach the top team level or level 4. Also, the first two levels through which an employee advances after hiring are tied to seniority as well as task accomplishment based on the UAW contract. After level 4, an employee can move to another team and begin to learn the jobs there. An employee acquires an increase in rate, then moves to another team and can progress up to level 6 within the new team. Level 6 means that an employee knows all of the jobs within two different teams.

In this program there was the issue of different teams having jobs requiring higher or lower technical skills due to the higher or lower technology involved in the work they perform. To address this, level 6 or the plant rate was established. An employee probably takes longer to advance on teams working with higher technology and advances faster on teams working with lower technology. An employee assigned initially to a higher technology team can transfer to a lower technology team and "catch up" while working toward the plant rate. This pay for knowledge system is tied to self-managing autonomous operating teams supported by technical and administrative teams.[23]

The increased knowledge pay system works in a similar fashion. There are also different levels with different rates, but these levels are all within a particular job category. The employee is not learning new jobs but is learning everything there is to know about her or his job.

WHAT MAKES PAY FOR KNOWLEDGE EFFECTIVE?

Work environments that have successfully implemented pay for knowledge systems have some common characteristics. Manufacturing operations using batch processing technologies are the most common situations in which pay for knowledge is found. Usually these systems have been established as part of overall startup of a plant. Local work culture values work itself and personal growth and development. Further, it has been best to try out such a system in favorable economic conditions.[24] Pay for knowledge is a relatively new phenomenon especially in unionized workplaces. Thus far most applications have been in manufacturing. How it will be applied in nonmanufacturing environments in both the public and private sectors is yet to be determined.

Pay for knowledge is most effective when certain organizational conditions exist. Management must value employee growth, worth, and quality of work life and be wholeheartedly committed to pay for knowledge. Also there must be other needed support mechanisms within the organization, including effective employee selection, job design to facilitate job rotation, training and development activities complementary to the pay for knowledge system, effective performance appraisals modified to be used in pay for knowledge, and clear and open communications overall.[25] The union should be prepared to experiment with the pay for knowledge concept, and employees should be receptive to being part of a pay for knowledge compensation system and involved in designing it. These conditions should represent the minimum requirements needed even to consider the system feasible. Further, the union and management partners should consider jointly specifying competencies and knowledge requirements, developing appropriate training curricula, and delivering the needed training to ensure maximum opportunities for learning and advancement for all employees. Finally, the partners will have to bargain over the pay levels and the advancement requirements.

WHAT ARE THE BENEFITS OF PAY FOR KNOWLEDGE?

The advantages to the employer of pay for knowledge are quite significant:

increased flexibility within the work force, higher quality of output, greater long-term productivity, leaner staffing, and lower absenteeism and turnover due to greater employee job satisfaction. The advantages to employees are related: increased employee motivation, greater feelings of self-worth, higher job security, and greater commitment and loyalty to the company.[26] Employees can pick up many more job skills and more money at the same time. Narrow job classifications are broken down and employers get greater flexibility in utilizing their human resources. This benefit was expressed well by Peter J. Pestillo, vice president for labor relations at Ford Motor Company: "I think pay for knowledge will ultimately do more to break down the burden of narrow classifications than anything else."[27]

Pay for knowledge can have financial benefits. At the GM Delco-Remy plant, the cost of car and truck alternators produced fell by 6 percent, attributed to the pay for knowledge system. Also volume has increased, and quality has improved. The plant hasn't hired any additional hourly workers and the salaried work force has shrunk by 18 percent.[28] Comparable pay for knowledge systems have had similar results.

WHAT ARE THE ISSUES AND POTENTIAL PROBLEMS WITH PAY FOR KNOWLEDGE?

The first two issues revolve around the questions of which employees and which jobs will be involved in pay for knowledge. Production jobs are better suited to pay for knowledge programs. Also organizational performance depends more heavily on teamwork and coordination in these jobs. It is not clear how this concept would be applied to service jobs at a comparable level. Also it must be determined how many jobs can be learned and retained and how much rotation can occur among which jobs. In a typical pay for knowledge setting, employees can learn up to four to eight jobs and rotate among them.[29]

The third issue concerns when and how the learning and training take place. In most pay for knowledge programs, the bulk of the learning and training takes place on the job. However, some programs require that employees study on their own. Also many employees have to do just that if they want to advance. Study on employee time raises several other issues. The first is that of compensation for time spent on "company business." Ideally, the employee obtains his or her reward or compensation for the amount of his or her own time the employee contributed by advancing to the next level and receiving higher compensation for it. The facts are that many employees will not have enough personal time to study because of family and union obligations, community involvement, and other job or educational obligations. This may limit the job advancement opportunities of working mothers, single heads of households, dual job holders, or people pursuing an education because they won't have the requisite time to devote to the additional study needed in their "off hours."

The last issue also involves the potential for discrimination. Studying to advance in the pay for knowledge system often requires that an employee have good study skills and be able to read reasonably well. However, ample statistics confirm that many of America's working adults are functionally illiterate. Furthermore, because of limited educational opportunities or discrimination by education institutions, many working adults do not have good study skills. Who will be responsible for ensuring that the participants in pay for knowledge have the requisite reading ability and study skills? Will pay for knowledge result in two classes or workers: those who are fairly well educated to begin with and can take full advantage of the pay for knowledge program and those who have been educationally disadvantaged and whose advancement through the pay for knowledge system is limited on that basis?

These are serious questions for union and management partners considering adopting a pay for knowledge program. The partners should consider providing remedial education and study skills training to ensure real equal opportunity for participants. Also the job training and study should be conducted on company time and be designed so that sufficient skills and knowledge for advancement are acquired by all employees regardless of background.

There are three fundamental problems for employees: holdups, maxing out, and supervisor dissatisfaction. "Holdups" refer to the situation in which an employee is ready to move to another job to learn it but there are no vacancies on that other job.[30] Some programs have devised a special holdup rate to compensate employees held back by the system itself. "Maxing out" occurs when an employee has literally learned all of the jobs he or she can in the system.[31] This employee has no where to go to obtain additional compensation through increased knowledge and competency. In some organizations merit or cost of living increases are given from that point onward. In others the multiskill-based and increased knowledge-based systems are combined to make maxing out take a very long time and/or eliminate it for all practical purposes. These two problems can reduce individual and group morale and diminish confidence in the pay for knowledge system.

The third employee problem is that of supervisors feeling threatened by pay for knowledge. They may become very unhappy as the pay, knowledge, and skills of their subordinates increase. The gap between supervisory pay and hourly pay may narrow. Further, a supervisor's perception that only he or she really knows the jobs and the work in the area will be seriously challenged. The roles of supervisor and subordinate are radically changed. Some adjustment may be needed in the terms and conditions under which supervisors work to make them promote and support the pay for knowledge program.

There are a number of potential organizational problems with pay for knowledge as well. In many situations, the supervisors are the only stable or permanent employees within a department. The other employees rotate in and out as part of the pay for knowledge system. This can make it difficult to build up teamwork within the department. It can also make the supervisor's job more taxing. Some organizations have developed assistant supervisor positions to provide more stability.[32]

Usually there are other employees at comparable levels within the organization who are not participating in the pay for knowledge program. These are often clerical or administrative employees. They may feel that they are dead-ended in their jobs with limited opportunities for increased pay. They may become demoralized as they see employees in other jobs rotating and advancing.

In organizations having other incentive-based bonus systems, employees may come to view pay for knowledge as adversely affecting their productivity and/or performance at times. As a result they think it will have a negative effect on the bonuses they would usually receive. Such employees may value the rewards that come to them through the other competing system more than they value pay for knowledge. This could result in employees resisting pay for knowledge or just marking time within it.

Costs of a pay for knowledge system can be substantial. Usually hourly labor costs are higher in a pay for knowledge compensation system than in the traditional wage setup. Employees try to progress to the highest level possible as quickly as possible. Further, wages are often higher in pay for knowledge workplaces than for comparable jobs in a traditional workplace.[33] Despite these facts pay for knowledge is often promoted as a way to reduce labor costs especially as a more acceptable alternative than concessions. The training costs for this program are significant, and productivity may suffer from the constant use of "trainees." The ratio of the length of time spent learning a job and the length of time spent doing it can be very high. Employees try to learn and move on as quickly as possible. Some organizations have set time requirements for how long a worker must perform a job learned.[34] The cost of keeping track of all of the information necessary for successful operation of the pay for knowledge program can also be significant. There is much more record keeping than in a traditional workplace with conventional job assignments and wage system.[35]

Last, labor conflicts may result from the adoption of a pay for knowledge system. This is particularly true in situations where the issues and problems described above have not been addressed prior to adoption of the program. While General Motors has had great success with its pay for knowledge program at its Delco-Remy plant, there was a strike at its Missouri plant over the pay for knowledge system in January 1985. Further, at its Orion Township plant in Michigan the pay for knowledge system was the number one bargaining issue from the UAW viewpoint during the 1984 negotiations there. The compromise reached allowed workers to opt out of the pay for knowledge program.[36]

For the union and management partners to be successful in a cooperative pay for knowledge program, they must determine exactly how to handle the issues and problems. It is also imperative that the performance standards be developed and monitored jointly to ensure that they are reasonable and fair.

Wage incentive systems hold out real potential for improving organizational performance. Recently, pay for performance and pay for knowledge systems have been most closely scrutinized by unions and management as avenues for changing organizations and addressing a range of workplace concerns. Both are complex wage incentive systems requiring favorable organizational conditions for their success. The union and management partners should proceed carefully when examining the potential of implementing these pay systems for their people and organizations.

ADDITIONAL RESOURCES

Heneman, Robert L. *Pay for Performance: Exploring the Merit System.* New York: Pergamon Press, 1984.

Jenkins Jr., G. Douglas, and Nina Gupta. "The Payoffs of Paying for Knowledge," *National Productivity Review* (Spring 1985): 121–130.

Katzell, Raymond A. and Daniel Yankelovich. *Work, Productivity and Job Satisfaction.* New York: Harcourt Brace Jovanovich, 1975.

Lawler III, Edward E. *Pay and Organization Development.* Reading, Mass.: Addison-Wesley, 1981.

Zager, Robert, and Michael P. Rosow, ed. *The Innovative Organization: Productivity Programs in Action.* New York: Pergamon Press, 1982.

19

Productivity Gainsharing:
Scanlon, Rucker, and Improshare Plans

Productivity gain-sharing programs (PGPs) are group-based financial incentive plans designed to improve both individual and group performance, thereby improving organizational effectiveness and productivity. These programs focus on enhancing organizational output and sharing the financial results of that enhancement with employees.

WHAT IS PRODUCTIVITY GAIN SHARING?

Productivity gain sharing refers to efforts to improve productivity by making "gains" over past and/or targeted organizational performance and then sharing the financial benefits from these gains between the employees and the organization. There are tailormade PGPs and standard PGPs, that is, Scanlon, Rucker, and Improshare. Both unions and management have become increasingly interested in gain sharing programs as an arena for cooperation. These programs often combine participation in various forms with financial returns.

There are four basic characteristics of any productivity gain-sharing effort that distinguish such an effort from individual incentive systems:

1. Productivity-based benefit sharing
2. Group administration, that is, focuses on and covers employees as a group rather than as individuals
3. Teamwork and cooperation throughout
4. Macromeasurements of a gross, overall nature based on the total group involved[1]

Any PGP will have eight different aspects: objectives; measurements; participant groups; performance period; sharing ratio, that is, how financial gains are shared between the company and employees; allocation basis, that is, how the financial benefits that go to the employees are shared among them; future changes, or how changes in operations and therefore in the program will be handled; and administrative provisions, or how all the paperwork and organization of the plan are to be accomplished.

Group-based incentive programs or PGPs have been successfully established in older organizations that may or may not previously have had individual incentive programs and in new plants as well. Productivity gain sharing can be adapted to virtually any private sector environment, but traditionally it has been used in small to medium-sized plants. Further, there have been very few applications of productivity gain sharing in the public sector. Recently, some public transit companies have tried out PGPs in garage and maintenance operations.

It has been common for older plants having individual productivity incentive plans to convert to group-based gain-sharing plans. A good example of this is in Holland, Michigan, at the Hart and Cooley metal stamping plant with IAM Lodge 1418. It had had a 40-year-old individual incentive plan covering 500 workers. Bonuses under this earlier plan ranged from 130 to 250 percent of base pay. Despite this, there were many serious problems, including high rework rates, high grievance rates, low productivity, high absenteeism, and a high accident rate. Updating the old individual incentive plan would have been costly and possibly would not have corrected many of the problems. Instead, a gain-sharing plan was installed with significant positive results: a 30 percent increase in productivity and a 9 percent reduction in the hourly labor costs with exactly the same work force. Furthermore, 65 percent of the employees are earning more under the new gain-sharing plan than under the old individual incentive plan. Hourly base pay was also upscaled to a level usually twice the previous base. The union and management partners are basically satisfied with the new group-based gain-sharing program.[2]

Many new plants institute productivity gain-sharing programs early in their operation. A new plant should operate for some time before undertaking a PGP so that operations can be debugged and a stable operation established. Then a history of operating results is available to establish a base performance level. In some new plants, the PGP is part of a total participative management system.

The role employee participation plays in productivity gain sharing is very important. Employee expertise is used to solve operational problems and increase productivity. Usually employee participation within the productivity gain-sharing context focuses on involving employees more fully with their actual work, with other employees with whom they work, and with the work of the entire organization.

HOW DOES PRODUCTIVITY GAIN SHARING WORK?

First, the goals and objectives of the gain-sharing effort are defined. Usually, the overall goal is to improve individual and group performance so that overall productivity is improved. In any PGP there may be other more specific objectives as well.

Specific gain-sharing plans vary widely in terms of which employees participate in them. In Scanlon plans usually all employees, including executives, participate. In Rucker plans hourly workers and sometimes supervisors, professional employees, technical employees, and administrative employees participate as well. In Improshare plans only hourly employees participate.[3] Determining who participates in the productivity gain sharing by receiving bonuses should take into account who to include to help foster teamwork directed toward improved organizational performance and who to include within the participating payroll for the calculation of the bonus.

Measurement must be done to establish a performance or productivity base. Later performance within the current period is measured and compared to the base. The performance base should include inputs that have the greatest impact on productivity and organizational performance as well as many inputs as possible to ensure that true productivity is being measured.[4] There are basically three ways to measure the productivity base: the history of the operations, standards developed by engineering formulas, work measurement or other mathematical techniques, and financial plans. Ideally, the proper point for establishing the productivity base is where prices, wages, and profits are at reasonably competitive levels. Various gain-sharing programs use different methods for calculating the productivity or performance base and for measuring current performance to compare with the base. The productivity or performance base may have to be modified when certain things change in the operation. Circumstances that may require such a change include new products with different labor and/or material content, major capital investments that affect other inputs, elimination of products, and major changes in marketing or pricing causing changes in the input/output ratio.[5] It is critical that great care be taken to establish the productivity or performance base and that accurate, complete data be gathered to compare current performance against the base.

The performance period must be established that is long enough for complete data to be collected in order to do the comparison with the base. At the same time, for bonuses to be motivating they shouldn't be too removed from the performance they are rewarding. This would support a relatively short performance period or bonus reward period. Some experts suggest that bonuses obtained through productivity gain sharing are a form of feedback from the organization to employees. They recommend regular, frequent feedback of this kind, usually on a monthly basis.[6] Some PGPs use weekly performance periods. The performance period should be chosen to best suit the work force.

How the company or organization and the participating employees split the financial value of the gains must be determined. Different PGPs use different sharing ratios. In Scanlon plans employees receive 75 to 100 percent of the labor productivity gains. In Rucker plans, employees receive 100 percent of the labor productivity gains. In Improshare plans, the company and the employees split the hours savings 50/50. The sharing ratio should be guided by a sense of equity or fairness and need not be permanent; in three situations it may have to be changed: when experience shows that there is a more equitable formula for sharing the gains, when business plans change that require a change in the sharing ratio to achieve new business objectives, and when economic or other external conditions are such that a larger share should go to either the employees or the company.[7] Changing the sharing ratio frequently may cause confusion, suspicion, and dissatisfaction with the PGP. Changes in the sharing ratio should be made to establish or maintain equity only.

There are three different ways to allocate the employee share of the gains among the participating employees: on the basis of hours worked, as a percentage of compensation, or in equal dollar shares. Percentage of pay and hours worked are the two most common allocation methods. There are sometimes problems with using percentage of pay as the basis for allocation because employees may consider the pay structure itself to be unfair. Also, under such an allocation, higher paid employees receive much higher bonuses regardless of their particular performance.

The size of the bonus is an additional consideration in how gain sharing works. Theoretically, the bonus is not a goal; it is a measure of the improvement accomplished. Some experts suggest that the size of the bonus will not be as important as it may seem if gain sharing results in better management, effective employee participation, and improved job security. Nevertheless, the rule of thumb is that bonuses must average in at approximately 10 percent of compensation to be significantly motivating or to have employees positively react to productivity gain sharing.[8] Union and management partners need to carefully examine how productivity gainsharing works both when assessing its feasibility and when designing a program.

HOW SCANLON PLANS WORK

Scanlon plans are the most common of the standard PGPs. Approximately 500 companies have used them with somewhere between 200 to 300 in operation at present.[9] The basics of the Scanlon plan were developed by Joseph N. Scanlon in the 1930s. He was local union president in a steel plant being closed due to competition from more efficient operations. By instituting the Scanlon plan with management, the plant was reopened and able to compete successfully. Initially, the basic feature of the plan was tying wages to plant productivity. Through discussions with Clinton Golden at the Steelworkers Organizing Committee, a suggestion committee system modeled on that at the B&O Railroad was added to the plan.

All Scanlon plans are characterized by a philosophy and practice of cooperation, an involvement system designed to increase efficiency and reduce costs, and productivity measurement based on sharing of the benefits.[10] Traditionally, a bonus is paid under a Scanlon plan when there is an improvement in the ratio of total labor costs to sales value of production:

$$\frac{\text{Total labor costs (inputs)}}{\text{Sales or market value of production (outputs)}}$$

Labor costs include direct and indirect factory labor, all other wages and salaries, overtime premiums, vacation and holiday pay, and hospitalization and workers' compensation. Usually salespersons' commissions, the employer's portion of social security, state and federal unemployment insurance, pension costs, and other miscellaneous employee costs are not included in the total labor costs.[11] Sales or market value of production commonly does include adjustments for fluctuations in inventories.[12] This productivity ratio is easily understood, doesn't require complicated additional record keeping, and allows employees to influence directly the input side of the ratio.

Not every Scanlon plan uses the traditional productivity ratio. For a productivity ratio to be useful with a Scanlon plan, it should be a good performance measure over time, be perceived as fair, be understandable by employees, be flexible enough to meet changing conditions, be easily administered, be useful in isolating problem areas, and be designed to orient employee effort in the desired direction.[13] In any case, once the productivity formula is developed, it should be tested out under actual organizational conditions before it is applied.

Several basic principles underlie measurement's role in a Scanlon plan. Measurement focuses on the group and thereby promotes teamwork. There is real education value to focusing on variables of critical importance to the company. Limiting the input side of the formula to labor costs links the work force to something over which they can exert control. The productivity standard is really set by the people themselves because the historical performance of employees is used as the basis for setting the standard. The bonuses are paid monthly to provide rewards as quickly as possible in order to be maximally motivating and are paid as a percentage of compensation to recognize individual skills and contributions to the organization. Last, measurement is an integral part of a comprehensive program for improving productivity.[14]

Employee participation is one of the basic elements of a Scanlon plan. To foster participation directed toward organizational improvement, there is a two-level system of suggestion committees. One is a network of Production Committees composed of a supervisor and two or three employee representatives. Suggestions for improvements are submitted by employees to the Production Committee in their area. This committee is empowered to implement suggestions that don't involve other departments or areas or costs above a certain specified amount. At the next level is a Screening Committee composed of representatives from all of the Production Committees, senior managers, and union officials. The Screening Committee meets monthly to discuss and evaluate suggestions referred to it by the Production Committees, to analyze current performance and determine bonuses, to administer the Scanlon plan overall, and to engage in troubleshooting, as needed. Also within the Screening Committee the basic economic health of the company is reviewed and discussed.

In most situations, the agreement-covered participants in the Production Committees are selected by elections held for this purpose. In that way all employees have the opportunity to participate directly in the suggestion committee system. Also all employees are asked to examine their work on a continuous basis in terms of quality improvement, quantity enhancement, and cost reduction.[15] Everyone participates through suggestions he or she may submit, teamwork is fostered by the program, and improvements are implemented as a result of suggestions and, of course, through the bonuses themselves. The Scanlon plan is more effective the greater the percentage of employees participating in it. Usually the only employees excluded are summer workers, part-time workers, new hires during their probationary period, and salespersons with their own incentive plans.[16]

The financial gains from the Scanlon plan are usually shared with 75 percent to the employees and 25 percent to the company. The rationale is that since the productivity formula is based on labor productivity and the company gets the full benefit of the savings, the employees should get a greater percentage of the benefits from the program. In most cases 25 percent of the gains are set aside in a reserve fund with the remainder being split 75/25 as described above. This reserve fund covers future deficits in the plan. It usually builds up over the year and is closed out at year's end with any surplus distributed according to the 75/25 formula. A deficit in the reserve fund is covered by the company so that the plan can start each year without having to overcome the previous year's losses.[17]

There are several other major features of a Scanlon plan. Often an employee survey is used to determine employee interest prior to instituting a Scanlon plan. Experts recommend conducting an annual survey to evaluate the impact of the program overall. Also a formal meeting prior to installing the plan is recommended. Employees discuss the plan and vote on whether to try it out for a one-year trial period with 80 percent acceptance as the standard to meet to start a Scanlon plan.[18] Many Scanlon plans hold a year-end meeting to bring closure to the year's efforts and involve employees.[19] Last, most Scanlon plans have a memorandum of understanding between management and the union or are included in the labor contract. A document like this usually covers what the plan is, how and why it got started, the principles of the plan, how the bonus calculation works, how the committee system works, and what the procedures for handling suggestions are.[20]

Scanlon plans are very sound in terms of employee motivation. Bonuses relate to factors in the workplace that employees can influence and are distributed as soon as possible after the performance period to which they relate. The plantwide nature of a Scanlon plan reinforces teamwork and organizational objectives. Through the suggestion committees system, employees develop an understanding of what makes for the success of the business and how their contribution is part of that success. Scanlon plans can complement overall organizational development efforts and profit-sharing programs.

Among the standard PGPs, Scanlon plans are the most widespread union-management cooperation vehicle. These plans can be a sound and viable cooperative approach combining real participation with financial incentives.

HOW RUCKER PLANS WORK

Another of the standard PGPs, the Rucker plan, was developed by Allen Rucker in its most basic form in the 1930s. Rucker is an economist who had observed that in the manufacturing sector labor costs as a percentage of value added remain stable over a long period of time. This stable relationship is not affected by the peaks and valleys of the business cycle.[21] He concluded that any change in the relationship of labor costs to value added or production value is very significant and does represent a change in productivity. It is from this observation that he developed the Rucker plan.

To determine productivity and calculate a bonus, the Rucker standard is established by calculating

$$\frac{\text{Labor costs}}{\text{Production value (value added)}}$$

Whenever actual labor costs in relation to value added or production value are less than the standard, then a bonus is paid. Production value or value added is calculated by adding net sales and inventory increases, then subtracting materials and supplies used. Employees receive the entire amount of the labor savings as a bonus. Usually bonuses are paid out monthly as a percentage of monthly earnings. There is a balancing account to handle months in which there is a deficit in the gains and therefore no bonus.

There are approximately 200 to 300 Rucker plans in operation, primarily in manufacturing. The Rucker plan is designed mostly for nonexempt operating employees. It is suggested that some kind of financial incentive for the excluded employees (executives, managers, supervisors, and professional staff) be paid out of the company's share from the results of the improvements. In terms of actual employee participation, Rucker plans can incorporate suggestion systems and

Rucker committees together with an extensive communications system to generate operational improvements to enhance bonus potential. Rucker committees are usually a single, plantwide committee but can also be a network of multilevel committees.[22] A complementary participative management philosophy and style support the use of the Rucker plan with rank and file employees.

HOW IMPROSHARE PLANS WORK

Improshare (Improved Productivity Through Sharing) plans were developed by Mitchell Fein in the early 1970s. The emphasis in these plans is on organizational performance and less on financial productivity measures, such as with Scanlon and Rucker plans. Improshare's goal is the production of more final products in fewer personhours. This PGP is meant to reflect the real changes in the workplace that occur especially in technology and the structure of work. Improshare plans are designed to reward group performance, include indirect workers in measuring and rewarding productivity due to the trend of increasing the ratio of indirect to direct workers, facilitate the introduction of new equipment, and avoid negative attitudes toward the Improshare plan.[23] The plan calculates performance based on the base productivity factor (BPF). This is determined using industrial engineering methods to set the performance standard. The basic formula is

$$\frac{\text{Actual time worked for all employees}}{\text{Total standard time earned for a base period}}$$

Gains are recorded as hours saved. These gains are divided 50/50 between the employees and the company. The employee bonuses are paid based on the actual time worked during the performance period, which is usually weekly. An Improshare plan includes a provision to adjust the base when new equipment or methods are introduced. Further, there are also procedures for the company to "buy" a permanent change in the BPF and for banking of bonuses to cover periods of low or nonexistent bonuses.[24]

Improshare plans traditionally had no formal employee participation program or tie-in to participative management approaches. Recently, in some situations, participatory elements have been added. Nevertheless, the vehicles for union-management cooperation within Improshare plans are less well developed.

WHAT MAKES PRODUCTIVITY GAIN SHARING EFFECTIVE?

There are a wide range of experiences from which to develop an understanding of the conditions that favor productivity gain-sharing programs. Edward Lawler, a recognized expert in financial incentive systems, identified the items key to a successful gain-sharing program. There are usually less than 500 employees in an organization old enough for an adequate performance history on which to develop standards. Product costs are controllable by the employees and the market for output is able to absorb additional production; otherwise the plan could result in increased productivity with no market for the additional production, resulting in layoffs. A participative style of management is applied in an open organizational climate with a high level of trust and open communications. There is limited use of overtime so that employees are not too dependent on overtime. Productivity increases could result in less overtime and therefore in reduced compensation for some employees. There is a high to moderate degree of work floor interdependence. The business is not seasonal and little capital investment is planned, which should make operations more stable and various measurements easier. Few product changes are planned, which should also make measurements easier.

Further, management is technically capable, supportive of participative management, open to new ideas and suggestions, and has good communications skills. The work force is interested in participation and greater compensation, technically skilled, and interested in organizational finances. The union is favorable to a cooperation effort. Engineering and maintenance groups are capable, willing, and able to respond to changes and improvements that grow out of the gain-sharing program and for which their skills are required during implementation.[25]

Probably no one PGP exists in an environment having all of these conditions. The union and management partners should consider these a kind of checklist to determine the applicability of gain sharing in their situation.

There are some additional factors relating to management's leadership in a PGP that are key to its effectiveness. Management must value participation, equity, and the partnership between labor and management. One gain-sharing expert expressed the importance of this aspect of management's leadership this way: "The organization that is serious about gainsharing must state clearly the value that labor and management not only are not adversaries but are, of necessity, partners in the enterprise."[26] Management must foster personnel policies that clearly demonstrate a commitment to people. It must also develop long-range goals that are clearly communicated and accepted by the organization and foster a climate characterized by open communications, effective decision making, and employee belief in their influence within the organization. Management must show respect for and be supportive of workers and believe in and practice teamwork.[27]

Finally, there is the role of employment security in effective gain sharing. Basic employee security must exist or be established for the full potential of effective gain sharing to be realized. Basically there must be a guarantee that no layoffs will result from the gain-sharing effort. Without this employees will be reluctant to participate fully in an activity that may result in the loss of their jobs.

WHAT ARE THE BENEFITS OF PRODUCTIVITY GAIN SHARING?

A successful gain-sharing program has diverse and significant benefits. One gain-sharing expert identified the following as direct benefits: better profits, better return on investment, higher rate of on-time deliveries, improved quality, reduced product costs, improved survivability and security, greater employee awareness of and understanding of what it takes to make a business successful, more effective change management, more and better teamwork, cooperation, and coordination, improved supervision, from production pusher to production facilitator, lower turnover and a wider selection of job applicants who are interested in employment because of the gain sharing, reduced absenteeism, greater job satisfaction, and declining frequency of grievances and better, quicker handling of them.[28] Such potential benefits as these are drawing increasing numbers of unions and managers to examine the utility of gain sharing in their situations. It is important to remember that such benefits can occur only when the necessary time and energy have been invested in developing and operating a truly effective gain-sharing program.

More research has been done on Scanlon plans than on the other two standard PGPs and tailormade PGPs. Experts in Scanlon plans state that there is a 90 percent acceptance of suggestions coming through the network of suggestion committees.[29] Research also demonstrates that in most cases such suggestions have led to significant improvements in productivity. In a study done in 1958 of ten applications of Scanlon plans the average productivity improvement over the two-year period studied was 23.1 percent with a minimum of 10.3 percent and a maximum of 39.2 percent. All but one of the companies involved in this study were unionized, and as a group they represented a sample of companies in manufacturing and fabricating using Scanlon plans.[30] In 1973 B. E. Moore and P. S. Goodman reviewed the literature on Scanlon plans and analyzed 30 cases of successful applications. They identified the following outcomes when a Scanlon plan is successfully applied:

1. The plan enhances coordination, teamwork, and sharing of knowledge at lower levels in the organization.
2. Social needs are recognized via participation and mutually reinforcing group behavior.
3. Attention is focused on cost savings, not just quantity of production.
4. Acceptance of change due to technology, market, and new methods is greater because higher efficiency leads to bonuses.

5. Attitudinal change occurs among workers who demand more efficient management and better planning as a result.
6. Workers try to reduce overtime, to work smarter not harder or faster, and produce ideas as well as effort.
7. More flexible administration of union-management relations occurs.
8. The union is strengthened because it is responsible for a better work situation and higher pay.[31]

The company benefits by having a better return to stockholders or owners, a reduction in complaints about spoilage or imperfect workmanship, and improvements in deliveries. Under a Scanlon plan supervisors truly lead their employees and can focus more on management of the work that is their responsibility.[32] While these result could be obtained through other PGPs, union and management partners should be clear that Scanlon plans have the power of the three basic elements: the philosophy and practice of cooperation, the employee involvement system, and the labor-based productivity measurement component as the basis for group sharing of gains. Other PGPs without these three powerful elements could not produce similar results.

HOW TO DETERMINE WHETHER PRODUCTIVITY GAIN SHARING IS FEASIBLE

As with any union-management cooperative program, the union and management partners should determine together whether such an effort is feasible for them to undertake. As recommended in Chapter 11, when considering a PGP, determine mutual goals and objectives for such an effort, examine the current organizational climate as it relates to union-management cooperation in general and gain sharing specifically, review other cooperative efforts undertaken, survey the range of options, and assess the risks and benefits.

It is helpful to simulate the financial incentive elements of any of the gain-sharing plans under consideration. To do this the various formulas for calculating the bonuses should be used on company data to determine where the company is and, if possible, to project likely bonus levels. This is probably the most important feasibility activity since it will indicate the potential that various gain-sharing plans might have in the workplace.

Also the partners must decide what is most appropriate and applicable: a standard PGP such as Scanlon, Rucker, or Improshare or a tailored gain-sharing program. To do this the three standard PGPs should be fully analyzed. Then consultants who design tailormade PGPs can explain what is involved and indicate the potential they see in that situation.

Last, the union and management partners must plan exactly how they are going to involve employees in the gain-sharing effort. At a minimum they should seek employee input about the program's objectives, measurements, participant groups, performance period, sharing ratio, and allocation basis. Also employees can be actively involved in designing a tailormade program or in designing implementation of a standard PGP.

Determining the feasibility of a PGP is no small task. In fact, the union and management partners would have to commit significant time, energy, and resources. Also the stakes are very high; the partners can have either an effective, successful gain-sharing effort that could become standard operating procedure for the organization in the future or they can have a costly, demoralizing failure that may make the use of any financial incentive programs in that workplace unlikely, if not impossible.

CRITICAL DECISIONS TO MAKE ABOUT PGPS

There are a set of critical decisions that the union and management partners must make together in designing a PGP: who participates, what the performance period for calculation of the bonus and what the payment period are, what input and output measures will be included in measuring performance, how the financial gains will be divided between employees and the company or organization, whether a reserve fund will be established and, if so, what portion of the gains will be held in reserve, and how the gains will be paid using what method. The union and management partners should talk through the possible options for each decision, focusing especially on the implications each option will have for everyone involved.

WHAT ARE THE CONCERNS ABOUT PRODUCTIVITY GAIN SHARING?

Even if PGPs are successfully implemented in a workplace, several real potential problems can develop in terms of measurement and people. Initially there may be problems in reaching agreement about what formula to use and which inputs and outputs to be included in that formula. There will probably be some inputs over which employees don't have control. If these inputs adversely affect employee opportunities for bonuses, then employees may become demoralized and discouraged with the PGP. Later there may be problems about the accuracy of the measurements. Having accurate and complete data is necessary to obtaining fair and equitable bonuses. Further, there can be conflicts if one or both parties want to change the formula to reflect changes in the organization.

The potential people problems revolve around the new roles a PGP presents to employees at all levels. Rank and file employees under a PGP are being asked to make a more focused effort on the job and in some cases to become more involved not only in their work but also in the organization as a whole. Supervisors in a PGP are being asked to renew their commitment to teamwork and to provide clear leadership out on the floor. Managers are being asked to be more attentive to planning and coordinating the work processes overall. The union is being asked to take a regular, active part in improving the operations of the organization. For some people these new or renewed roles are a welcome relief; for others they are suspect or too demanding. The success of any PGP, whether standard or tailormade, rests on the reaction of and acceptance by the work force. Also, because gain sharing is group-based, excessive peer group pressure can develop as well as other negative group dynamics. Less skilled, handicapped, or older workers may be made to feel undesirable because other workers perceive that they are holding the group back. Sometimes a PGP is promoted with promises that it can't possibly keep. When employee expectations aren't fulfilled, the credibility of the program is damaged.

The final problem occurs when gain sharing is seen as a substitute for something else: for adequate and equitable wages and benefits, for a strong union organization, and/or for a competent management team. Gain sharing has value in and of itself, but it cannot solve all of the problems of the workplace. Nor should it be a substitute for other necessities for workplace success.

FACTORS NECESSARY FOR SUCCESS

Several factors can limit the applicability of Scanlon plans: organization size, performance measurement, measurement complexity, administrative costs, and worker characteristics. They work best where there are less than 500 employees; in larger organizations it may be difficult for employees to see the relationship between what they do and the impact on the bonus. However, a Scanlon plan has been successfully applied in 11 plants of the Dana Corporation involving more than 2,000 UAW members. An organization must have good performance measures and some reasonable performance history to have accurate productivity measurement. Further, if organizational performance can only be measured in very complex ways, then a Scanlon plan won't work well. If the costs of administering the plan are too high, then the return on investment may be too low to justify the plan. Last, a majority of the workers have to want to participate and to earn more money in order for the plan to succeed.[33] These factors can also limit the applicability of the other PGPs. The fact that PGPs exist in slightly more than 1,000 U.S. companies after 50 years of promotion attests to the difficulty of implementing and maintaining such a program.

When considering a standard PGP, such as the Scanlon, Rucker, or Improshare plan, or a tailormade PGP, eight factors are necessary for success:

1. Labor and management must make a commitment to the success of the PGP at all levels.
2. All participants should have realistic expectations from the beginning. No PGP will be the solution to all of an organization's problems and ills.
3. A properly designed formula that is easy to understand and acceptable to both the union and management must be developed.
4. There must be adequate wages and benefits prior to implementing a PGP. It cannot be a substitute for inadequate wages and benefits.
5. There must be proper planning from the beginning. A joint planning process strengthens the program and gets it off to the best possible start.
6. There must be an effective employee education process. Being well informed is the first step toward making a commitment.
7. There must be an effective communications system through which continuous information about the PGP can flow.
8. There must be accurate, accessible accounting and record keeping for the program.

Having these factors present in a workplace ensures that the productivity gainsharing program undertaken will be built on a solid foundation.

CONCLUSION

The combination of financial incentives and participation within the framework of union-management cooperation can be a powerful mechanism leading to bottom-line improvements for both employees and employers. There are three key opportunities for common action within this context. Joint study teams can develop the productivity or performance formula. The union and management partners can design and develop the participation system to be combined with financial incentives. To do this they should pursue the steps covered in Part Three of this book. Currently the participation systems are often not as sophisticated as the measurement systems. However, much of the energy for the PGP comes from the participation system and that system needs to be as encompassing and effective as possible. Third, the implementation and administration of the measurement system should be a joint activity. If the union and management partners act together in these ways they will harness significant energy and power inherent in their situations to their mutual benefit.

ADDITIONAL RESOURCES

Doyle, Robert J. *Gainsharing and Productivity: A Guide to Planning Implementation, and Development.* New York: AMACOM, 1983.

Frost, C. F., J. H. Wakely, and R. A. Ruh. *The Scanlon Plan for Organization Development, Identity, Participation and Equity.* East Lansing: Michigan State University Press, 1974.

Lawler III, Edward E. *Pay and Organization Development*. Reading, Mass.: Addison-Wesley, 1981.

Lesieur, Frederick G., ed. *The Scanlon Plan: A Frontier in Labor Management Cooperation*. New York: Technology Press of Massachusetts Institute of Technology and Wiley, 1958.

Moore, Brian E., and Timothy L. Ross. *The Scanlon Way to Improved Productivity: A Practical Guide*. New York: Wiley, 1978.

Ringham, Arthur J. "Designing a Gainsharing Program to Fit a Company's Operations," *National Productivity Review* (Spring 1984): 131–144.

Slichter, Sumner H., James J. Healy, and E. Robert Livernash. *The Impact of Collective Bargaining on Management*. Washington, D.C.: Brookings Institution, 1960.

20

Taking Stock:
ESOPs and Employee Ownership

In its ideal form, employee ownership is an attractive concept. It provides for sharing in the success of the company and offers an avenue to influence the governance of an organization that theoretically could affect all aspects of its operation. Its real form falls far short of this. Voting rights are rarely provided to worker-owners, and even so, that amount of stock owned by any one employee provides little sense of ownership leading to real influence. The degree of ownership and the actual dollar returns are often so diluted as to have little motivational effect much less provide any control over corporate direction. In these situations employee ownership is valuable primarily as a corporate financing tool and not as a vehicle for union-management cooperation.

It is a promising avenue for cooperation when there is sufficient stock vested in the employees, when the employees can vote their stock, when there is employee/union representation on the board, when there is clear communication and solicitation of employee input into board level decisions, and when additional steps are taken to involve employees and the unions in decision making and operational improvements. Unfortunately, few employee stock ownership plans (ESOPs) meet these criteria. Rarely will highly profitable firms elect to become democratically employee-owned. Many, if not most, employee buyouts will work in marginal firms. However, simply becoming employee-owned will not transform a loser into a winner in the marketplace. Real participation in an ESOP in such a buyout could mean the difference between failure and success and may carry the firm into viability. In addition, companies whose return on investment does not satisfy corporate finance departments may be successfully converted into employee-owned enterprises. Still even these firms will have to grapple with the issues of long-term profitability and the ability to generate capital for expansion and modernization. All this is to say that employee ownership is not impossible but only difficult. As an arena for union-management cooperation around financial participation, it is the most challenging one.

There are two categories of worker ownership: direct ownership by which employees actually own their shares and beneficial ownership by which employees own their shares through the vehicle of a trust. Direct ownership includes direct stock ownership plans through stock bonus or stock purchase plans and producer cooperatives. Beneficial ownership includes a variety of employee stock ownership plans.

There is a long history of worker ownership in America. Between 1791 and 1940 almost 400 companies were established with a large portion of their stock directly owned by employees. Today there are more than 100 companies in which employees own a majority of the stock. More than 7,000 firms have various kinds of ESOPs. Worker ownership is very much in the news as many organizations approach employee ownership in whatever form as a strategy for ensuring organizational survival.

WHAT ARE ESOPS AND HOW DO THEY WORK?

Ten million workers in the United States are enrolled in ESOPs at this time; ten years ago there were only 500,000 enrolled in ESOPs. The annual growth rate for new ESOPs is 10 percent, largely due to the lucrative tax incentives given to ESOPs in 1984. At this pace, by the year 2000 25 percent of all American workers will own part or all of their companies. Since 1980, 100 major firms have been rescued by ESOP-financed buyouts. In fiscal year 1986 the U.S. government will lose $2.5 billion in tax revenues to the tax benefits granted to ESOPs. By 1990, it is estimated that $4.4 billion per year in lost federal tax revenues will be attributable to ESOPs.[1] Clearly, ESOPs are among the fastest growing business strategies in the U.S. economy. In fact the Employee Benefit Research Institute asserts that ESOPs are the fastest growing employee benefit in the United States.

In the 1920s many stock purchase and bonus plans were established as part of the welfare capitalism approach to labor-management relations. Most of these plans were destroyed by the 1929 crash and the resultant Great Depression when stock values plummeted. Louis Kelso, an investment banker, has been promoting ESOPs as a way to equalize the distribution of wealth since the 1950s. He suggests that by broadening capital ownership through employee stock ownership, the return to capital would rise to the "true" competitive market level, the return to labor would drop, and labor wage incomes would be lower, but workers would have a second income from their stock.

Essentially an ESOP is a way for employees to acquire the stock of their employer without having to put up any of their own money. Usually management gives employees equity in the company in exchange for something else, often some other form of compensation. Technically, an ESOP is an employee benefit plan. All cash and stock contributed to the ESOP are allocated to individual accounts of the participating employees. These allocations are held in an employee stock ownership trust (ESOT) that oversees and invests the assets of the ESOP. The ESOT is administered by a trustee or trustee committee. Theoretically, the ESOT is a legal entity existing independently of the employer specifically for the purpose of acquiring stock for the benefit of employees.

There are three basic types of ESOPs: leveraged, nonleveraged, and the tax credit or payroll-based stock ownership plan. A leveraged ESOP is one that borrows money to purchase stock in the company. The company in turn promises to contribute to the plan so that the loan will be paid off. As the loan is paid off, stock is allocated to employees participating in the plan according to the chosen formula. The company treats all ESOP contributions as business expenses, thereby writing off both the principal and the interest on the loan for tax purposes. This leveraged ESOP is a significant business financing tool through which companies obtain cheaper capital with few strings attached.

The nonleveraged ESOP is one in which the company contributes the stock to the ESOP or gives it cash to purchase the stock. The stock is allocated to the employees according to some formula, and the company contribution is a tax deductible business expense.

Tax credit employee stock ownership plans, or TRASOPs, are also called payroll-based stock ownership plans, or PAYSOPs. These types of ESOPs cannot borrow money and must pass voting rights through to the participating employees. Companies with TRASOPs or PAYSOPs receive generous tax credits. Companies can have both TRASOPs and the more conventional ESOPs, thus gaining both tax deductible business expenses and tax credits.

Participative or cooperative ESOPs are an adapted form of ESOPs in which the ESOT is organized as a cooperative. The voting rights are separated from the equity value that employees have. In these ESOPs each employee gets only one vote rather than voting in proportion to the stock owned.

All of these ESOPs can be analyzed by examining six variables: the level of corporate contribution and how corporate contributions are made, the amount of stock held by the ESOT, voting rights, the formula for allocation to participating employees, the vesting process, and the handling of dividends. There are essentially three different methods whereby corporate contributions are made to the ESOP: on the profit-sharing basis whereby a portion of profits is diverted, on the cost principle basis whereby a fixed percentage of labor costs is contributed, or on the fixed contribution principle whereby a certain dollar amount is transferred. ESOPs vary in terms of the amount of stock held. In TRASOPs the stock holdings are very small, and often in closely held companies the stock holdings of the ESOT are relatively small. In approximately 10 to 15 percent of all ESOPs, employees hold a majority of stock, and 10 to 20 percent hold very a small percentage of stock. In the rest employees own between 15 and 50 percent of the stock. In ESOPs established to prevent plant shutdowns, usually a majority of the stock is held by the ESOT.

Commonly the trustee or trust committee votes the stock according to some procedures, and voting rights are not passed through to employees. More often than not, the real owners of the company and/or management retain control by restricting the voting rights of the employee-stockholders. In some ESOPs non-voting stock is held. In 85 percent of all ESOPs the worker-owners do not have direct voting rights.[2]

Voting rights are attached to the vesting of ownership interest, that is, the rate at which employees gain ownership over their shares. Employees gain greater rights to their shares as they accumulate tenure with the company. The vesting timetable will vary from plan to plan. In general, vesting starts at two to three years at the 20 to 30 percent level and continues until 100 percent vested at ten years. Usually stock is allocated to employees based on their compensation or is equally distributed among participants. In most cases an employee is vested 100 percent by the time he or she retires. At that time employees can do anything they want with their stock. In some cases the ESOP has the right of first refusal on all shares an employee owns in the event the employee wants to sell them. Employees pay no tax on their stock while it is in trust and pay very minimal tax when they receive their stock upon retirement or termination.

Dividends are paid on stock held by the ESOT. These dividends are either allocated to the employee's account or passed through and paid directly to the participants. There is no tax liability for the dividends held in the trust.

Government assistance to ESOPs has been a significant factor in their growth. This assistance has taken three forms: tax benefits in the form of favored treatment, tax credits, and loan subsidies. Since 1974, there have been 16 tax laws that give favored treatment and support to ESOPs.[3] Until recently the two most significant benefits have been the company's right to deduct both principal and interest on the loan in a leveraged ESOP and to deduct ESOP contributions equaling from 15 to 25 percent of the compensation paid to participants. In 1984, three equally significant benefits were granted to ESOPs: commercial lenders can deduct 50 percent of the interest on loans to ESOPs from their income, corporations can deduct the cash dividends paid out on shares already allocated to ESOP participants, and the owner of a closely held business can sell stock so that the ESOT owns at least 30 percent of the company and then defer capital gains taxes by reinvesting proceeds from the stock sale in other securities within one year.[4]

Last, while ESOPs are considered a kind of pension plan, they are exempt from many of the more costly protections under the Employee Retirement Insurance Security Act (ERISA). ESOPs can invest primarily in the employer's securities and are not limited to the 10 percent limit on other pension plans. ESOPs are not subject to the funding requirements of other pensions and are not covered by Pension Benefit Guarantee Corporation Insurance. Clearly, ESOPs are not a good substitute for traditional pensions; ESOPs mean taking significant risks with employees' deferred wages.

HOW HAVE ESOPS BEEN USED IN AMERICAN INDUSTRY?

ESOPs have been used in seven major ways:

1. As a means of *corporate financing* through the leveraged ESOP
2. As a form of *deferred compensation,* that is, as a substitute for more conventional pensions and/or to provide remuneration in place of other wages and benefits
3. As a method for *transferring ownership* of companies, especially failing ones, to workers
4. As a means to create an *in-house market for the stock* of a closely held company
5. As a strategy for *fighting hostile corporate takeovers*
6. As a way to *raise worker motivation* and therefore positively affect profitability, productivity, and overall performance, which may in turn save jobs

As more ESOPs are being established, two uses stand out: companies are using ESOPs to give employees stock ownership in exchange for wage concessions and closely held or privately held companies are using ESOPs to sell out to their employees rather than conglomerates.

There are many clear advantages of ESOPs for employers. ESOPs provide cheap capital for refinancing of corporate indebtedness. They also provide a new market for stock that allows the company essentially to protect itself from outside control and limit worker control as well. ESOPs can create new stockholders who have ownership but little or no control and therefore management increases its power relative to stockholders. ESOPs allow a closely held company to raise capital without having to go public to do so. ESOPs can eliminate pension plan costs and reduce the pressures for upgrading pension plans and/or increasing wages.

Through ESOPs, employees can obtain stock without any initial outlay. Where employees have voting rights with their stock, they can have input into corporate decision making. Also employees can share in the financial gains of the company.

Often ESOPs are promoted as avenues for increasing worker motivation and thereby improving profitability, productivity, and performance. As with some of the other financial incentives, the motivational potential of ESOPs may be limited by the relatively small dividend income gains. However, some research does show that ESOPs do have these desirable effects. When the National Center for Employee Ownership studied 360 high technology companies, it found that companies having employee ownership grew two to four times as fast as companies without employee ownership. It also studied 52 employee-owned companies throughout American industry and found that the best performers were those that made the largest stock payments to workers' ESOP accounts. These companies also gave workers a voice in decision making and had strong "ownership culture."[5] Research also shows that profitability in worker-owned firms is often higher with the greater profits directly tied to a greater proportion of stock owned by workers.[6] Additional studies by the National Center for Employee Ownership concluded that publicly traded companies at least 10 percent owned by employees outperformed 62 to 75 percent of comparable competing companies by various performance measures.[7] While no absolute conclusions can be drawn it is fair to say that ESOPs may have a positive impact on worker motivation and organizational profitability, productivity, and performance.

Two examples of how American companies and unions have actually used ESOPs show the range of features such plans can have.

In 1982, all Pan Am employees gave up 10 percent of their wages in exchange for a nonleveraged ESOP and one seat on the board of directors. The company donated 10.8 million shares or an average of 450 shares worth less than $3 per share for each of the 24,000 participants in the plan. Plan participants were fully vested from the beginning and have full voting rights. The ESOP holds 13 percent of the stock of the company and operates alongside a profit-sharing plan. Over time the ESOP will acquire between 20 and 35 percent of Pan Am's stock.

Chrysler Corporation's ESOP was mandated by Congress as part of the bailout of the company. Ninety-four thousand employees received more than $40 million worth of stock through the ESOP. The voting stock was allocated equally among employees with each receiving 66 shares worth about $441 at the beginning of the plan. As of 1984, the ESOP held approximately 15 percent of the company stock, making it the largest bloc stockholder. The ESOP board consists of two United Autoworkers representatives and two company representatives. In 1984, the .ESOP was terminated by mutual consent. The stock in the ESOP was then worth approximately $487.5 million.

ESOPs have been used in American industry in a variety of ways to serve a number of different purposes. In a survey conducted in 1983, the National Center for Employee Ownership determined that only 7 percent of all ESOPs would exist if there were no tax benefits.[8] Also, it is estimated that 40 percent of all ESOPs have been established primarily for tax purposes.[9] One important fact does stand out, that ESOPs are not a "free lunch." Taxpayers pay for the tax benefits ESOPs receive. Existing stockholders pay for the establishment of the ESOPs by the dilution of their stock and/or the costs of making the contribution to the ESOP. Employees pay for the ESOPs when they accept them as substitutes for existing wages and benefits or in place of increased wages and benefits. The important issues for union and management partners regarding ESOPs are who benefits, who pays, and how.

WHAT ARE EMPLOYEE BUYOUTS AND HOW DO THEY WORK?

Employee buyouts occur when a company is sold to its employees. Very often such a company is in severe economic difficulty or failing. At other times the corporate parent may want to sell the company off because it is not profitable enough or no longer fits into the overall corporate business strategy. Many closely held companies are sold off to their employees when the owner and/or major investors don't want to continue with it. The "new" company is usually reorganized in one of three forms: direct employee ownership, an ESOP, or a producer cooperative. ESOPs are by far the most common form of employee buyouts.

All three forms have advantages and disadvantages. What is really happening is that employees are agreeing to give up financial security gained through collective bargaining to take on some of the employer's entrepreneurial risk in order to maintain their jobs and the company. Direct stock ownership fundamentally means that each employee takes on the risk of his or her own investment. This may lead to conflicts among employees, which can lead to conversion back to nonworker ownership.

Employee-owners will often disagree over the use of the company's financial resources, such as higher wages or greater dividends in the short term versus reinvesting in the company to ensure its long-term success. This was the case with both Chicago Northwestern Transportation Company and the Vermont Asbestos Group. ESOPs with their tax benefits may significantly help a failing firm. At the same time they are not the answer in and of themselves, especially when they do not include a high enough degree of worker control. Employees and their unions may be sold short without adequate control, which was the case at South Bend Lathe.

Last, producer cooperatives can experience problems as the value of employee-held stock increases; retiring employees may have to sell their shares to nonemployees to obtain their market value. Younger employees may not be able to afford to purchase a share in the company when hired. Nonshareholding employees and nonemployee shareholders result. Over time this changes the worker-owned co-op until it is no longer a producer co-op. This has been true of many of the plywood cooperatives in the Northwest. The union and management partners need to commit themselves to getting a good feasibility study done and to using the process outlined in Part Three of this book for structuring their joint work around the buyout.

HOW HAVE EMPLOYEE BUYOUTS BEEN USED?

Often control is divorced from ownership in employee buyouts. This means some companies are employee-owned but not employee-controlled, even though employees own a controlling interest of stock. There are many examples of closely held companies being purchased by their employees in which there was no immediate financial crisis. But the buyouts involving larger companies have usually been conducted in a crisis environment in which employees are literally buying their jobs. This has led to some serious flaws in the construction of those buyouts.

The following examples of employee buyouts are a mix of success and failure. They are not meant to be representative but are descriptive and to some extent prescriptive.

O&O Supermarkets: United Food and Commercial Workers created these worker cooperatives when A&P closed its stores in Philadelphia. Each store is a co-op with one worker having one vote. The employees elect a board of directors, which in turn hires the store manager. To join the co-op the worker must pay an equity share of $5,000. Decision making regarding all store business is divided among the store manager, the store workers, and the board of directors. The O&O Supermarkets have regularly outsold the A&P markets they replaced.

Weirton Steel Company: This was a division of National Steel that was not making enough money to meet corporate goals. National Steel offered to sell the company to the employees in 1984. A joint study committee did a feasibility study. A leveraged ESOP was established with 100 percent employee ownership. The employees are represented by the Independent Steelworkers Union. Initially, the ESOP trustee votes the stock in the ESOP, but eventually employees will vote their shares on a one-person one-vote basis for all issues. The union selected three of the twelve members of the board of directors. Eventually employees will be electing a majority of board members. Weirton has probably the most open communications system in the steel industry and has full-blown employee participation programs at all levels. It has become one of the most profitable integrated steel makers in America. For the 7,000 employees who purchased this company, it has been a welcome success. Not only did they save their jobs but they also now own a profitable company.

Rath Packing: This is a participative or cooperative ESOP begun in 1979 by the local union, UFCW Local 46, and the company. Wage reductions and pension plan termination were exchanged for 60 percent of the company's stock. Union members elect the entire board of directors. Employees have control and real power as well as a system of employee participation at all levels. The union has veto power over changes in the plan or termination of the agreements that created the plan. Rath had a very rough time in the marketplace due to factors that the partners couldn't control. As a result, in 1983, Rath filed for bankruptcy and was reorganized into a smaller, regional packer. This illustrates very clearly that even the best ESOP cannot necessarily salvage a deteriorating company faced with serious market challenges.

Hyatt-Clark: In 1981, the employees purchased this division of General Motors for $53 million through a leveraged ESOP. A key element of this buyout was that GM is obligated to purchase a portion of all of its bearing needs from Hyatt-Clark through November 1987. However, this division had been unprofitable for five years prior to the sale, had declining product demand combined with obsolete equipment and plant layout, and had a history of poor labor relations. The employees took a 25 percent wage cut and a 50 percent reduction in benefits and accepted new work rules in exchange for 100 percent ownership.

The workers don't have voting rights, but the union, the UAW, controls three seats out of twelve on the board of directors. The union-management relationship under employee ownership has been a rocky one with conflicts over how much authority workers have in the selection and compensation of management and over how monies are to be spent. At the same time a productivity bonus system and profit sharing have been established.

In September 1985, the board of directors unanimously voted to authorize the sale of the company to someone other than the employees. Essentially GM had refused to lend Hyatt-Clark much needed funds for equipment and modernization. Also Japanese bearing makers have penetrated the U.S. market, driving down the price GM had had to pay for bearings purchased from Hyatt-Clark. Last, the partners didn't overcome their poor relationship, as indicated by Corey Rosen, executive director of the National Center for Employee Ownership: "Hyatt was one of the first major buyouts of a failing company and there was a lot of groping around. They did some things right and they did some things wrong, but mostly they didn't ever resolve the bad labor relations."[10]

Employees will probably continue to try to save their jobs through buyouts whatever form they may take. In areas with high unemployment and a concentration of high seniority employees with few other employment prospects, there may be no better alternative. Also, owners of closely held firms will continue to sell to their employees for many reasons, not the least of which is the attractive tax incentives an ESOP offers. A number of labor unions are pursuing their interest in preventing plant shutdowns by examining employee buyouts as an alternative. It is especially important to correct the flaws and address the problems that have marred such buyouts in the past.

UNIONS AND EMPLOYEE-OWNED FIRMS

Collective bargaining occurs in employee-owned firms because most employees are not the majority owners, and in almost all such situations there is still a management organization. There are relatively few unionized companies in which the employees are rank and file employees, managers, and owners simultaneously. There are an array of issues regarding collective bargaining within employee ownership. However, most of these are primarily concerns for the union.

Unions have been skeptical of employee ownership. This skepticism has focused on the questions of whether employee ownership is feasible and whether it really serves worker interests. In many employee ownership situations management takes the lead in making the conversion. Union attitudes toward employee ownership are varied. ESOPs are usually not considered an acceptable substitute for conventional pension plans because they lack many of the protections afforded to conventional plans and because they mean taking significant risks with workers' deferred wages. Collective bargaining is considered the proper arena in which to determine the detailed structure for any employee ownership opportunity. Unions are concerned that employee ownership arrangements may break down worker solidarity. They may pit workers who want to maximize their short-term gains (take-home pay or current dividends) against workers who want to maximize their long-term gains (return on and value of their stock). Unions have had limited recent experience with employee ownership. Additional experiences over time will shape union attitudes further.

Several significant issues that relate to what the union does vis-à-vis employee ownership are the following:

1. *Duty of fair representation*: In several instances union members have charged their unions with inadequately representing them in the development of ESOPs. Duty of fair representation liability exists if the union provides loans or other financial assistance to some locals and not to others. Further, there can be some liability when unions give advice about the feasibility of an ESOP. If it fails after the union presented it as a good business proposition, then members may feel that they were not fairly represented.[11]

2. *Union representation on boards of directors*: Unions may represent workers on the boards of competing firms in the same industry. This may raise some antitrust issues, especially around the motivation and opportunity for price fixing. Unions can limit the risk by having different people serve on the competing boards and by having these representatives appointed or elected by stockholders, which removes them to some extent from union control and responsibility. The value of being involved at the board level in critical investment decisions would usually outweigh these risks.

3. *Conflicts of interest*: The Landrum-Griffin Act and other antitrust regulations establish a series of things that union officials must avoid in order to be free of conflict of interest. Some of these relate to things that can happen under worker ownership: accepting payments or fees paid by the employer where the union represents employees, investing union funds in employer stock, and holding employer stock.[12]

These issues describe real risks that the union partner may take on in representing the employee-owners. Union officials need to check carefully whether these risks apply to their situation when they become involved with employee ownership. Sympathetic management partners need to understand how they can avoid unintentionally compromising their partners in these ways as well. Also, union and management partners need to recognize that in some cases the employee ownership framework has been used to break bargaining units or to counter union organizing drives. Only through careful planning and honest dealing can the union and management partners avoid the appearance, or the reality, of union busting using employee ownership.

The last consideration is the impact of a single plant buyout. When a single plant is bought out, it is separated from the master contract. This sets up wage competition between the worker-owners of the newly created company and the workers within the former parent company. This may weaken the union's national contract. At the same time this may be the only way to maintain jobs. This is probably one of the most serious dilemmas faced by the union partner. A comprehensive assessment of the risks and benefits at the beginning of such a venture is the only protection the union and management partners have against making mistakes that later threaten not only the collective bargaining relationship but also the very survival of the company.

EMPLOYEE PARTICIPATION IN ESOPS AND EMPLOYEE BUYOUTS

It is important to examine the indicators of employee influence in an employee-owned company. These include percentage of equity owned by workers; whether workers have voting rights, what kind, and to what degree; and whether workers have representation on the board of directors. These indicators relate to participation by employees as owners or shareholders. By these indicators, participation is often quite limited. It is estimated that in 85 percent of all ESOPs workers don't have the very basic participation opportunity of voting rights.

Another way to examine employee participation in the context of employee ownership is to look for specific participation programs designed to enhance the role of rank and file employees as workers and shareholders. Many ESOPs and most TRASOPs have no such programs combining participative management with greater employee involvement. Too often it is assumed that with employee ownership there will be greater involvement of employees in the running of the business. Unfortunately, that is probably the most common misconception, especially in employee buyout situations. By contrast, in producer cooperatives and participative ESOPs, employee involvement activities are a critical part of the employee ownership framework.

In any case, the union and management partners cannot ignore what other companies know about the value of employee participation. For employee-owners to obtain the best possible return on their stock the company has to be the best performer it can be. Employee participation approaches provide avenues for a company to enhance its performance greatly.

FACTORS NECESSARY FOR THE SUCCESS OF EMPLOYEE BUYOUTS

Three general factors are necessary for the success of employee buyouts: maximizing voting rights, separating voting rights and equity accumulation, and having a training or resocializing process. Voting rights are a key indicator of the real power that employee-owners have or don't have. Voting rights are also the avenue by which employees exercise control over their equity. Employees need a way to act on their interests in companies in which they have a share. Separating voting rights and equity accumulation injects a more democratic structure into the decision-making arena in an employee-owned firm. Participative or cooperative ESOPs do this by applying the one-person one-vote rule while employees accumulate different amounts of stock. A training or resocializing process moves the employee-owned organization closer to industrial democracy. It helps employees at all levels to obtain the expertise necessary to function actively as employee-owners in a successful enterprise. It could be complementary to employee participation programs. All three of these factors relate primarily to situations in which employees have a majority or controlling interest in the company. Having these three factors at work would mean that that interest would be maximally directed toward the success of the company as a whole.

The National Center for Employee Ownership has conducted extensive research into what makes an ESOP successful. It determined that the company must make a significant contribution to the plan, at least 5 percent annually and preferably 10 percent of the covered employee payroll. It also must be strongly committed to employee ownership, must treat employees as owners, and must bring employees into company decision making. The company must have an active ESOP communications program through which employees know what their ESOP means. The National Center has also concluded that a financially successful company is in a better position to accomplish those things that make an ESOP work well. Financially troubled firms usually cannot afford to do what it takes to make the ESOP successful unless they turn their financial situation around quickly.[13]

PITFALLS OF ESOPS AND EMPLOYEE BUYOUTS

Serious organizational problems may be related to employee ownership. It may be difficult for employee-owned firms to obtain the necessary capital, especially in buyout situations, due to biases against employee ownership and against small business. Many employee-owned firms are in fact small to medium-sized businesses that may experience a range of difficulties in the marketplace due to their size as much as their form of ownership. ESOPs are a risky form of pension plan and may also be an unstable form of employee compensation. Employees deserve to be adequately compensated for their effort and paid for their long-term contribution to the company through an adequate pension plan.

Employee ownership in no way ensures labor-management harmony or peace. A positive union-management relationship has to be developed over time by working successfully together around cooperative activities. An employee-owned firm can provide opportunities for the union and management to work together, but a structured process for doing so must be established. Too often employee ownership results in increased management power and control at the expense of stockholders and employees. Voting rights and board of directors control are two key areas in which employee interests should be well represented to balance management interests. Sometimes stock is sold to the ESOP at inflated prices, or management purchases stock at much lower cost than the stock purchased through the ESOP for employees. Neither of these occurrences helps build the union-management relationship.

Expectations about the power or control employee-owners will have, about the likely stock dividends, or about the profitability and survival of the company can become problems when they are not borne out by reality. Sometimes employee ownership is oversold in terms of the positive results it will bring. When expectations are unmet, dissatisfaction and disillusionment with employee ownership can result.

Finally, those responsible for running the company may not have the entrepreneurial capacity and expertise to do so. Employee ownership may enhance organizational effectiveness, but it is no guarantee that the company will be a success in the marketplace. The union and management partners need to figure out how they can avoid the pitfalls while getting the maximum benefits from employee ownership.

Since ESOPs are by far the most common form of employee ownership and are growing much faster than any of the other forms, the key question is how can management and unions overcome the common pitfalls. Deborah Groban-Olson, executive director of the Michigan Center for Employee Ownership, recommends these strategies:

1. The terms of the ESOP should be a mandatory subject for collective bargaining.
2. All stock held by the ESOP trust should have full voting rights; the rights should be passed through to employees in closely held firms; an advisory committee elected by the employees should direct the voting of the stock by the ESOP trustee.
3. Diversification of ESOP trust funds should be required where there is no other pension plan.
4. If the company already has a pension plan qualified under ERISA, then it should not be able to replace that plan with an ESOP.
5. Regulations should be developed to prevent ESOPs from paying inflated prices for the stock of closely held firms.
6. Vesting schedules should be shortened to provide full vesting after three years of employee participation.[14]

Employee ownership is one of a number of approaches that the union and management partners can take to improve organizational effectiveness, save jobs, and enhance the quality of work life. Financial success flows from organizational success. The key, as with other approaches, is to pursue employee ownership jointly in a careful and organized fashion.

ADDITIONAL RESOURCES

Clark, Dennis, and Merry Guben. *Future Bread: How Retail Workers Ransomed Their Jobs and Lives.* Philadelphia: O&O Investment Fund, 1983.

General Accounting Office. "Initial Results of a Survey on Employee Stock Ownership Plans and Information on Related Economic Trends." Washington, D.C.: U.S. General Accounting Office, 1985.

Groban-Olson, Deborah. "Union Experiences with Worker Ownership: Legal and Practical Issues Raised by ESOPs, TRASOPs, Stock Purchases, and Cooperatives," *Wisconsin Law Review* (1982): 732–823.

Institute for Social Research, University of Michigan. *Employee Ownership: Report to the Economic Development Administration.* Washington, D.C.: U.S. Department of Commerce, 1977.

Rosen, Corey M., Katherine J. Klein, and Karen M. Young. *Employee Ownership in America: The Equity Solution.* Lexington, Mass.: Lexington Books, 1986.

Saltzman, Gregory M. "Employment Stock Ownership Plans: An Economic and Industrial Relations Analysis." Washington, D.C.: U.S. Department of Labor, 1979.

21

Conclusion

Union-management cooperation is really an issue of choice. It is neither inevitable nor impossible. It is the choice of the union and management partners to opt for cooperation or confrontation. Once that commitment is made there is an enormous range of choices bounded in large part by institutional imagination about what forms cooperation can take. The parties must carefully choose the approaches best suited to their own particular circumstances and needs. The range includes reorienting the collective bargaining arena to tackling important topics for labor-management committees to establishing new organizational and work design to revenue and growth-centered agendas to strategic planning for the future to new pay and ownership possibilities. In each of these, we have outlined some alternatives. We recognize that beyond those are other possibilities that space did not allow us to discuss or that need to be invented by union-management efforts. Yet the choices do not end with selecting an approach, for within each one are a number of choices about how it should be developed and nurtured. At the end, the choice emerges again about whether the cooperation was worthwhile, should it continue, and, if so, how can it be improved or extended.

Each party needs to address these issues in its own way and for its own purposes. As we have stressed throughout this book, commonality of purpose doesn't preempt particular agendas, it subsumes them. Union-management cooperation is a legitimate forum for seeking improved government, more profitable enterprises, and better pay and working conditions for union members.

TRADE UNION MOVEMENT

The union movement needs to grab hold of the cooperative possibilities and pursue them as far as possible. For the membership that makes up the backbone of the labor movement, this is essential if new benefits and better working environments are to be gained. To recruit a new generation of union membership, a new clarion that calls for a better deal, a better workplace, and greater inclusion of the work force is a necessity. Sitting by the wayside and carping about the difficulties or screaming at the barricades will scarcely change things for the better. The union movement needs to exercise imagination in how to propose cooperative ventures rather than waiting to be called upon. This means exploring the frontier areas of job creation, product development, new technology, work redesign, strategic collective bargaining, and other similar innovations. Unions should challenge management to see how far it is willing to go in generating mutual gains. In doing so, a new form of unionism will emerge. The range of issues where union leadership is conversant and involved will expand greatly. The advocacy of workers' interests will span the entire range of issues inside the workplace as well as outside.

MANAGEMENT AND EMPLOYERS

Management should exercise good judgment and good sense and join hands with the unions that represent its employees. Continuing the battle only drains energy and resources that could be funneled into constructive, mutually beneficial activities. Management's refusal to work with responsible labor gives credence to radicals who assert that management is at best a presumptuous elite and at worst acting in ways antithetical to the broader concerns of workers.

Most important, cooperation provides an essential aid to effective management. It is always easier to manage when the work force is pulling in the same direction. Finding common direction and goals with the work force can harness common potential. By framing the collective bargaining process cooperatively as much as possible, industrial relations can take on a new tone and make a new contribution. By getting the workers involved in more efficient use of energy, resources, machinery, and other inputs, the process of work can be more effectively managed. By getting workers involved in customer service, marketing, product development, and new facility decisions, new markets and expanded business can be generated. Overall, by garnering the ideas and energy of all of the people who work in a location, the organization that managers are to manage will work more smoothly, more imaginatively, more enjoyably, and more profitably for everyone.

GOVERNMENT

Governments do have a useful role to play in the cooperation equation. They can serve as a catalyst to bringing unions and management together in as many forums and for as many purposes as possible. Where government policy seems to divide the parties and fan tensions, then those areas should be examined to see if initially more cooperative approaches can be used. The nation as a whole will benefit from improved industrial relations and a new relationship at the workplace between unions and employers. Aimed in the positive direction we have laid out in this book, this can only improve the financial health of enterprises, the operations and revenues of government organizations, and the quality of life of the citizenry. Government as employer should model what is best in private enterprise not the worst. The best is not represented by foot dragging or obstinate approaches to collective bargaining but by the enlistment of civil servants and their unions into a common enterprise. Government as employers should be as involved or even more so with their unions in cooperative activities than the private sector. Since collective bargaining laws support trade union activity, government managers should support the broadest and best application.

All too often, function has gotten obscured by position. Union-management cooperation offers each party the opportunity to do what it should do best. For managers, cooperation provides an opportunity to manage. They can help define the plans, marshall the resources, apply their knowledge and expertise, and coordinate the people that "managing" truly implies. For trade unions, rather than being caught up solely in the means of their mission, cooperation provides an additional avenue to advance the interests of their membership. For government, rather than just policing the conflicts, it can serve to promote the general welfare of employers and its working citizens.

We hold no illusions about the difficulty of the task. On the other hand, we still marvel at its possibilities for change. Union-management cooperation will not occur in all places, at all times, and in all ways. Cooperative approaches do not guarantee industrial utopias or wonderful workplaces. Cooperation engages the principal parties in the common struggle for significant betterment. By pointing the finger in the direction of a better way, joint efforts can make important and tangible improvements for all concerned. A union and management can do almost anything they set out to do when they summon common imagination and dedication to quality application.

Notes

CHAPTER 1

1. Frederick Harbison and John R. Coleman, *Goals and Strategy in Collective Bargaining.* (New York: Harper and Brother, 1951), p. 20.
2. Ibid., p. 54.
3. Ibid., p. 90.

CHAPTER 2

1. *American Federationist*, May 1919. In *Labor and the Employer*, Samuel Gompers (New York: E. P. Dutton, 1920), p. 305.
2. *AFL-CIO News*, press conference, Tulsa, Okla., July 13, 1985.

CHAPTER 3

1. Federal Mediation and Conciliation Service, *Labor-Management Committee: Planning for Progress* (Washington: D.C.: GPO, 1977), pp. 6–7.
2. Charles G. Burck, "Working Smarter," *Fortune*, June 15, 1981, p. 73.
3. S. Andrew Carson, "Participatory Management Beefs Up the Bottom Line," *Personnel* (July 1985): 47.
4. Ibid., p. 48.
5. Karl Frieden, *Workplace Democracy and Productivity* (Washington, D.C.: National Center for Economic Alternatives, 1980), pp. 21–22.
6. Ibid.
7. Robert Zager and Michael Rosow, eds., *The Innovative Organization: Productivity Programs in Action* (New York: Pergamon Press, 1982), p. 60.

CHAPTER 4

1. Carroll E. French, *The Shop Committee in the United States*, dissertation, Johns Hopkins University, 1922, p. 8.
2. William Leavitt Stoddard, *The Shop Committee* (New York: Macmillan, 1919), p. 93.
3. "Cooperation of Trade-Unions with Employers." *Monthly Labor Review* 27 (October 1928): 657–79.
4. Report of the AF of L Railways Employee Conference, Seventh Annual Conference, 1928, pp. 19–20.
5. Ibid., p. 19.

6. Otto S. Beyer, *Wertheim Lectures on Industrial Relations: 1928* (Cambridge, Mass.: Harvard University Press, 1929), pp. 3, 4.

7. Quoted in Milton Derber, *The American Idea of Industrial Democracy* (Urbana: University of Illinois Press, 1970), pp. 208–209.

8. Milton J. Nadworny, *Scientific Management and the Unions: 1900–1932* (Cambridge, Mass.: Harvard University Press, 1955), p. 130.

9. *American Federationist*, April 1925, p. 227.

10. *American Federationist*, June 1927, p. 729.

11. Clinton Golden and Harold Ruttenberg, *Dynamics of Industrial Democracy* (New York: Harper and Brothers, 1942), p. 233.

12. Ibid., pp. xvii, xviii.

13. Clyde E. Dankert, *Contemporary Unionism in the United States* (New York: Prentice-Hall, 1948), p. 475.

14. "Management Looks at the Labor Problem." *Business Week*, September 26, 1942, p. 90.

15. Ernest Dale, "Employee Cooperation to Increase Productivity" (New York: American Management Association, 1944), p. 165.

16. Charles A. Meyers, "Conclusions and Implications." *Causes of Industrial Peace* (New York: Harper and Brothers, 1953).

CHAPTER 5

1. Robert Kuttner, "Blue Collar Boardrooms," *New Republic*, June 17, 1985, p. 21.

2. *Resource Guide to Labor-Management Cooperation* (Washington, D.C.: U.S. Department of Labor, GPO, 1983), p. 118.

3. Ibid., p. 143.

4. Ibid., p. 140.

5. Susan G. Clark, Kathleen D. Warren, and George Greisinger, *Assessment of Quality of Work Life Programs for the Transit Industry* (Washington, D.C.: Transportation Research Board, National Academy of Sciences, 1983), pp. 35–40.

6. Analysis of the public sector entries in the *Resource Guide to Labor Management Cooperation* published by the U.S. Department of Labor, October 1983.

CHAPTER 6

1. Asian Productivity Organization, *Labour-Management Consultation Mechanism* (Tokyo, 1984), p. 189.

2. Suzanne B. Lincoln, "Indianapolis/Tokyo Work Commitment Survey" (Bloomington: Indiana University, 1982).

3. Robert Cole, "Participation and Control in Japanese Industry," USAID Conference on Productivity, Ownership and Participation, May 24–25, 1983, p. 8.

4. H. Okamoto, in *Towards Industrial Democracy: Europe, Japan and the United States* (Montclair, N.J.: Allanheld Osmun, 1979), p. 202.

5. Ibid., p. 203.

6. Johannes Schregle, "Codetermination in the Federal Republic of Germany: A Comparative View," *International Labour Review* 117 (January–February 1978).

7. *Workers Participation in Decisions Within Undertakings* (Geneva: International Labour Office, 1981), p. 96.

8. Stafan Aguren, Reine Hansson, and K. G. Karlsson, "The Volvo Kalmar Plant" (Stockholm: Rationalization Council, 1976), p. 5.

9. Oyvind Skard, "Organizational Change and Job Design" (Oslo: Cooperation Council LO-NAF, November 1976), p. 12.

10. For further discussion, see Edward Cohen-Rosenthal, "Working Together: An Overview of Worker Mutual Assistance Organizations," Contract No. AID/SOD 147-0464 (Washington, D.C.: U.S. Agency for International Development, July 1981).

11. C. P. C. Thakur, "Toward Industrial Democracy in Asia: The Indian Case." In *Industrial Democracy in Asia*, edited by Freidrich Ebert Siftung (Bangkok, Thailand: 1980), p. 88.

12. Indian National Trade Union Congress, "Participative Management," mimeo, December 30, 1980.

13. Tata Iron and Steel Company, "Working Together: Closer Association of Employees with Management in TATA Steel" (Jamshedpur, 1973), p. 2.

14. Eliezer Rosenstein, "Worker Participation in Israel: Experience and Lessons," *AAPS Annals* (May 1977): 113–122.

15. Daniel Zwerdling, *Workplace Democracy* (New York: Harper Colophon Books, 1980), p. 160.

CHAPTER 7

1. David Lewin, "Collective Bargaining and the Quality of Work Life," *Organizational Dynamics* (Autumn 1981): 37–52.

2. David A. Nadler and Edward E. Lawler III, "Quality of Work Life: Perspectives and Directions," *Organizational Dynamics* (Winter 1983): 30.

3. Ibid., p. 28.

4. John J. Popular, "Labor-Management Relationships by Objectives," *Industrial Relations Guide Service* (Englewood Cliffs, N.J.: Prentice-Hall, 1982), sec. 42, 184.

5. Robert R. Blake, Herbert Shepard, and Jane S. Mouton, *Managing Intergroup Conflict in Industry* (Houston: Gulf Publishing Co., 1964), p. 144.

6. Robert R. Blake, Jane Srygley Mouton, and Richard L. Sloma, "The Union-Management Intergroup Laboratory: Strategy for Resolving Intergroup Conflict," *Journal of Applied Behavioral Science* 1 (1965): 31.

7. Robert R. Blake and Jane S. Mouton, "Developing a Positive Union-Management Relationship," *Personnel Administrator* (June 1983): 23–32.

8. Richard Walton and Robert E. McKersie, *A Behavioral Theory of Labor Negotiations* (New York: McGraw-Hill, 1965), p. 11.

9. Ibid., p. 128.

10. Ibid., p. 137.

11. Ibid., p. 139.

12. Lane Tracy and Richard C. Peterson, "Tackling Problems Through Negotiation," *Human Resource Management* (Summer 1979): 23.

13. Walton and McKersie, op. cit., p. 152.

14. Ernest J. Savoie, "The New Ford-UAW Agreement: Its Worklife Aspects," *The Work Life Review* 1 (1983): 5.

15. Roger Fisher and William Ury, *Getting to Yes: Negotiating Agreement Without Giving In* (New York: Penguin, 1983).

16. Ibid., p. 59.

17. Ibid., p. 91.

18. Arthur A. Sloane and Fred Witney, *Labor Relations* (Englewood Cliffs, N.J.: Prentice-Hall, 1977), p. 224.

19. For an analysis of the categories of grievances and their disposition, see Dan R. Walton and William D. Tudor, "Win, Lose, Draw: The Grievance Process in Practice," *Personnel Administrator* (March 1981): 25–29.

20. K. L. Sovereign and Mario Bognanno, "Positive Contract Administration," in Dale Yoder and Herbert G. Heneman, eds., *Employee and Labor Relations* (Washington, D.C.: Bureau of National Affairs, 1976), p. 7–177.

21. William L. Batt, Jr., "Canada's Good Example with Displaced Workers," *Harvard Business Review* (July–August 1983): 4–11.

22. *Plant Closing Checklist: A Guide to Best Practice* (Washington, D.C.: U.S. Department of Labor, 1985); see also Gary B. Hansen, "Ford and the UAW Have a Better Idea: A Joint Labor-Management Approach to Plant Closings and Worker Retraining," *AAPS Annals* 475 (September 1984): 158–174.

CHAPTER 8

1. Paul J. Champagne and Mark Lincoln Chadwin, "Joint Committees Boost Labor-Management Performance and Facilitate Change," *SAM Advanced Management Journal* (Summer 1983): 20.

2. Robert W. Ahern, "Positive Labor Relations, Plant Labor-Management Committees and the Collective Bargaining Process," prepared for the Buffalo-Erie County Labor Management Council, April 1976.

3. *Starting a Labor-Management Committee in Your Organization* (Washington, D.C.: National Center for Productivity and Quality of Working Life, Spring 1978).

4. Robert P. Quinn and Graham L. Staines, "The 1977 Quality of Employment Survey" (Ann Arbor: Survey Research Center, University of Michigan, 1979), p. 178.

5. *Major Collective Bargaining Agreements: Safety and Health Provisions*, Bulletin No. 1425-16 (Washington, D.C.: Bureau of Labor Statistics, 1976).

6. Kevin M. Sweeney, *Building an Effective Labor-Management Safety and Health Committee* (Washington, D.C.: American Center for the Quality of Work Life, 1984), p. 5.

7. Thomas A. Kochan, Lee Dyer, and David Lipsky, *The Effectiveness of Union-Management Safety and Health Committees* (Kalamazoo, Mich.: W. E. Upjohn Institute for Employment Research, September 1977).

8. Sweeney, op. cit., p. 6.

9. Gerald G. Gold, *Employment-based Tuition Assistance: Decisions and Checklists for Employers, Educators and Unions* (Washington, D.C.: National Institute for Work and Learning, 1985), pp. 3, 11.

10. Thomas Pasco and Richard Collins, "A Program in Action," in *From Vision to Reality: The UAW and Ford Create New Directions in Employee Development and Training* (Dearborn, Mich.: UAW-Ford National Development and Training Center, 1985), p. 16.

11. Wayne Weagle and Gordon Skead, *Maintaining and Enriching Your EAP: The Role of the Joint Committee* (Troy, Mich.: Performance Resource Press, 1984).

12. Edward Cohen-Rosenthal, "QWL and EAPs: Making the Connection," *EAP Digest* (May/June 1985): 42–52.

13. Hy Kornbluh, James Crowfoot, and Edward Cohen-Rosenthal, *Worker Participation in Energy and Natural Resources Conservation: A Final Report* (Ann Arbor: University of Michigan Institute of Industrial and Labor Relations, December 1984).

14. Edward Cohen-Rosenthal, James E. Crowfoot, Roger Kerson, and Hy Kornbluh, "Preliminary Conference Report of U.S. Survey Data," presented at Employee Participation in Conservation: The U.S. and Japan Experience conference, Ann Arbor, Mich., September 1983, pp. C-7 and C-8.

15. Cynthia E. Burton, "Participation in Conservation: Maryland Department of Health and Mental Hygiene," in *United States Case Studies* (Ann Arbor: University of Michigan Institute of Labor and Industrial Relations, 1983).

16. Dennis Chamot and Michael D. Dymmel, *Cooperation or Conflict: European Experiences with Technological Change at the Workplace* (Washington, D.C.: Department of Professional Employees (AFL-CIO), 1981)); see also Steven Deutsch, "International Experiences with Technological Change," *Monthly Labor Review* 109 (March 1986): 35–40.

17. Doris B. McLaughlin, *The Impact of Unions on the Rate and Direction of Technological Change*, NSF Grant No. PRA 77-15268 (Detroit: University of Michigan Institute of Labor and Industrial Relations, 1979).

18. Richard Walton, "Challenges in the Management of Technology and Labor Relations," in Richard Walton and Paul R. Lawrence, eds., *HRM: Trends and Challenges* (Boston: Harvard Business School Press, 1985), p. 215.

19. John Auble, Jr., "Giving the United Way," *St. Louis Globe Democrat*, September 16–17, 1967.

CHAPTER 9

1. Robert Cole, "Some Principles Concerning Union Involvement in Quality Circles and Other Employee Involvement Programs," *Labor Studies Journal* 8 (Winter 1984): 221–229.

2. For a fuller discussion, see Cynthia Burton, "How to Do Quality Circles in a Unionized Workplace," *International Association of Quality Circles Transaction* (1983): 48–58.

3. Resolution adopted by IUE International Executive Board, January 1982, and IUE 20th Constitutional Convention, September 1982.

4. Owen Bieber, "UAW View Circles: Not Bad at All," *Quality Circles Journal* 5 (August 1982): 6.

5. Barry A. Stein and Rosabeth Moss Kanter, "Building the Parallel Organization: Creating Mechanisms for Permanent Quality of Work Life," *Journal of Applied Behavioral Science* 16 (1980): 373.

6. Dale Zand, "Collateral Organization: A New Change Strategy," *Journal of Applied Behavioral Science* 10 (1974): 63–89.

7. Stein and Kanter, op. cit., p. 384.

8. For a good discussion of task forces in general, see James P. Ware, "Making the Matrix Come Alive: Managing a Task Force," in David Cleland, *Matrix Management Systems Handbook* (New York: Van Nostrand Reinhold, 1984), pp. 112–131.

9. T. G. Cummings, "Sociotechnical Systems: An Intervention Strategy," in William A. Passmore and John J. Sherwood, *Sociotechnical Systems: A Sourcebook* (San Diego: University Associates, 1978), p. 169.

10. Albert Cherns, "The Principles of Socio-technical Design," *Human Relations* 29 (1976): 783–792.

11. Drawn from Fred Emery and Einar Thorsrud, *Democracy at Work* (Leiden: Martinus Nijhoff Social Sciences Division, 1976), p. 159.

12. Cherns, op. cit., p. 792.

13. Ontario Quality of Working Life Centre, "Starting Up a Redesign Project," *QWL FOCUS* 1 (March 1981): 7.

14. Calvin H. P. Pava, *Managing New Office Technology: An Organizational Strategy* (New York: Free Press, 1983), p. 26.

15. Ibid., p. 27.

16. Ibid., p. 28.

17. Randall B. Dunham, "The Design of Jobs," in Wendell French, Cecil Bell, and Robert Zawacki, *Organization Development: Theory, Research and Practice* (Plano, Tex.: Business Publications, 1983), pp. 301–314.

18. Richard E. Walton, "From Hawthorne to Topeka and Kalmar," in French, Bell, and Zawacki, op. cit., pp. 292–300.

19. David A. Nadler and Edward E. Lawler III, "Quality of Work Life: Perspectives and Directions," *Organizational Dynamics* (Winter 1983): 20–30.

20. Thomas C. Hayes, "At G.M.'s Buick Unit, Workers and Bosses Get Ahead by Getting Along," *New York Times*, July 5, 1981.

21. Stephen H. Fuller, "How Quality-of-Worklife Projects Work for General Motors," *Monthly Labor Review* (July 1980): 38.

22. Harry C. Katz, Thomas A. Kochan, and Mark R. Weber, "Assessing the Effects of Industrial Relations Systems and Efforts to Improve the Quality of Working Life on Organizational Effectiveness," *Academy of Management Journal* 8 (1985): 509–526.

23. Edward E. Lawler III and Gerald E. Ledford, Jr., "Productivity and the Quality of Working Life," *National Productivity Review* (Winter 1981–82): 23–36.

CHAPTER 10

1. This section is drawn extensively from Edward Cohen-Rosenthal, "Orienting Labor-Management Cooperation Towards Revenue and Growth," *National Productivity Review* (Autumn 1985): 385–396.

2. Hilary Wainwright and Dave Elliot, *The Lucas Plan* (New York: Allison & Busby, 1982).

3. Interview in *Trowel* 2 (Winter 1984): 5.

4. *Starting a Labor-Management Committee in Your Organization: Some Pointers for Action* (Washington, D.C.: National Center for Productivity and Quality of Working Life, Spring 1978), p. 11.

5. Norman Halpern, "Organization Design in Canada: Shell Canada's Sarnia Chemical Plant," in A. Brakel, ed., *People and Organizations Interacting* (New York: Wiley, 1985), pp. 117–151.

6. Louis E. Davis and Charles S. Sullivan, "A Labour-Management Contract and Quality of Working Life," *Journal of Occupational Behavior* 1 (1980): 33.

CHAPTER 11

1. Much of this section elaborates on a manual prepared by the authors for the United Paperworkers International Union titled *QWL: Buzzword or Breakthrough*. This workbook, available through ECR Associates, provides flowcharts and worksheets to help local organizations develop cooperative programs.

2. Robert Guest, "Quality of Work Life: Learning from Tarrytown," *Harvard Business Review* (July–August 1979): 76–87.

CHAPTER 14

1. For one version of the process, see *The Participative Problemsolving Workbook*, available through ECR Associates, which lays out steps and procedures in the problem-solving process.

CHAPTER 17

1. Edward E. Lawler III, *Pay and Organization Development* (Reading, Mass.: Addison-Wesley, 1981), p. 152.

2. Robert J. Doyle, *Gainsharing and Productivity: A Guide to Planning, Implementation, and Development* (New York: AMACOM, 1983), p. 19.

CHAPTER 18

1. Ralph M. Barnes, *Motion and Time Study Design and Measurement of Work* (New York: Wiley, 1980), pp. 482–483.

2. Garth L. Mangum, *Wage Incentive Systems* (Berkeley: University of California, Institute of Industrial Relations, 1964), pp. 5–7.

3. Barnes, op. cit.

4. Barnes, op. cit., p. 629.

5. Mangum, op. cit., pp. 12–13.

6. Robert Zager and Michael P. Rosow, ed., *The Innovative Organization: Productivity Programs in Action* (New York: Pergamon Press, 1982), pp. 196–197.

7. Mangum, op. cit., p. 16.

8. Barnes, op. cit., pp. 487–488.

9. Edward E. Lawler III, *Pay and Organization Development* (Reading, Mass.: Addison-Wesley, 1981), p. 4.

10. Ibid., p. 8.

11. Ibid., pp. 197–198.

12. "Pay for Performance Works, Most Firms Say," *Miami Sun Sentinel*, June 12, 1984, p. 12C.

13. Robert L. Heneman, *Pay for Performance: Exploring the Merit System* (New York: Pergamon Press, 1984), p. 9.

14. Heneman, op. cit., pp. 4–5.

15. Lawler, op. cit., p. 89.

16. Ibid., p. 131.

17. Ibid., pp. 88–89.

18. Ibid., p. 108.

19. Heneman, op. cit., pp. 11, 17.

20. Lawler, op. cit., pp. 94–96.

21. G. Douglas Jenkins, Jr., and Nina Gupta, "The Payoffs of Paying for Knowledge," *National Productivity Review* (Spring 1985): 121.

22. Ibid., p. 122.

23. Zager, op. cit., pp. 136–137, 298.

24. Jenkins, op. cit., pp. 126–127.

25. Ibid., p. 125.

26. Ibid., pp. 122–123.

27. "A Work Revolution in U.S. Industry," *Business Week*, May 16, 1983, p. 110.

28. Leonard M. Apcar, "Work Rule Programs Spread to Union Plants," *Wall Street Journal*, April 16, 1985, p. 6.

29. Jenkins, op. cit., p. 128.

30. Ibid.

31. Ibid.

32. Ibid.

33. Ibid., p. 124.
34. Ibid.
35. Ibid., p. 129.
36. Apcar, op. cit.

CHAPTER 19

1. Arthur J. Ringham, "Designing a Gainsharing Program to Fit a Company's Operation," *National Productivity Review* (Spring 1984): 132.
2. Robert Kearns, "Gainsharing Tempers Wage Inequities," *Chicago Tribune*, October 17, 1983, sec. 3, p. 3.
3. Robert J. Doyle, *Gainsharing and Productivity: A Guide to Planning, Implementation and Development* (New York: AMACOM, 1983), p. 123.
4. Ibid., p. 97.
5. Doyle, op. cit., p. 129.
6. Ibid., p. 125.
7. Ibid., p. 133.
8. Ibid., p. 136.
9. Ibid., p. 5.
10. Brian E. Moore and Timothy L. Ross, *The Scanlon Way to Improved Productivity: A Practical Guide* (New York: Wiley, 1978), p. 1.
11. Ibid., p. 62.
12. Ibid., p. 7.
13. Ibid., p. 22.
14. Frederick G. Lesieur, ed., *The Scanlon Plan: A Frontier in Labor Management Cooperation* (New York: Technology Press of the Massachusetts Institute of Technology and Wiley, 1958), pp. 73-76.
15. Moore and Ross, op. cit., p. 6.
16. Ibid., p. 98.
17. Doyle, op. cit., p. 9.
18. Moore and Ross, op. cit., p. 37.
19. Ibid., p. 132.
20. Ibid., p. 40.
21. Doyle, op. cit., p. 11.
22. Ibid., pp. 11-13.
23. Ibid., pp. 15-16.
24. Ibid., pp. 17-19.
25. Edward E. Lawler III, *Pay and Organization Development* (Reading, Mass.: Addison-Wesley, 1981), p. 144.
26. Doyle, op. cit., p. 57.
27. Ibid., pp. 57-60.
28. Ibid., pp. 23, 25-29, 31-35.
29. Lesieur, op. cit., p. 49.
30. Ibid., pp. 110-111.
31. Sumner H. Slichter, James J. Healy, and E. Robert Livernash, *The Impact of Collective Bargaining on Management* (Washington, D.C.: Brookings Institution, 1960), pp. 866-868.
32. Ibid., pp. 875-877.
33. Lawler, op. cit., pp. 150-151.

CHAPTER 20

1. "ESOPs: Revolution or Ripoff?" *Business Week*, April 15, 1985, p. 94.

2. Elaine Hopkins, "Peoria Has ESOP: Management Has Control," *The Guild Reporter*, June 7, 1985, p. 7.

3. "ESOPs: Revolution or Ripoff?" op. cit., p. 96.

4. Leonard Sloane, "Your Money: Pros and Cons of ESOPs," *New York Times*, April 20, 1985, p. 32.

5. "ESOPs: Revolution or Ripoff?" op. cit., p. 94.

6. Institute for Social Research, University of Michigan, *Employee Ownership: Report to the Economic Development Administration* (Washington, D.C.: U.S. Department of Commerce, 1977), pp. 2–3.

7. Corey M. Rosen, Katherine J. Klein, and Karen M. Young, *Employee Ownership in America: The Equity Solution* (Lexington, Mass.: Lexington Books, 1986), p. 2.

8. Rosen, op. cit., p. 26.

9. Ibid., p. 46.

10. Douglas R. Sease, "Worker-Owned Hyatt Clark Industries Looks for Buyer After GM Refuses Loan," *Wall Street Journal*, September 10, 1985, p. 7.

11. Deborah Groban-Olson, "Union Experiences with Worker Ownership: Legal and Practical Issues Raised by ESOPs, TRASOPs, Stock Purchases, and Cooperatives," *Wisconsin Law Review* (1982): 796–797.

12. Ibid., pp. 800–803.

13. Rosen, op. cit., pp. 138, 145.

14. Groban-Olson, op. cit., pp. 772–773.

Index

About the Authors

Edward Cohen-Rosenthal is President of ECR Associates in Baltimore, Maryland, which he founded in 1979. Previously, he was Associate Director of the American Center for the Quality of Work Life and a faculty member at the Rutgers University Labor Education Center. He was also Project Advisor for the Trade Union Study of Alternative Working Patterns in Europe. He has published and lectured extensively on new working and learning arrangements. He holds a Masters in Education from Harvard University and a B.A. from Rutgers College.

Cynthia E. Burton is currently Vice President of ECR Associates, a position she has held since 1980. She also consults to small businesses and nonprofit organizations to improve their organizational effectiveness. Prior to her work at ECR Associates, she was Program Associate at the Maryland Center for Productivity and Quality of Working Life and Co-Director of Strongforce, Inc., a Washington, D.C. economic development organization. In addition to publications on union-management cooperation, Ms. Burton is also coauthor of a book on women and economic development and a workbook on equal education for women. Ms. Burton holds a B.S. degree from Western Michigan University, Kalamazoo, Michigan.

Cohen-Rosenthal and Burton have consulted for a wide variety of union, government, corporate and educational organizations to investigate and implement joint union-management projects. Working with management and labor unions, they have developed programs in the areas of employee participation, QWL and productivity improvement, strategic bargaining, resource conservation and new technology.